Rebellion
and
Repression
in the
Philippines

Rebellion and Repression in the Philippines

RICHARD J. KESSLER

Yale University Press   New Haven and London

Excerpts from *Soldiers and Stability in Southeast Asia*, edited by
J. Soedjati Djiwandono and Yong Mun Cheong (1988), reproduced with
kind permission of the publisher, Institute of Southeast Asian Studies,
Singapore. Acknowledgment is also made to The Stanley Foundation
for permission to include material based on "U.S. Policy toward the
Philippines after Marcos" by Richard J. Kessler for The Stanley
Foundation, Policy Paper 37, June 1986.

Designed by Richard Hendel and set in Times Roman type
by Marathon Typography Service, Inc., Durham, North Carolina
Printed in the United States of America.

Library of Congress Cataloging-in-Publication Data
Kessler, Richard J. (Richard John)
Rebellion and repression in the Philippines / Richard J. Kessler.
    p.   cm.
Bibliography: p.
Includes index.
ISBN 0-300-04406-2 (alk. paper)
1.–Philippines—History—1946-1986.   2. Philippines—History—
1986.   3. Insurgency—Philippines—History—20th century.
4. Philippines—Armed Forces—History—20th century.   I. Title.
DS685.5.K46   1989   89-30536
959.9'04—dc19   CIP

The paper in this book meets the guidelines for permanence and
durability of the Committee on Production Guidelines for Book
Longevity of the Council on Library Resources.

10 9 8 7 6 5 4 3 2 1

Pamela, Tristan, and Catriona

Contents

Tables and Figures

Preface

The Philippine insurgency may be the last great Communist-led peasant rebellion in Asia. Yet too little information is publicly available on the insurgency — its historical roots, cultural links, and contemporary setting — and on the Philippine military.

A 1985 article about the Philippine insurgents by *Time* reporter Ross Munro in *Commentary* entitled "The New Khmer Rouge" is characteristic of most reporting on the subject; though provocative and useful, it stirred interest without clarifying the situation. Insufficient attention has been paid to the Philippine military as well, which to its detractors was thoroughly venal under Ferdinand Marcos but to its supporters had been praiseworthy for its professionalism prior to the Marcos period. I thought it important to write about these two antagonists side by side because, like scorpions, they are locked in a deadly embrace.

It is a conflict in which the United States is intimately involved. American strategic interests, most prominently Clark Air Base in Pampanga and Tarlac provinces, and Subic Naval Base in Bataan (as well as several secondary facilities), will be directly affected by the struggle's outcome.

In the same way that American military aid was instrumental in Marcos's ability to impose his authority under martial law, American aid is now essential to Corazon Aquino's effort to rebuild the Armed Forces of the Philippines. Should the conflict threaten the new democratic government, the United States may become even more deeply involved, perhaps to the extent of sending American troops.

My work has been aided by a number of research assistants who have borne with my search for obscure details and helped bring together the information needed to write this study. They include Monica Mahoney (Georgetown University, 1984), Philip S. Wellman (Trinity College, spring 1985), Leah Buenaventura (Mount Holyoke College, summer 1985), John Gershman (Colgate University, summer 1985), Wendy Trainer (Colgate University, January 1986), Amy Clayton (Georgetown University, spring 1986), and Kathy Bazoian (Pomona College, summer 1986), who deserves special mention for having helped prepare the glossary. I hope they found the work as useful as I found their contribution to it.

I was aided also by the keen insights and useful corrections provided by a number of academic and government colleagues. Some must remain nameless, but in particular I appreciate the kind criticism and advice of Benedict Kerkvliet, Eduardo Lachica, David Rosenberg, Stephen Walt, Eric Willenz, Raymond Bonner, Ross Munro, Robert Manning, Nayan Chanda, Carl Lande, Mely and Ed de Jesus, Larry Niksch, David Wurfel, and my careful editors at Yale, Otto Bohlmann, Caroline Murphy, and Cecile Watters. Of course, any mistakes there may be are mine.

My deep appreciation goes to Thomas L. Hughes and the trustees of the Carnegie Endowment for International Peace, whose wise and gentle nurturing of an intellectually creative environment made my work possible during my stay there from 1985 to 1988.

Finally, special thanks to my wife, Pamela Cox, who has helped me cope with computer technology, my son, Tristan, who brought me notes of cheer, and my daughter, Katy, who taught me so much about compassion.

1 The Social Context of Philippine Insurgencies

On August 21, 1983, Philippine opposition leader Sen. Benigno S. Aquino, Jr., stepped out of the China Airlines plane returning him to Manila after three years of exile and was shot in the head by his military escort. The press and Aquino's supporters were penned up in the plane, blocked by government security forces. They could see nothing of the events occurring just a few feet away. The agony was intense.

As news of the killing spread, the entire nation seemed to express a collective sense of horror. Aquino's body was placed on public view for ten days and paraded in a final funeral procession in which thousands participated. The assassination marked a turning point in the dictatorship of Ferdinand E. Marcos, which culminated in his fleeing the country on February 25, 1986, and entering exile in Hawaii.[1]

Marcos's departure did not, however, bring to an end the long-standing Communist-led insurgency in the Philippines, the causes of which are rooted deeply in the nation's history and culture. These complex causes fall generally into two categories. The first concerns the historical relationship of the elite class and the military with the peasantry; the second concerns the traditional cultural and religious character of the Filipino people. The nature of the peasant rebellion and of its preconditions has changed little over the past two centuries, despite its added intensity following the injustices of the Marcos era.

These injustices became more and more flagrant as Marcos strengthened his position during almost eighteen years of unchallenged power as president. His rule was not devoid of impressive accomplishments, however. He oversaw the creation of a modern Philippine military, directed a decade of significant economic growth in the 1970s, and brokered the important strategic position of the island nation to Philippine advantage. As late as 1981 he won reelection as president in a landslide.

But the Marcos years were clouded by allegations of corruption, nepotism, and fiscal mismanagement. An ostentatious display of personal wealth became the hallmark of his presidency. Hundreds of millions of dollars of U.S. military and economic aid, Japanese aid, and World Bank loans were reportedly skimmed from government coffers to finance the ventures of the Marcos family and friends. In partial consequence, the economic growth of the 1970s stalled at the turn of the decade, and much of the country (especially its rural population) was plunged into a severe depression. Against this background, a Communist-led but peasant-based rebellion spread throughout the archipelago, becoming a serious military threat by the early 1980s.

Few observers doubted Marcos's complicity in the Aquino assassination and in the subsequent cover-up that blamed his murder on an alleged Communist gunman named Rolando Galman, who was conveniently shot seventeen seconds after Aquino left the plane under military guard. Bowing to domestic and international pressure, Marcos appointed a special fact-finding board under the direction of Justice Corazon Juliano-Agrava, a sixty-eight-year-old specialist in juvenile delinquency. Known as the Agrava Board, it concluded in late 1984 that Aquino's murder was the result of a military conspiracy. Twenty-four military personnel (including the armed forces chief of staff, Gen. Fabian Ver) and one civilian were tried for the crime in 1985 and acquitted in December. Galman, the judges decided, had been "the soulless assassin."

Outrage but not amazement greeted the trial's outcome. There was no outpouring of protest in the streets, however, for by that time Marcos had once again proven himself a master political tactician and had changed the rules of the game. Under pressure from the United States to stabilize the political and economic situation—which was rapidly deteriorating under the onslaught of opposition groups galvanized by Aquino's murder—Marcos had announced to an American television audience on November 3, 1985, that a presidential election would be held "in three months or less." The date of February 7, 1986, was soon established. (Marcos considered seven his lucky number.)

The campaign season prior to February's snap election was stormy. A united opposition fielded Benigno Aquino's diminutive widow, Corazon Cojuangco Aquino, for president under the political banner of the United Nationalist Democratic Organization (UNIDO), the party of her vice president, Salvador Laurel. It was an alliance of convenience. Laurel, a former senator, had spent years building a national political organization in the hopes of one day becoming president, but he lacked the popular appeal of the martyr's wife. Marcos chose as his running mate moderate Arturo Tolentino, recently ousted from his post as foreign minister for disagreeing with Marcos over diplomatic appointments. It was an electoral battle between traditional elites, with little chance given to the Aquino-Laurel ticket. Nevertheless, the people participated in droves.

Aquino and Laurel drew larger and more enthusiastic crowds than Marcos but were denied access to state-controlled television and radio. Their campaign funds were modest, whereas Marcos gave away large sums of money to individuals in his effort to win votes. Violence marred the election, with at least fifty-one election-related deaths (mostly of Aquino supporters) reported before February 7. The Communist Party of the Philippines (CPP) decided on January 6 to boycott the election, claiming that "the possibility that the opposition would win is a remote one"; but its military wing, the New People's Army (NPA), was significantly less active during the campaign.

By all nongovernment accounts, the election was stolen. Not content just to buy votes and stuff ballot boxes, Marcos supporters tampered with central computerized returns in Manila, provoking a walkout by programmers. Amid charges of fraud and election-day violence that left another twenty-six dead, Marcos claimed victory. Aquino called for a national protest strike on February 16, and on February 22 the Marcos government began to unravel. On that day the defense minister, Juan Ponce Enrile, and the deputy chief of staff of the armed forces, Lt. Gen. Fidel Ramos, took control of the military's headquarters at Camp Aguinaldo in Manila, announcing their support of Aquino. Jaimé Cardinal Sin, archbishop of Manila, called on the people to protect the military rebels. Thousands of civilians surrounded the base in a show of "people power," preventing soldiers from penetrating the installation. Although some units were able to position themselves —one artillery unit had its guns sighted on Ramos's office—and Marcos ordered them to fire, no attack ever materialized.

On February 24 Marcos declared a state of emergency. Early the next morning both Aquino and Marcos were sworn in as president at separate ceremonies. By nine o'clock that evening events in the streets as well as pressure from the United States finally persuaded Marcos to leave the country. Shortly after two in the morning helicopters lifted Marcos, his family, and loyal retainers (including General Ver) from the grounds of Malacañang Palace to Clark Air Base, and gunboats carried boxes of Marcos's loot down the Pasig River for reshipment to aircraft at Clark. Then Aquino supporters stormed the palace, and hundreds of thousands of Filipinos took to the streets in celebration of the overthrow.

In the days immediately following victory, President Aquino appointed a cabinet and sought to consolidate her new government. One of her first official actions was to release almost five hundred political prisoners, four of whom were prominent leaders of the Communist insurgency. Aquino hoped this gesture of goodwill and national reconciliation would help bring an end to the conflict with the Communists, but few rebels took advantage of her offer of amnesty, and subsequent peace negotiations in the fall of 1986 failed. This failure grew into a significant stumbling block during her first two years in office. Some military coup attempts were motivated at least in part by dissatisfaction with her reconciliation policy, and fighting continued after a temporary cease-fire collapsed.

To casual Western observers of the struggle, the persistence of the Communist insurgency after the departure of Marcos from the country is perplexing. It is understandable that the CPP boycotted the 1986 election, just as they (along with all other parties) had boycotted the penultimate 1981 sham presidential election in which essentially only Marcos ran. They believed that a fair election was impossible so long as Marcos controlled the electoral machinery. But with an open, democratically elected government in place, and a new constitution and congress in 1987, why did the rebels not simply throw down their weapons and return home? To understand the causes of the present conflict, and to grasp the reasoning behind the strategies chosen by the leadership of the insurrection and by the government in response, we need to understand the historical pattern of rebellion in the Philippines. Thus I will first give a short account of that pattern before returning to an examination of the present struggle.

The nature of the struggle has not changed very much over the past two hundred years. The desire for a nation free of foreign influence, with wealth distributed equitably, although often voiced, is still unfulfilled. The CPP recognizes the importance of this historical tradition, dating the peasant struggle from Raja Sulayman's resistance in 1564 to Spanish encroachment on what later became Manila.[2] As a 1981 classified report from the American embassy notes, "the NPA portrays itself as inheritor of a revolutionary tradition, a force of destiny capable of leading the Filipino masses to victory in their long struggle for Kalayaan (freedom)."[3]

Revolt of the Masses

The Philippines is a socially and geographically fragmented nation. It has more than a hundred tribal groups and seventy languages dispersed over a mainly mountainous terrain of about 7,100 islands, volcanic in origin. These islands form the western boundary of Southeast Asia, sitting on the edge of the Mindanao Trench; the Pacific stretches beyond. The Philippines extends for almost 1,150 miles, but its land mass is comparable to Italy's.

The country comprises three major regions: the island of Luzon, which includes Manila; several smaller but significant island groupings in the central part of the archipelago known as the Visayas, including Cebu, Palawan, Samar, Negros, Leyte, Panay, and Bohol; and the southernmost island of Mindanao, similar in size to Luzon.

Geographic fragmentation reinforced social fragmentation, particularly after Magellan discovered the islands in 1521 and named them for the Spanish crown prince, the future Philip II. Politically and economically the Philippines remains atomized. Geography also fostered discontinuous development: some areas prospered, such as Bicol because of the nineteenth-century trade in abaca, whereas others, such as Samar, remained economic backwaters. Only gradually has the Philippines knit itself into a nation—a nation still in the process of being formed.

The country is most unified in its elites. Spanish and American occupation fostered the development of a national elite and the consequent centralization of power in Manila. The process began when the Spanish formalized the positions of Malay tribal chieftains (known as *datus*) as a means of administering Spanish rule in the villages and towns, creating a new class of native tyrants. But no matter how strong

Manila grew, geography impeded direct application of its power. The social distance between the elite and the masses tended to increase over the years, as did the disparity between the central power in Manila and its ability to influence events in distant provinces.

Periodic peasant revolts were a response to the social transformation and abuse imposed by Spanish civilian and church authorities, by their own native elite, and by economic conditions. The peasants' complaints were numerous. In 1649 they revolted on Samar when the Spanish tried to impress them to build shipyards in distant Cavite. In 1745 they rebelled in Cavite because of continuing demands for corvée labor and the expropriation of land by the Dominican order. In 1762 they rose up in Cagayan against native officials who had treated them " 'as slaves, beating them without mercy for the slightest fault.' "[4]

A classic example of peasant rebellion was the revolt of the Brotherhood of Saint Joseph (Cofradía de San José) in Quezon (then called Tayabas) province in 1841.[5] Begun by a Catholic laybrother of peasant stock, Apolinario de la Cruz, who was refused permission by church authorities to become a priest, the Cofradía sponsored masses for the natives who paid membership dues. These services grew quickly in popularity. Alarmed by the success of the movement, Catholic church leaders importuned the Spanish authorities to suppress it. Apolinario was fired from his job as a laybrother in a charitable hospital and went underground. Orders were issued to arrest other members, but these arrests only incited Apolinario to expand the brotherhood's activities, ultimately leading to an outright conflict between Spanish troops and bolo-swinging peasants. Initially the struggle favored the natives, who killed the Tayabas governor, but reinforcements from Manila eventually overwhelmed the rebels' camp. Although Apolinario escaped, he was later betrayed by several followers disillusioned by his failure to protect them from Spanish bullets with magic amulets (known as *antinganting*). He was executed and his body dismembered.

The Cofradía rebellion was noteworthy in several respects. First, it occurred in an economically prosperous area with no previous history of revolt. The region was underpopulated and had no large church estates or absent landlords. Second, the quasi-Christian and pagan overtones of the brotherhood's religious practices demonstrated the "organizational and revolutionary potential" of religion to facilitate peasant revolts. And, third, the movement spread quickly, with followers deeply committed to its success. What made peasants rebel? What made them join the Cofradía? As David Sweet remarks, "such a movement could only occur among a people subject to severe deprivation—a people chronically frustrated in the effort to achieve what it thought of as the normal satisfactions of life."[6] Repeated personal humiliation, taxes, corvée labor, arbitrary use of church and government authority, and prohibitions on pagan rituals may all have contributed to the desire among peasants to join the brotherhood and ultimately fight to the death when authorities tried to suppress the movement.

The tendency toward these "little" rebellions, sporadic and geographically isolated, did not disappear as the Philippines developed. Nor did they completely merge into the nationalist movements of the nineteenth century. Instead they intensified, taking on some characteristics of nineteenth-century nationalism while remaining in many ways unique. The reasons for this lay both in the evolution of an indigenous elite whose perception of and motivation for instigating revolution were different from the peasantry's and in a culture that bound the peasantry together, giving them the means and method to rebel.

The development of the modern Philippine elite began in the late eighteenth century. Until then, smallholder agriculture had been the dominant form of land tenure. This began to change as the growing involvement of the Philippine economy in world trade fostered the rise of a native middle class that put its wealth into land for export crops.[7] Land ownership gradually became concentrated in large estates, known as haciendas, many of which were owned by church orders or by mainly Chinese or Spanish mestizos (people of mixed ancestry).

Although different regions experienced different patterns of growth, the general trend was toward the commercialization of agriculture and the alienation of the peasants from their land. By the nineteenth century a rural hierarchy had developed of the *hacenderos* (landowners), noncultivating tenants, and sharecroppers. So long as new land was available, the peasants could migrate. But in the mid- to late nineteenth century, increasing population growth and limits to land availability intensified social pressures. Peasant revolts in the eighteenth century had been caused mainly by oppressive measures, such as corvée labor, imposed by local and Spanish authorities. By the late nineteenth century, land tenure (with concentration of ownership in haciendas) had become the major source of tension, and changes in the economic and political system worsened rather than alleviated the conflicts. A period of economic prosperity was ending, the hacienda system was spreading (thus disenfranchising farmers), and Filipino nationalism was on the rise. Daniel Doeppers characterizes the years between 1890 and 1914 as "disastrous for the peasantry because of epidemics of man and beast, locusts, wars, changes of regime, banditry, collapse of foreign sugar markets, and general economic depression. The landowners reacted to all these threats to their economic interests by squeezing tenants harder."[8]

Naturally enough, the latter part of the century saw the rise of a number of significant peasant-based religious movements similar to the Cofradía. The first was Mary's Honor Guards (Guardia de Honor de Maria), established in 1872 as an orthodox lay group in a Manila convent. Dedicated to the Blessed Virgin, the movement soon gained thousands of members both in Manila and in the provinces, where the church could exercise less strict control over the group's practices. In 1882 the church withdrew its approval of the movement's Ilocano branch, but the group continued nevertheless, its adherents fired by the promise of salvation after an approaching apocalypse announced by the Guardia's leaders, Julian Baltasar and his blind wife, who were later regarded as living deities.[9]

Spanish efforts to eliminate the organization drove it into the mountains, where it undertook a guerrilla campaign. By 1898, the Guardia had sizable military strength, which both the new Philippine independence army under Gen. Emilio Aguinaldo and the recently arrived American troops treated with respect. After the movement established a communelike existence in Cabaruan, in the province of Pagasinan, it attracted even more adherents. The organization's concentration in a single locale, however, facilitated its dispersal in 1901 by American military forces who, having defeated the Spanish in the Spanish-American War of 1898, were now in the process of consolidating American colonial rule of the Philippines. The Guardia's most prominent leaders were hanged.

A similar group was the Church of the Saint (Santa Iglesia), organized in 1894 from the remnants of an association like the Cofradía initially called Gabinista by a middle-class man from Bulacan Province named Felipe Salvador. The Santa Iglesia endured until Salvador's hanging by American colonial officials in 1914. Declaring himself "immune to the weapons of the Spanish Army,"[10] Salvador affiliated himself with Filipino nationalists in their battle with the Spanish in 1896 and subsequently against the Americans until 1902. He won support by robbing the rich and distributing some of the bounty to the poor while propounding (in clerical garb) a vision of utopia. From his base on Mount Arayat in central Luzon, the site according to peasant beliefs of relics from Noah's Ark, Salvador preached the news of an impending cataclysm from which only true believers could be saved.

At the same time another rebellion with loose ties to the nationalist movement was being led by a self-proclaimed "Pope Isio" in Negros. Isio, whose real name was Dionisio Sigobela, had lost his farm to one of the wealthy hacenderos who were accumulating property and riches during the sugar boom of 1890–1900. A mix of nationalist rhetoric and liturgy, Isio's movement grew rapidly, attracting refugees and bandits to his mountain hideouts from which he raided the haciendas. When American forces appeared on the scene and local plantation owners switched allegiance to the new rulers, Isio gained even more support among the poor. As Sturtevant points out, "he began to stress the glories of independence—a highly desirable condition which would usher in a 'communistic paradise'".[11] Despite this support, Isio was finally forced to surrender in 1907 after a long-term effort by the American-led constabulary to regain peasant support. But rather than being hanged, he was given clemency.

Religion was a powerful bond in all these chiliastic peasant movements, suggesting a deeper cause for rebellion than just oppression or economic deprivation. The Philippine nation can be understood as an Eden lost when the nation was first colonized—an Eden that could be regained only through participation in the country's religious tradition.[12] As the ideals of nationalism and independence grew, especially in the late nineteenth century, they found expression in religious forms that peasants easily understood and accepted. These native movements promised their followers something more than land reform and higher wages: they offered salvation and independence (kalayaan) of the inner self (*loób*) in a greater brotherhood.

The ideals ascribed to in today's Communist struggle can be interpreted in more secular terms as an effort to restore the lost heritage of a failed Filipino nationalist revolution of the late nineteenth century known as the Katipunan. Today peasants join the NPA for many of the same reasons that their ancestors joined the Cofradía or the Guardia. But their leaders may prefer to see the roots of their struggle in the betrayal of the Katipunan by the elite, who deserted the independence movement's nationalist principles in favor of a collaboration with the Americans that preserved their privileged position, but not before they had created a new force for rebellion.

The nationalist revolution was directed by the Highest and Most Respectable Society of the Sons of the People (Kataastaasang Katipunan nang manga Anak Bayan), a secret society advocating Philippine independence. Formed in 1892 by the lower-class clerk Andres Bonifacio, it had only three hundred members in 1895, but by August 1896 it had attracted ten thousand. Wary of the Katipunan's increasing strength and hearing rumors of a plot to overthrow the government, the Spanish moved to suppress it but succeeded only in provoking a general uprising in August 1896. The Katipunan became involved in a protracted war with the Spanish but was rent by internal disputes over leadership and direction. In an incident still clouded in dispute, Bonifacio was executed in May 1897 by troops under Emilio Aguinaldo, former mayor of Kawit in Cavite and a general in the rebellion. Aguinaldo surrendered to the Spanish later that year in return for 800,000 pesos and exile in Hong Kong, after having been elected president of the new Republic of the Philippines in November 1897. In 1898 Aguinaldo returned to Manila with Rear Adm. George Dewey's invading American forces, and on June 12, 1898, he declared Philippine independence. But the failure of the United States to recognize the country's independence at the conclusion of the Spanish-American War precipitated a second struggle to liberate the Philippines that was not finally suppressed until 1903.[13] The Katipunan movement, however, was a historic watershed in the linking of nationalism with peasant unrest, bringing together peasant aspirations for religious salvation and bourgeois yearnings for national independence.

The development of more secular movements beginning with the Katipunan must be viewed in the same cultural context as the millenarian movements. Although the nationalist groups espoused more secular goals—independence, land reform, redistribution of wealth, and so forth—and embraced diverse social and geographical groups, the transformation of spiritual movements into national political organizations cannot be placed easily on an evolutionary continuum.[14] Although the newer groups represented a more sophisticated organizational structure, capable of uniting the peasantry and the middle class, the same cultural glue of mysticism and search for personal liberation held them together.

The concept of independence did gain a more precise, secular meaning during American colonial rule. "Independence" was both a political slogan of the elite and part of the rhetoric of peasant movements. As one rebel in a peasant organization of the 1930s stated:

> I want independence. I want our country to be free. . . . I am opposed to the present leaders because they put in the Commonwealth. I don't want it. It would be sweet to my heart to have independence even if I with my children must suffer every kind of hardship. . . . We didn't settle this like they do in America . . . because in America they count ballots fairly. Here I have no confidence in the ballots being counted. Under independence they would be . . . because everyone would purify himself inside.[15]

The pre–World War II urban nationalist radicals, convinced that "American power constituted the primary obstacle to effective reform,"[16] sought to free themselves of American bondage partially because they thought independence would make it possible to define what it meant to be Filipino—in much the same way that millenarian movements promised a new definition of self in a spiritual rebirth. Elite-based politicians also argued for independence, but as a means of enlarging their power base. For them, independence promised a paradise of riches. Even under American rule, members of the elite were able to amass more wealth and power as the Spanish were displaced.

During the American colonial period in the early twentieth century, many of the Catholic church's estates, which were spread throughout the islands, were broken up, and more land was acquired by the native elite. These new hacenderos continued the process begun in the previous century of concentrating wealth and power, first creating multiple tenancies and then converting leasehold tenants into sharecroppers by imposing higher rents. Dividing land into smaller and smaller plots reduced productivity, increasing the tenant's dependence on the landlord for financial support. "In extending credit to his tenants the hacendero was more interested in power than profits. . . . It was through debt—short term, long term, and the interest on both—that the landlord controlled the tenant and held him to the land."[17]

The situation was worse where full commercialization of agricultural production was particularly rapid. In Negros, where the richest sugar haciendas were established, peasants were completely disenfranchised from the land. Workers were regularly whipped, and the police patrolled the highways at night to prevent workers from escaping. "The Negros hacienda worker was . . . a wage or debt slave who owned, quite literally, nothing more than his clothes and cooking utensils." At the same time, landlords were becoming less interested in their land, moving to Manila's bright lights and leaving daily operations to an overseer who "set the stage for intimidation of the peasants." The result was a breaking down of the affection induced by the special patron-client bonds between a peasant and his landlord, permitting the landlord "to expropriate so much of the fruit of others' labor."[18]

Urban growth in the years before World War II led to an increasingly sharp division between the wealthy "landed-cum-urban elite" and the working class.[19] There was little obvious evidence of a middle class becoming increasingly bifurcated and alienated from itself; the full impact of this trend did not become apparent until the 1970s. But the signs of continued peasant and worker frustration and alienation were very clear.

The pre–World War II period was one of frequent urban and rural turmoil. Labor unions and peasant associations were created to promote social reform, existing alongside peasant millenarian movements, now referred to generically as *colorums* (after the liturgical expression "per omnia secula seculorum," or "world without end"). Typical of the colorums was Pedro Kabola's Association of the Worthy Kabola (Kapisanan Makabola Makasinag), established in 1923. Kabola claimed to have had spiritual communication with the Santa Iglesia's Felipe Salvador, who had instructed him to liberate the Philippines. Pledging ritual oaths, holding initiation rites, and charging membership dues, Kabola established a broad base of support within two years and in March 1925 attempted an insurrection, during which he was killed. But significant though the colorums were, the secular groups had a more permanent impact on the organization and substance of peasant protest.

The nationalist movements of the 1920s and 1930s nominally drew their inspiration from the Katipunan. In fact, one of the early leaders of one of these movements, Artemio Ricarte y García, had been a general in the war of independence of 1896–1903. Yet the strength of these groups came from the slowly emerging middle class and from urban and rural workers who felt they were being excluded from power and exploited by the elite.[20] The leaders of these groups were well educated. Ricarte, for example, had been a provincial schoolmaster in Cavite. Another radical *supremo* (or leader), Patricio Dionisio, was trained as a journalist and lawyer. A third, Benigno Ramos, had also been a schoolteacher before becoming a journalist and minor government official.

General Ricarte refused to acknowledge American conquest of the Philippines, and he engaged in numerous plots to overthrow the Americans. He was repeatedly exiled or jailed for his efforts. From exile in Hong Kong he conspired with Japanese intelligence to gain information on American defenses, and after one large-scale attempt at insurrection in 1914 he was pursued by American officials from his Hong Kong base into China, from where he escaped to permanent exile in Japan.[21] From this vantage point he acted as an inspiration for others disgruntled with the oligarchy and American rule. One whom he inspired was Patricio Dionisio.

In 1927 Dionisio established a secret society called the National Association (Katipunan ng Bayan), which by 1930 was not so secret, having acquired ninety-seven members in both local and regional branches. Then, in an effort to obtain official recognition, he changed the name to Association for an Offensive for Our Future Freedom (Kapatiran Tangulang Malayang Mamamayan). Immediate independence was the association's rallying cry, bringing it into conflict with the authorities. Stories began to circulate of supplies of Japanese arms and imminent revolution. Anticipating such actions, the government arrested the group's leaders, tried them for sedition, and found them guilty—although no actual conflict had occurred, nor had weapons been recovered. In one of the few signs of enlightenment, Dionisio was paroled and given a position in the Labor Department (from which he retired in 1955) to investigate the causes of rural unrest.[22]

A less satisfactory outcome attended the Sakdal uprising in 1935. *Sakdal*, meaning "to strike or accuse," was the name of a small newspaper chartered in 1930 by Benigno Ramos, a former minor government functionary. Ramos had been dismissed for making an issue of an incident of American racism (in which an American teacher had called Filipinos "monkeys") that his patron, Manuel Quezon, president of the Senate, had tried to hush up. In his new paper, Ramos attacked "our so-called leaders growing fat and rich on money amassed from taxing the poor."[23]

Promoting social reform and independence, Ramos gained a popular following among the rural poor and even formed tacit links with Dionisio's Tangulang. In 1933 he established the Sakdal party. His popular movement gained so much support that in the 1934 elections Sakdal candidates won several seats in the new House of Representatives.

But the party's initial success was also its downfall. Sakdal's increasing popular support among the rural and urban poor eroded the party leadership's control of its mass base. "Village true believers," Sturtevant points out, "were transforming a bourgeois challenge to the Nacionalista [the dominant political party] oligarchy into a rampant patriotism of a millennial variety."[24] True to form, the government tried to suppress the movement. In May 1935 sixty thousand Filipinos revolted. While Ramos hid out in Japan, the outbreak was suppressed at the cost of sixty dead. Yet the movement was a landmark event in the secularization of the spiritual themes of personal and national salvation, just as the Katipunan had been central to the popularization of nationalism.

These revolts were not the only signs of congruence among social unrest, nationalism, and religion. Union organizing was strong in the 1920s and the 1930s. The construction of sugar centrals in Negros and Panay provided new opportunities for unionizing workers, to the consternation of planters and mill owners. Peasant tenant unions were also formed, such as the Brotherhood of Farmers (Kapatiran Magsasaka). The brotherhood had elaborate initiation rites, including branding, which "brought a euphoric sense of unity and common purpose to the villagers." Members were described as holding "syncretic folk-Marxist ideas, adapted through the earlier idiom of folk-catholic ideas." Although busted by landlord thugs, brotherhood members later joined other groups, such as the Sakdals. Manila also had its share of trouble, notably from a three-month-long cigar makers' strike in 1934 involving more than eleven thousand workers. It was "the most notable example of workers' solidarity, evident proletarian class consciousness, and active yearning for socioeconomic change."[25]

Insurrections typically grew rapidly, outstripping their original bases and expanding into other provinces and social sectors. Each movement's self-perception as an inevitable wave of the future increased its support exponentially. The kinship system, in which family ties were created by both blood and ceremony (through baptism or marriage, for example), enabled cults to expand by accretion, spreading beyond linguistic boundaries. Many of the movements in this century started out as mutual-aid societies. Sometimes organized in secrecy and noted for their complex initiation rites, these groups only gradually became radicalized. Their initial demands were rarely outrageous—lower taxes, higher wages, land reform, and so on. It was only after violence had erupted that they began placing emphasis on overthrowing the government and, in the words of one mystic leader of Negros at the turn of the century, forming a "communistic paradise."[26]

Describing followers of Entrencherado, self-proclaimed "Emperor of the Philippines" and leader of one of the many colorum movements, the *Manila Tribune* of May 18, 1927, noted: "Some enlisted from ignorance. . . . Another small portion joined for plunder and power. . . . The greater portion [however] joined for revenge of accumulated wrongs and pent-up grievances . . . between the rich and the poor."[27]

Owing in part, perhaps, to the country's diffuse island geography, the government failed to pay heed to the rebellion until it had taken deep root among the Philippine people. When the authorities did respond, they did not address the people's basic grievances but applied repressive measures that deflated the insurrections without eliminating their underlying causes. Violent confrontation became part of the pattern, triggered not so much by the movements themselves as by government efforts to contain the spread of discontent. Reform never extended beyond the sphere of rhetoric.

By attacking the movements piecemeal, identifying and destroying their leaders, the government broke them down and isolated them from their mass base. Leaders were played off against one another; bribery, deceit, and treachery were commonly used tactics. After a period of tumult, the government suppressed the rebellion, and the rebels merged back into the fabric of rural society.[28]

The Huk rebellion of the 1940s and 1950s, the immediate precursor to the current insurrection, was also part of this historical framework. As with the previous struggles, the Huk revolt had a twisted past. It first emerged after 1941 as the Hukbalahaps, or People's Anti-Japanese Army (the Hukbo ng Bayan laban Hapon). Later, after forming an alliance with the Manila-based Philippine Communist Party (Partido Komunista ng Pilipinas, or PKP), it became known as the HMB, or People's Liberation Army (the Hukbong Mapaspalaya ng Bayan). But Huk origins lie in the rural terrain of peasant movements that prevailed in the 1930s.

Luis Taruc, at one time the Huk supremo, was a peasant from Pampanga Province in central Luzon who often seemed more content to commune with nature than lead a Communist agrarian revolution.[29] Like the Sakdalistas, the Huks struggled against an indigenous elite —but with a precise set of objectives: agrarian reform and political power. The Huks peaked in 1951, even threatening to invade Manila, but they slowly faded away as their members tired of the struggle against an increasingly effective counterinsurgency campaign led by the charismatic defense secretary (and later president) Ramon Magsaysay. A few remained in the hills and formed part of the nucleus of the NPA several years later.

World War II provided some respite for the peasants, as wartime conditions helped loosen the landlords' control over them. Peasant participation in the anti-Japanese guerrilla movement and the prospect of national independence from American rule following the war offered some hope of political power. This hope was quickly dashed in 1946, when congressmen elected under the peasant- and Communist-supported Democratic Alliance banner were expelled from the new congress. This paralleled to some degree the situation in the 1987 congressional elections, when leftist candidates under the People's party (Partido ng Bayan, or PNB) found broad electoral support for their cause, but not enough to ensure their election votes. Overall, the peasants' lot was not improving.

The postwar period brought an acceleration of previous trends, as Philippine agriculture became more commercialized. Capital demands of modern agriculture—with its fertilizers, insecticides, and so forth —increased peasant dependence on moneylenders, placing them in greater bondage. In the 1960s peasant society became more differentiated, consisting of smallholders, large tenants, small tenants, and non-agricultural laborers.[30]

Differentiation was a sign of social decay, not progress. Although agricultural productivity increased between 1970 and 1980, it did not benefit the peasants. In the 1980s productivity then began to decline, becoming negative in 1983. By 1985, of the estimated 62 percent of all Filipinos in rural areas, 63 percent lived below the poverty line. In urban areas 52 percent were poor.[31] The land-reform program had proven to be more rhetoric than reality: 61 percent of farms were smaller than three hectares, accounting for only 24 percent of arable land. High population growth continued to reduce farm size and constrict incomes. Economic policies, such as capital-intensive industrialization, provided few opportunities for surplus labor. As one scholar has noted, "Philippine economic growth has been characterized by very little mobility into the elite and a lack of diffusion of entrepreneurial skills."[32]

The lack of mobility and the failure of economic policies to promote a large middle class were not the only consequences of economic developments in the latter part of the twentieth century. Equally important was the concentration of elites in Manila, who in effect turned their backs on their rural roots. This hindered provincial cultural cohesion and the effectiveness of local government. In addition, the pattern of economic and population growth created a larger pool of discontented rural workers.

Economic growth in the Philippines had always been regionally segmented. For example, Cagayan prospered with tobacco in the eighteenth century, Bicol with abaca in the nineteenth, Negros and Panay with sugar in the early twentieth, and Mindanao with timber, mining, and fruit products in the late twentieth century. This regional and time-specific development spawned "a series of distinct regional elites with divergent, if not conflicting, economic interests."[33] Arguably, it contributed, too, to the lack of national identity that afflicted Filipino consciousness.[34] It also meant that local political elites could wield national political power through both the purse and the ballot box.

But this pattern of economic segmentation began to change in the 1950s and 1960s, as economic policies favoring agricultural commercialization and industrialization lured elites away from the provinces toward Manila, where they could more easily secure access to credit and other important commercial tools (such as import licenses). Rather than broadening the economic class base of society, the new growth

TABLE I.I
Top Filipino Families' Shares of Nation's Income

Year	Percentage of Nation's Total Income
1956	27.0[a]
1961	28.9[a]
1971	52.9[b]
1975	55.0[b]
1980	58.0[b]
1983	58.8[b]
1985	37.0[a]

a. Top 10 percent of Filipino families.
b. Top 20 percent of Filipino families.
Sources: World Bank, *The Philippines: Recent Trends in Poverty, Employment and Wages* (Washington, D.C., June 20, 1985), 16; Thomas C. Nowak, "Class and Clientelist Systems in the Philippines: The Basis for Instability" (Ph.D. diss., Cornell University, 1974), 103. National Economic Development Authority, *Highlights of the Draft Medium-Term Philippine Development Plan, 1987–1992* (Manila, October 1986), 12.

increasingly concentrated wealth among a few. A 1974 study found that the top 15 percent of stockholding families controlled 84.3 percent of the corporate assets, and a study of income shares (see table 1.1) shows a continuation of this trend.[35]

Elite families did not completely forsake their rural roots but maintained political control by leaving some family members in the provinces. This system, however, began to disintegrate after Marcos declared martial law in 1972. Marcos also worked at concentrating even more economic decisions in Manila, by which he could reward his friends and punish his enemies,[36] destroying the rural political machines that threatened his power.

The isolation of elites from their roots had begun even before martial law, which then accelerated the process and exacerbated rural anomie. The breakdown of an implicit social contract between the elites and the peasantry whereby the landlord (or patron) cared for his peasants (or clients) was apparent at least by the 1930s, when peasant discontent was partially attributed to "landlord urbanization and declining involvement with former tenant-clients."[37] Landlords were in essence commercializing their ties with their serfs without giving them the means to commercialize themselves in turn as blue- or white-collar workers. They remained serfs but without the previous security of cultural values that had stressed the landlord's responsibilities to his tenants.

So long as there were frontier areas with arable land to absorb additional population growth, a system in which the elites stayed rich and the poor stayed poor could be stable, inequitable though it was. But rather than remaining constant, the social chasm between the Manila-based elite and the mass of Filipino peasantry widened as the economy was modernized and the population grew, putting increasing pressure on the traditional feudal system. This was especially evident in rural areas. The failure of several attempts at land reform, including one under Marcos, resulted in even more unfavorable land distribution, with most of the rural population gaining no access to land. High population growth also led to further reductions in farm size and greater use of land unsuitable for cultivation. Large-scale deforestation weakened the rural ecosystem, and economic policies promoting capital-intensive industrialization reduced opportunities for labor.[38]

Although growth rates of real gross domestic product averaged 6 percent per annum in the 1970s, growth did not improve the lot of the poor, whose numbers multiplied.[39] In the 1980s, with lower economic growth rates and thus fewer benefits to distribute among more people, the social system became less capable of coping with the increasing tension. This failure was one reason Marcos could not capture a victory in the February 1986 presidential elections despite an enormous expenditure of funds and other rewards: the trickle-down approach did not trickle far enough.

Another reason for the system's collapse that can be attributed to elite dominance was the erosion of government effectiveness. Central government control has historically been weak in the Philippines,[40] despite efforts by the Americans to improve it. But weak central government did not translate into strong local government. The local government was actually weaker, since the central government held the right to collect taxes and distribute revenues. Once wealth was transported to the capital it was almost impossible to return it to the provinces, in part because of the weak provincial bureaucracies, thus perpetuating a cycle of local-government poverty.

The state of government in the 1970s and 1980s recalled conditions during the Philippine-American War of 1898 to 1903, when "rampant graft and corruption characterized the administration of many a municipality, exacerbating the grievances of the peasant masses and contributing to their radicalization." Again, despite positive growth rates, the central government did not invest in local government at high enough levels to keep pace with the expanding population base. A deterioration in local government capabilities was an obvious consequence. Another effect was a further loss of legitimacy for the national political system with the closing of the "civil service frontier"—that is, career opportunities in the national bureaucracy, a traditional outlet for surplus labor.[41] Because government jobs were no longer available, support for the government began to weaken. At the same time, Marcos's efforts to disenfranchise competing power centers, coupled with the increasing concentration of elite interests in Manila, removed protection for the peasants. This vacuum provided an opportunity for the Communists to establish themselves in rural areas.

Economic development patterns helped create a large pool of rural unemployed and/or landless poor. By the mid-1970s the rural landless (people without land to live on or to farm) accounted for a significant portion of the population, at least 3.5 million. By 1987 they numbered an estimated 6 to 8 million, according to U.S. aid officials. The existence of such a large group of disenfranchised poor was another signal of the breakdown of social cohesion in rural areas.

A study of central Luzon by Pilar Jimenez and Josefa Francisco in the late 1970s concluded that "the most important underlying factor in the decline of armed peasant movements is the emergence of a fast-growing new class within the village—the landless labourers."[42] The authors argued that the landless constituted in effect a new class that exacerbated intravillage tensions, making it difficult for outside revolutionaries to mobilize the village as a group. Yet by the 1980s even central Luzon was the scene of Communist activity. Clearly the landless rural poor have added a new dimension to conflict; they have become a source of cannon fodder for both sides in the insurgency. The government draws on them to form anti-Communist vigilante groups, and the NPA draws on them for its assassination teams and regular forces.

A 1984 study by the same authors of the rural poor in Leyte found that most were landless farmers, working as tenants or leaseholders, while an increasing proportion were forced to migrate to upland or urban areas. "The poor generally do not have access to social services in health, nutrition, and education; their households continue to exhibit poor health, malnutrition, and little education. Institutional services in terms of extension services do not as a whole reach most of them because of poor physical infrastructure and limited manpower in the extension agencies."[43] The existence of the rural poor signified not so much a restructuring of social classes as a failure of society to maintain effective local government.

Thus, the environment for revolution was a long time in the making and not a direct result of Marcos's rule, although his regime undoubtedly enhanced the spread of revolution. The strongman had helped destroy the social equilibrium by permitting one group to dominate the resource allocation system. He and his cronies controlled the distribution of all the rewards, creating regional inequalities and encouraging indifference and greed. They upset the delicate balance by going beyond what was considered *delicadeza*. Ultimately, this monopoly formed an environment susceptible to the explosive situation that led to Marcos's overthrow.

But the factors that caused Marcos's fall should not be confused with those that contributed to the rise of the NPA, whose insurgency continues despite Marcos's absence. Marcos was deposed because he upset the balance among members of the Manila elite; the NPA are revolting against a society that permits the elites to exist. The same problem now afflicts the post-Marcos Philippine government's efforts to stabilize the situation as it attempts to replicate the apparent social equilibrium of the past. In the past, reforms were promised but not implemented. As the momentum of uprisings dissipated under repressive action, the government was able to avoid change.

The cyclical pattern of rebellion encouraged a certain complacency among the ruling elite and contempt for the peasantry. Peasants were seen as petulant children, easily manipulated by a few charismatic leaders.[44] The elites adopted the rhetoric of change out of political expediency and self-preservation, with no real commitment to reform. The continued failure to cope with peasant frustration has bred ongoing discontent.

The peasants, however, still see the struggle in less secular terms. Some are not even aware of the presence of American military bases. Said one NPA soldier, "The purpose of the movement is to get a smooth flow in society" — still engaging, in other words, in the traditional quest for a spiritual wholeness.[45] Thematic continuities are a peculiar function of Philippine culture with its distinctive system of social relations.

The Cultural Context

Philippine society, then, had been in a state of revolt or internal war long before the 1968 creation of the Communist Party of the Philippines. Historically, elites had been able to repress revolutionary momentum but had never been able to eliminate the source of discontent, because to do so would have eroded their own power base. Thus, corrective action in response to peasant complaints was precluded. But the revolutionary impulse was sustained by factors indigenous to Philippine culture and religion.

Philippine behavior is popularly seen as being based on an intricate value system emphasizing reciprocity among individuals and the smooth functioning of personal relations. The kinship circle that facilitated the expansion of cults is based on blood ties and ritual kin relations. Effective blood ties extend to the third cousin through both parents, creating a series of overlapping family circles. Identity is established within this "we-they" network of extended familial ties that induces Filipinos to act in concert rather than alone.[46] Likewise, the culture encourages Filipinos to perceive the world as hostile so that safety can be found only by belonging to a "strong in-group." Individual relations are governed by a value system that has commonly, although perhaps inaccurately, been characterized by the acronym SIR, for "smooth interpersonal relations."[47]

The basis for Filipino interaction is often viewed as determined by four concepts: *utang na loób*, *pakikisama*, *amor propio*, and *hiya*. The first, *utang na loób*, or debt of prime obligation, refers to a system of social exchange in which one person offers something, not requested, to another, who then incurs a debt that must be repaid. To have the offer of aid refused is to incur *hiya*, or shame, and thus the offer is not made unless it is sure to be accepted. Shame acts as a sanction on behavior. The system of *pakikisama*, or getting along together, requires concern for *amor propio*, or personal dignity and esteem of others, so that damage is not caused to individual honor. This system of mutual ties overlays and overlaps the kinship system. Thus, the social system encourages cooperation both vertically and horizontally. But it is fragmented cooperation, among individuals rather than groups, favoring particularistic behavior and dyadic alliances and making the concept of national welfare difficult to accept. The culture tends to isolate groups; rather than bridging social gulfs it increases social distance, with cooperation among individuals intensifying rather than reducing conflict between individual alliances. As George Guthrie has remarked, "severe want and poverty do not produce cooperation but rather seem to encourage indifference and greed."[48]

Such selfish behavior is not surprising when one views the society dynamically rather than in the static terms characterized by the SIR concept. Some Philippine social science research "pictures groups living in fear for their safety and fighting for survival amid eternal conflict." Ideally, dyadic ties have given elites the means to control the peasants, while the peasants have benefited from a "system of personal exchange."[49] The system has been in constant tension and has repeatedly broken down, partly for economic reasons. The commune-style system promoted by millenarian movements can thus be seen as the peasantry's reaction to the negative effects of a social system that encourages selfish behavior and conflict.

The culture also promotes a virulent struggle for power among individuals as they fight to raise their status. Higher status confers greater control over resources and hence greater rewards. Elites distribute benefits downward through their particular in-group and vie for a share of distributable resources to ensure the continued allegiance of their supporters. So long as the political system permits change, no group is able to dominate the resource base. Elites become skilled at distributing benefits rather than at promoting social change because change alters the balance of power in society. Thus, politics and economics have become intertwined in the Philippines.

As the long history of religion-based rebel movements testifies, Philippine religion—Catholicism inlaid with traditional beliefs—also provides a sophisticated channel for expressing discontent. Religious themes, often utopian, have exerted a strong influence on Philippine life since the introduction of Christianity by the Spanish in the sixteenth century. The Catholic church allowed the peasantry the means of channeling discontent through charismatic, Christ-like leaders who promised salvation through allegiance to them and gave their adherents a sense of identity and status. The theme of salvation was easily absorbed into a more secular nationalist movement during the nineteenth century, linking issues of poverty and injustice to independence from colonial rule. Ironically, the Catholic church, whose large estates were the source of some peasant grievances under Spanish rule, also gave the peasants the liturgy for revolution. It is ironic, too, that the conservative church of the nineteenth century became a force for dynamic change in the latter part of the twentieth century with the introduction of liberation theology.

The Passion texts in particular speak to the Philippine peasant experience. Rather than promoting docility and acceptance of the status quo, they propose a separation from one's family by joining a rebel leader. Jesus is a subversive figure who teaches the peasantry to form a brotherhood through commitment to a cause. Social status based on wealth and education has no value in such a brotherhood; having a "beautiful loób" (soul) is all important.[50] The search for kalayaan (independence) has become the society's motivating force, providing a means of reestablishing a previously disturbed social equilibrium and recovering an idealized pre-Spanish condition of wholeness.

Although the importance of religious themes in peasant rebellions may have diminished during the twentieth century, they have not been extinguished. The theme of the Passion story, for example, still gives the peasantry a language for understanding their social condition and a rationale for questioning their fate. The strength of religious traditions even in the current Communist insurgency shows in the CPP's efforts to distance itself from past insurrections by portraying its Communist revolution as one of the proletariat and by attacking efforts to interpret the movement in less secular themes.

Although the Communist insurgency has criticized the Katipunan insurrection of 1896 as a "national-democratic revolution of the old type" whose leadership did not possess a "proletarian ideology" and has disparaged the Huk leaders as "the black bourgeois gang . . . [who] kept on sabotaging the people's war,"[51] the present uprising has been more effective than previous rebellions because of its ability to draw on the strength of the religious and secular themes of the past. The potency of the Philippine revolutionary tradition comes from the mingling of these two strains of thought, the spiritual search for liberation and the political search for independence, into the overarching quest for a Filipino identity.

Founded by Manilan intellectuals—descendants in a sense of the *ilustrado* (enlightened) elites of Spanish times—the CPP has created a formidable national organization whose strength is in the rural areas. Today it deliberately aims to bridge the historical gap between the ilustrado-influenced Katipunan and the peasant-based Huks, claiming their movement is led by the "Filipino working class."[52] The current insurgency draws consciously on the nationalist frustration of the elites and unconsciously on traditional peasant yearnings for utopia. Even in the postcolonial period independence from American domination remains a central theme of the CPP's leaders, who often refer to the need to free the Philippines from the "IMF–World Bank–U.S.–Marcos Dictatorship." In effect, the Communist political cadres are continuing the secular tradition of past bourgeois struggles for nationalism,[53] whereas their followers are responsive to the implicit religious themes of personal liberation.

A complex structural and behavioral force fuels the insurgency. Deteriorating political and economic conditions have been influential but are not the only contributors to the conflict. The rapid economic growth experienced by the Philippines in the 1970s was followed by a significant decline in the early 1980s, culminating in negative growth rates in 1984 and 1985. "By 1986 real wages had been falling for a period of 18 years," observes economist Richard Hooley. "In terms of magnitude this decline is surely impressive: a fall of 50 percent or more from the peak reached in the early sixties to a level *below* that of the thirties and only a little higher than the level of 1903. . . . This is the only period in Philippine history in which real per capita income rises consistently while real wages are falling."[54] Figure 1.1 depicts this trend since the Huk rebellion peaked in the early 1950s.

Clearly, too, the political and social systems were becoming dysfunctional under Marcos's authoritarian rule. Social conflict surfaced among elites and between elites and other social strata, and the government's ineffectiveness at suppressing rebellion spurred the conflict's

FIGURE I.I.
*Real Wages and National Income Trends in the Philippines. Source:
Derived from statistics collated by the National Economic
Development Authority,* Philippine Statistical Yearbook *(Manila).*

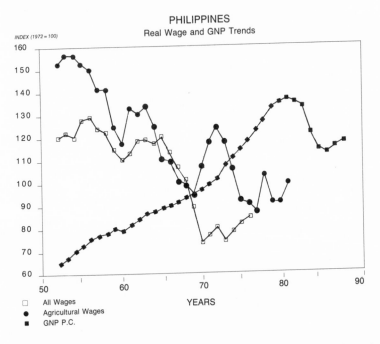

PHILIPPINES
Real Wage and GNP Trends

INDEX (1972 = 100)

☐   All Wages
●   Agricultural Wages
■   GNP P.C.

YEARS

growth. Idiosyncratic variables, such as the appearance of charismatic revolutionary leaders imbued with Marxist rhetoric, also played a role.

But the reason primus inter pares for rebellion in the Philippines is the historical Filipino search for a national identity. Emilio Aguinaldo expressed that yearning when he once said: "Let us leave behind all these parties and other things that cripple our unity, and let us all be one name—Filipinos—a sign that we are one nation, one loób, one Katipunan."[55]

Benigno Aquino's death in August 1983 seemed to bring about just such a welding together of the nation. In the heavy heat of Manila's typhoon season rich and poor passed by the open coffin to see the decomposing body: the dried blood caked on Aquino's clothes, the bullet hole in his head with its exit hole in his chin. From Tarlac to Manila the coffin was paraded. The final funeral procession from Santo Domingo Church in Quezon City to the Manila Memorial Park cemetery took eleven hours because of the crowds, most of whom were poor city dwellers. At the funeral mass Corazon Aquino spoke to great applause, saying in part: "Ninoy, who loved you, the Filipino people, is now loved in turn."

Through his death Aquino, an elite scion, became a martyr to the poor. During his widow's presidential campaign, she drew on the same source for her support. Her obvious deep personal faith, simplicity of dress and manner, and serenity in the midst of turmoil were strongly appealing. In one sense she was an instrument of the people's revenge against the Marcos regime; in another, she offered the promise of a new Philippine society. She told the people, "I don't seek vengeance, only justice, not only for Ninoy, but also for the suffering Filipino people. . . . Join me," she said, "in my crusade for truth, justice and freedom. . . . Think less of ourselves, think more of our country."[56] These, too, are the themes of the Communist insurgency and a source of its popular appeal. President Aquino's failure to deliver on these promises after Marcos had been toppled could once again strengthen the country's revolutionary forces—in particular, the Communist Party of the Philippines.

2 Origins of the Communist Party of the Philippines

In the years preceding the overthrow of Ferdinand Marcos, the Communist Party of the Philippines (CPP) became a formidable political and military force. *Ang Bayan* (*Nation*), the CPP's official newspaper, reported in December 1984 that over thirty thousand Filipinos were members of the party and that the New People's Army (NPA) had twenty thousand troops with ten thousand high-powered rifles active on fifty-nine guerrilla fronts in fifty provinces. Additionally, there were more than six thousand barrio revolutionary mass organizations and more than sixty thousand national democratic mass activists. This assessment was substantiated by American defense officials.

The American assistant secretary of defense for international security affairs, Richard Armitage, testified in November 1985 that the CPP controlled or influenced about 20 percent of the Philippine population, and in testimony in June 1986 he reported that the "NPA remains a serious threat to the Philippine Government, with a strength of more than twenty-two thousand five hundred armed troops and fifteen support personnel."[1] Estimates in 1987 placed NPA strength at 24,400.

These figures indicate the organizational effectiveness of the CPP, which in 1969 had only a few armed supporters.[2] Indeed, present figures underestimate the military potency of the CPP, as its definition of armed forces refers only to combat personnel. They also underestimate the CPP's strength, especially among its mass base, since the organization of military units is predicated upon first developing a local stronghold. Since its formation in 1968, the CPP has grown steadily and systematically from a core base of eleven,[3] to a large organization with military forces spread throughout the archipelago to almost all the major island groups, including the distant island of Palawan. Unlike previous revolutionary movements, the CPP did not try to ignite a false fire that would quickly spend its flames. By emphasizing political mobilization of a mass base, the party hoped instead to stoke the fires of rebellion sufficiently to withstand efforts to extinguish it.

The CPP and the Huks

The organization and leadership of the CPP are descended from the Hukbalahap movement, which developed out of the agrarian reform and urban socialist movements of the 1920s and 1930s. Gradually these movements had coalesced into the Hukbalahaps and the Philippine Communist Party (Partido Komunista ng Pilipinas, or PKP), which in turn formed an alliance in the early 1940s and 1950s. There are many points of comparison between the PKP-Huk and the CPP-NPA organizations.

The difference between the PKP and the Huks is exemplified in the background of their leaders: Luis Taruc, the Huk supremo, was a peasant from Pampanga, whereas the Lava brothers (Vicente, Jose, and Jesus), leaders of the PKP, were well-educated members of a wealthy Bulacan landowning family. (The question of who controlled whom is still open to debate.)[4] A similar comparison can be made between the CPP's and the NPA's founders: Jose Maria Sison, the CPP's leader, was a university lecturer, and Commander Dante of the NPA, a peasant. The PKP and the Huks cooperated closely, but their objectives never entirely coincided, and in the mid-1950s, after many in the PKP's Politburo had been captured, the alliance broke apart. The recombination of the urban socialists with peasant movements made possible the rejuvenation of the Philippine Communist movement under the CPP after 1968. Unlike the PKP-Huks, the CPP-NPA has proven to be stronger than the personalities of its founders.

The CPP's foundation however, was also marked by some of the ideological currents of nationalism that distinguished the Huk-PKP alliance. Although neither the CPP nor the PKP originated this sentiment, they drew on it for some of their ideological strength. Numerous labor and peasant groups formed during the early Commonwealth period were reflective of the power of personality, and consequently factionalism, in Philippine politics. In many instances elites manipulated these groups as part of the "new national pastimes of electoral maneuvering,"[5] following the creation in 1935 of a commonwealth to govern the Philippines during a ten-year transition to independence. But a second nationalist tradition was also current—that of the *Propagandistas* and *Filibusteros* of the nineteenth century.

The Filibusteros risked death or exile for advocating independence from Spain. Jose Rizal's novel *El Filibusterismo* (*The Subversive*) popularized the term and the movement. Rizal, along with Marcelo H. del Pilar and Lopez Jaena, was a leading member of the Propaganda movement—a group of ilustrado reformists who, though not advocating secession as did the Filibusteros, agitated for political reform.[6] Indeed, the Spanish inability to distinguish between the two led to Rizal's execution and consequent martyrdom because of a mistaken belief that he was a revolutionary Katipunan—and just as he was about to join Spanish forces as a doctor in the Spanish-American War.

The urban intellectuals and union organizers of the twentieth century were the spiritual descendants of the Filibusteros and Propagandistas. Because many writers also were printers, the printing trade became a focus of union organizing and radical nationalist thought. Crisanto Evangelista, the PKP's founder, helped establish a printers' union in 1906 and in 1913 a labor movement, the Philippine Labor Congress (Congress Obrero de Filipinas, or COF). Only later—after he had visited the United States as a member of the first Philippine Independence mission in 1919—did he convert to Marxism.[7]

Still, Evangelista did not immediately establish a Communist party. First he attempted to run for political office as a member of the Nacionalista party. When he failed to be nominated, he and others established their own party, the Labor Party of the Philippines (Partido Obrero de Filipinas), in 1924. After Evangelista was ousted from the COF in 1929, he formed the Congress of Philippine Workingmen (Katipunan ng mga Anak–Pawis ng Pilipinas, or KAP) dedicated to implementing a "Soviet system in the Philippines."[8] At an organizing conference in August 1930 this group became the basis for the PKP, which a year later was banned and its leaders arrested.

Concurrently, another ilustrado, Pedro Abad Santos, whose large legal practice in Pampanga aided the peasants, founded the Socialist party in 1929. Santos had been a young man during the Propaganda movement, later serving with the revolutionaries in the Philippine-American War. The Americans imprisoned him—a key event in his life that confirmed his animosity toward American rule. The Pampanguenos constituted his political power base, which enabled his party to win eight congressional seats in the 1940 elections. By this time Luis Taruc was the party's general secretary. Abad Santos organized the peasants and rural workers for mass actions—protests and strikes—declaring in words later echoed in the CPP's policy of self-criticism, "Every strike must be a school, even if it is lost."[9] Although the Socialist party established for the first time a "viable form of secular radicalism,"[10] it was still a political organization based on personal ties and largely the creation of Abad Santos. In October 1938 the PKP and the Socialist party merged.[11]

Members of Abad Santos's entourage disagreed with the decision to unite with the PKP. They opposed it because they believed that Communist "godlessness" would antagonize the peasantry and that Abad Santos's position in the new coalition would be secondary.[12] Although the reason for the merger may be of only historical note, the rather abrupt and uncharacteristic action suggested the difficulties that lay ahead for the coalition. Combining a Pampangueno peasant-based protest movement mainly interested in tenancy reform with a more ideologically oriented, outlawed, urban, intellectual group was difficult.

The onset of World War II delayed the appearance of inevitable schisms within the new PKP. Both Evangelista and Abad Santos were arrested by the Japanese. Evangelista was executed, and Abad Santos died in 1945 after a long illness. Vicente Lava succeeded as the party's chief executive with Luis Taruc becoming chairman of a military department that was organized as the People's Anti-Japanese Army (Hukbo ng Bayan Laban sa Hapon). By the war's end, estimates of Huk forces ranged from ninety-five hundred to twelve thousand.

Although the Huks were active in the war, their size and contribution have been exaggerated, and their targets were not always the Japanese. Peasants joined for protection from the Japanese, the local police and Philippine Constabulary, bandits, and landlords. Some enlisted for nationalist reasons; others, because friends or relatives were members. Following Lava's replacement as a party executive for his disastrous decision to "retreat for defense" by dividing Huk units into small bands in an effort to escape through Japanese lines, the PKP, meeting in September 1944, decided to change the Huks from an anti-Japanese guerrilla group to a movement for broad political reform.[13]

Yet the Huks did not emerge from the war, as did others elsewhere in

Southeast Asia, as a nationalist revolutionary force seeking to liberate their country from all foreign oppressors. The Huks actively aided the U.S. war effort and welcomed the American liberators. But the Americans arrested the Huk leaders in early 1945, including Taruc, and tried to disarm their men. Despite this, and symptomatic of the primacy of personality over ideology in traditional Philippine politics, a "Democratic Alliance" was formed in July 1945 of Communists and liberals on an anticollaboration platform, proclaiming support for the Nacionalista party in the 1946 presidential elections.[14]

The main target of the alliance was Manuel Roxas, the Liberal party's presidential candidate, who had collaborated with the Japanese but was cleared by Gen. Douglas MacArthur. With MacArthur's blessing, Roxas won the 1946 election, defeating Sergio Osmeña.[15] The Huks emerged as a revolutionary force against this postwar backdrop of extreme political animosity, a ready supply of weapons, and economic deprivation. Peasant earnings did not reach prewar levels in absolute terms until the early 1950s; thus they experienced a substantial decline in real terms—a situation comparable to that of agrarian income in the 1980s.[16] Given the history of grievances, especially in central Luzon, and the conditions then prevailing, it would have been strange if rebellion had not broken out.

Rebellion was not immediate, though. Taruc and others, including Jesus Lava, won congressional seats as Democratic Alliance members in the 1946 election, though they were not allowed to take their seats by the elite-controlled government. In August 1946 one of the Huk leaders, Juan Feleo, while under military police escort, was murdered, and by the end of that year, the peasants were rejoining the Huks and rebellion was spreading. Presaging the formation in 1986 of anti-Communist vigilante groups, the Philippine Constabulary went on "Huk hunts" with the private guards of local officials and "spread terror throughout local populations.[17] Still, despite these provocations, the PKP, then under Pedro Castro, continued to emphasize the "legal struggle" over the "armed struggle," even supporting some of Roxas's candidates in the 1947 election. Only after the party and the Huks were declared illegal in March 1948 and the Lava brothers, Jose and Jesus, had wrested party control from Castro in May did the focus shift back toward armed struggle.[18]

This strategic shift can be too easily attributed to ideological considerations, if one forgets that the Lava brothers themselves had earlier favored a coalition with the Nacionalistas.[19] More probably, ideology was used as a justification by the Lavas, first, to regain control of an apparatus they thought was theirs by natural right and, second, as a means of continuing their struggle against their bitter enemies, the collaborationists, represented by President Roxas and his successor, Elpidio Quirino.

The party under the Lavas also had difficulty in differentiating between its own interest in developing a proletariat movement based on the Manila trade unions and the peasants' interest in ending repression and procuring agrarian reform. As interviews among both peasants and party cadres showed, little connection was made between their plight and American imperialism.[20] Nevertheless, partly because of Roxas's close ties to the Americans, the PKP made freedom from imperialist domination an objective.

Perhaps the PKP leadership never really wanted to build a mass party. The Lava brothers and their supporters were enamored with the *form* of revolution, the dialectical rhetoric, rather than the actuality of warfare.[21] The PKP Politburo remained based in Manila partly because Jose Lava, who worked as a clerk in the Philippine National Bank, refused to join his troops. But on October 18, 1950, the Politburo was discovered and arrested by government forces. In December 1952 the Central Committee officially renounced armed struggle in favor of legal, parliamentary means.

Thus, the peasant rebels were abandoned in the field, and the revolution was left to Luis Taruc. Although the Huks changed their name to the People's Liberation Army (Hukbong Mapagpalaya ng Bayan, or HMB), they remained more interested in settling scores with local tyrants and effecting some measure of political and economic reform than in overthrowing the central government (although at one point they were able briefly to capture the provincial capital of Nueva Ecija).[22]

By 1951 the Huk armed struggle was losing momentum as a new defense minister, Ramon Magsaysay, toured the provinces promising change. The military became more effective in tracking Huk units to their hideouts, repression of the peasants declined, and the 1951 congressional elections—which were supervised by the military—provided an opportunity for peaceful political change. Because of the new government programs and military reforms of the time, it would seem that government actions were instrumental in defeating the Huks. But it is still unclear what really brought about their downfall. Were they destroyed or did the peasants just abandon their struggle temporarily?

Clearly some reforms were implemented by the government. When the military was reorganized in 1950, the Philippine Constabulary (its reputation weakened by human rights abuses) was integrated into the regular armed forces and its primary responsibility for the campaign against the Huks given to the army. The army too was reorganized and increased in size. Command changes permitted young officers with actual combat experience to be promoted. Small units were deployed: seven-man Scout Ranger teams collected intelligence, set up ambushes, and conducted psychological warfare against the Huks.[23] Magsaysay inspired his men, promoting, demoting, and decorating them in the field. If after being named defense secretary, he had not implemented these command changes, the military might have collapsed under the weight of its own ineptitude.

Still, military operations in themselves contributed the least to defeating the Huks. Most important was the confidence Magsaysay exuded and the spirit of reform he represented that offered an alternative to rebellion. The military provided medical services in the rural areas, and the office of the Judge Advocate General gave legal advice to tenant farmers. An Economic Development Corps (EDCOR) was established to resettle surrendering Huks, and although only about 20 percent of those so designated were really Huks, the program had considerable impact. The hallmark of the Magsaysay program was well-publicized small projects, such as health clinics, extension services, wells, and roads, although they appeared more important than they actually were.[24] The United States aided the effort, providing weapons, training, and funds to the military, including monies to purchase weapons from surrendering rebels. The well-digging program was also funded by the Americans, and the U.S. Information Service organized the military's psychological warfare and public relations programs. American military officers even went on combat operations as "noncombatant observers." All these efforts dampened enthusiasm for rebellion.

That elites never understood the need for substantive reform to disrupt the cycle of conflict is apparent from their approach to the Huk rebellion. Although Magsaysay reorganized the military and inaugurated showcase programs that gave the appearance of reform, they were never implemented on a broad enough scale to make fundamental change possible. And the EDCOR program, the medical teams, and legal aid were merely effective public relations efforts. None of the changes entailed structural reform. Magsaysay probably never intended real change, for like other elites, he was concerned more with appearance than substance. Ultimately the "reforms" only deepened the peasants' suspicion of the government and fanned their discontent with social conditions.

Most important in defeating the rebellion, however, were the Huks' own problems, stemming from a variety of sources: The military's psychological warfare effort fostered mutual suspicion within the rebel leadership (in some ways paralleling problems in the CPP's Mindanao Regional Commission in 1985 when government infiltrators were discovered). The Huk killing in April 1949 of Manuel Quezon's widow weakened their popular image. The appearance of a seemingly more legitimate government made it harder for the Huks to justify their rebellion. Government pressure contributed to the Huks' battle fatigue, their weariness with the decade-long conflict. And finally, the Politburo's capture in October 1950 effectively split the movement's leadership in half, isolating forces in the field.[25] Although the problems that had caused the rebellion had not been resolved, the Huks could not adapt their tactics and strategy to a changed environment. In an important sense, they defeated themselves.

Units of the Huks remained, however, although most reverted to simple banditry (later becoming the basis for the NPA). And the PKP, now under Jesus Lava, remained active in intellectual circles but with so little impact it was possible for one American scholar to write in 1966 that "today there are few socialists among Filipinos."[26] But there was considerable ferment beneath the apparent normality. Out of the intellectual fervor on Philippine campuses in the 1960s emerged the Communist Party of the Philippines.

Formation of the CPP

The roots of the CPP lay in the remnants of the PKP and in the deeper tradition from which the PKP itself had emerged—that of the Filibusteros and Propagandistas. The student leaders of the 1960s who were the CPP's founding fathers had spent their formative years in the 1950s under the tutelage of the venerable senator Claro Recto.[27] Many had worked on his 1957 presidential campaign with Sen. Lorenzo Tanada of the Nationalist Citizens' party (Lapiang Makabansa).

Recto had acquired his strong nationalist credentials during the period of the Commonwealth as had many Philippine politicians. Attacks on the United States and demands for independence were the standard repertoire of almost every aspiring Philippine leader in the prewar period. Anti-American rhetoric was used by the ilustrado elite to gain popular followings while they jockeyed for power without upsetting the status quo. But Recto did not survive the Japanese occupation as easily as some. He collaborated, serving briefly as secretary of education, health and public welfare.

Recto was not the only elite collaborator, but he was one of the few who were punished by the Americans. He and Jose P. Laurel, who had served as puppet president, were the most notable among those who were imprisoned and tried. Although Recto was granted amnesty in 1948, the experience embittered him toward the Americans, leaving an emotional scar similar to that of Abad Santos's.[28] When Recto tried to regain office in the 1949 elections, he lost and was unable to win a Senate seat until three years later. During the 1950s, he refined his anti-American attacks, condemning the continued presence in the islands of American military bases and charging the United States with neocolonialism, economic domination, and subversion of the political system. The neoimperialist themes he sounded are still popular among Philippine nationalists and the CPP.

Recto's influence was as important as external ideological influences in determining the agenda of the CPP. Jose Maria Sison, for example, the party's leading theoretician, was already active in student movements when, at twenty-three years of age, he made his first trip to Sukarno's Indonesia, where it is likely that he made contact with Indonesian Communist leaders.[29] Sison was the CPP's founder and, under the nom de guerre of "Amado Guerrero" (Beloved Warrior), the principal author of *Philippine Society and Revolution*, the essential theoretical basis for the CPP.[30] It was his early organizational work and his political disputes within nationalist circles that led to the formation of the CPP.

Jose Maria Sison ("Joema") was born into a middle-class family on February 8, 1939, in Cabugao, Ilocos Sur. His mother was a teacher, and his father, Salustino, who died in 1958, was part of the landed elite, growing maguey (a succulent fiber plant) on his plantation. An uncle became a bishop and a brother, a doctor, who emigrated to Los Angeles to practice. After graduating from Letran College in 1956 and then earning a B.A. cum laude from the University of the Philippines (UP) in 1960, Sison taught briefly at UP. Student politics was his primary occupation, however.[31] He was a man in search of an organization to lead.

In 1959 Sison, along with Francisco Nemenzo, later to be dean of the UP College of Arts and Sciences, formed the Students Cultural Association of UP (SCAUP) in order, according to Nemenzo, to promote Recto's nationalist ideas and attack American "imperialism." The group was created originally to counter charges of Communist leanings brought against the UP faculty by a retired Philippine military officer. The accusations had resulted in a controversial investigation by the Philippine House Committee on Anti-Filipino Activities.[32] Nevertheless, campus radicalism only increased.

The SCAUP group and others provided opportunities for a new generation of student radicals to interact with PKP members, spreading their views to other campuses. But the formation of the CPP did not logically progress out of this network. Sison was neither the only student leader nor the best liked, and controversy and factionalism followed him everywhere, much as it had other Philippine politicians.

In November 1964 Sison, Jose Lansang (dean of the Manila Lyceum School of Journalism), and other colleagues at the Lyceum, formed the Patriotic Youth (Kabataang Makabayan, or KM). The KM chose Andres Bonifacio as its patron saint because of his "proletarian revolutionary courage."[33] Sison also became vice president of the Workers or Labor party (Lapiang Manggagawa, or LM) founded by trade union organizer Ignacio Lacsina in 1962. Sison was trying to develop a broad-based national front through which he could dominate nationalist politics. With its principal theme of anti-Americanism, the KM organized anti–Lyndon Johnson demonstrations during the president's Manila visit in October 1966. Despite his initial success, however, Sison was forced out as its chairman in 1967.

Other important organizations in existence at this time were the

Bertrand Russell Peace Foundation; the MPKP (Malaysang Pagkakaisa ng Kabataang Pilipino; founded on remnants of the KM after Sison's expulsion); the MAN (Movement for the Advancement of Nationalism); and MASAKA (Malayang Samahang Magsasaka; a peasant group). In 1968, when the first issue of the CPP's paper *Ang Bayan* was published, it attacked some of these groups. A few of the organizations, especially MASAKA, had close ties to the PKP, but the others did not.[34] A consistent thread running through all these groups was Sison's effort to dominate them.

Sison succeeded in alienating both members of his own generation and older members of the PKP. A historical critique of the party was "commissioned" which Sison either wrote or helped prepare.[35] This critique excoriated the Lava family, tracing each brother's strategic failures and blaming them for the Huk defeat. But Lava supporters blocked the report's acceptance, and in April 1967 Sison was expelled from the PKP.[36]

In reaction Sison established an alternative Politburo, which, in its first public statement on May Day, 1967, hailed China's Cultural Revolution, condemned the Soviet Union, and depicted "the so-called 'Lava clique' as the bearers of modern revisionism in the Philippines." The May Day Statement, which came on the heels of several trips Sison made to China in 1966, was later broadcast by both the Hsiuhua News Agency and Radio Beijing.[37]

Sison continued participating in other political groups, serving as general secretary to MAN with Sen. Lorenzo Tanada as its chairman. But when Sison tried to gain additional power, he was opposed by moderates, such as Francisco Nemenzo. Later Sison claimed that MAN was an "instrument of the Lava revisionist renegades." Juan Tapales, a leading member of the Bertrand Russell Peace Foundation and the MPKP, attempted to mediate a peace between Nemenzo and Sison but was unsuccessful.[38] In early 1970 Sison founded yet another united nationalist front structure, the Movement for a Democratic Philippines, to replace MAN which had collapsed.[39]

Although the extent of Chinese and Soviet influence on both the PKP and the CPP is debated, it is known that the two countries' ties to the Philippine Communist movement were established in the 1920s.[40] Chinese military advisers were rumored to have helped the Huks during the Japanese occupation,[41] and both the Chinese and Soviets began actively promoting contacts with Filipinos in the early 1960s, when trade and cultural exchanges were encouraged.[42] In December 1965 Radio Beijing began broadcasting in Tagalog, a major dialect of central Luzon and the basis for the national language, Pilipino.[43] Nemenzo states that "Guerrero" (Sison) solicited Chinese support when he broke with the PKP in 1967 and that the PKP did not begin openly attacking Mao until 1971. Revisionist thinking within the CPP, according to Nemenzo, later concluded that the split with the PKP in 1967 had not been inevitable, again attesting to the importance of personality struggles over ideological factors in the movement's early days.[44]

Certainly Chinese Communism was the central ideological influence on the thinking of the CPP's founders, as indeed the thought of Mao Tse-tung influenced radicals worldwide. In its early years the party appended the letters "M-L" (for Marxist-Leninist) or the phrase "Mao Tse-tung Thought" to its name to differentiate itself from the PKP. *Quotations from Chairman Mao Tse-tung* (the *Little Red Book*) had recently been published internationally to great success, and the CPP adopted verbatim many of Mao's strictures. Thus there was no need for Filipinos to have had direct or even indirect contact with the Chinese to have been influenced by him.[45] The ideological divergence between the Soviet-oriented PKP and the Chinese-oriented CPP did not reflect the Sino-Soviet split or differences in doctrine so much as the CPP's need to justify its own existence, given the continued presence of the PKP. The PKP had a revolutionary history, whereas the CPP needed one.

In many ways the formation of the CPP was thus less a revolutionary response than an act of revenge against those who had opposed Sison. Rejected by mainstream radical groups, Sison had only one other to turn to: the peasants. After his expulsion from the PKP in April 1967, he and a small band meeting in an obscure barrio of Pangasinan Province formed the CPP on December 26, 1968. The movement would probably not have lasted long except for several fortuitous events.

First, the government's own actions radicalized society, which multiplied recruitment opportunities for the group. Without governmental repression and anticommunist hysteria, the CPP would likely have gone the way of the PKP under Jesus Lava—purveying cheap tracts and secret communiqués to members of a moribund organization. But in 1969 the Philippine Armed Forces (AFP) captured CPP documents that appeared to indicate that a new, more dangerous threat to national security loomed. The AFP's view of communism was extremely reactionary—a right-wing counterpart of the Philippine left's almost pathological obsession with the American CIA. The reasons for the AFP's attitude toward communism were both practical and imaginary. The AFP's early experiences with the Huks and later with the North Vietnamese in the Vietnam War, as well as their training under American military personnel, had contributed to a 1950s McCarthy-like perception of communism and the radical left. For that matter, some of the same views about student radicals were widely accepted in the United States, too. There was also a more practical consideration: the defense budget.

President Marcos had used Philippine involvement in the Vietnam War as leverage to procure more American military aid, but by 1969 this source of funds was drying up. A U.S. General Accounting Office report in 1973 declared that the Philippine government had not "provided adequate support for a number of years" to its own military.[46] The AFP thus seized upon the "threat" presented by the CPP to justify its demands for a larger share of the national budget. But by so publicizing the CPP—it went so far as to publish CPP documents that had not until then received wide circulation—the AFP mythologized the group, investing it with a revolutionary aura that only attracted more supporters.

The government fueled the fire further with a crackdown on mass actions in the Manila streets during late 1969 and early 1970. Students and workers—outraged by the fraud surrounding Marcos's winning an unprecedented second term in November 1969—had begun street demonstrations, aided in part, no doubt, by Marcos's political opponents in the Liberal party. Four demonstrators were killed on January 30, 1970, in the Battle of Mendiola (named after the Manila bridge where a major confrontation occurred). Rather than quieting the protests, the so-called First-Quarter Storm of 1970 further enraged the demonstrators and split the PKP between those advocating armed struggle and those favoring a parliamentary approach. Veteran Philippine journalist Eduardo Lachica wrote that the student riots never really endangered the government but only incited "momentary public hysteria." He also found, however, that CPP influence had spread deeply into the upper and middle classes of central Luzon (although the extent of upper-class penetration is difficult to document).[47]

Marcos polarized the country with his declaration of martial law on September 21, 1972, allegedly because the nation was "imperilled by the danger of violent overthrow."[48] Possibly no other act was as instrumental in legitimating the CPP in the minds of the discontented. Marcos then arrested most of the political opposition, including congressmen, businessmen, journalists, and academics. Others went underground. The legal opposition was similarly destroyed. The powerlessness of the traditional elites in the face of Marcos's actions discredited them in the eyes of some of the younger generation, and others, already radicalized, joined the armed struggle. The institutionalization of Marcos's martial-law rule over the next decade paralleled the rise of the CPP. If martial law had not been imposed, some of the government's opponents might have been co-opted by the political system (as indeed some were even under martial law), and the CPP might have degenerated into a quixotic band of aging revolutionaries slowly tiring of life on the run. As the CPP noted in an October 1972 policy statement: the situation was "far more favorable to the revolutionary movement than ever before."[49]

The second major event contributing to the formation of the CPP was the link-up between a group of scared urban radicals and an experienced jungle fighter—Bernabe Buscayno, or Commander Dante. Although Dante was about the same age as Sison and his fellow radicals, he had already spent sixteen years in the field with an aging Huk supremo, Commander Sumulong (Faustino del Mundo). The latter, after starting out in the Huks, had become a petty racketeer in a town next to Clark Air Base. Sumulong, Dante, and other so-called Huks were well known and popularized by the Manila press. They were not suppressed by the government because they had their political uses and they offered protection from high-level racketeers. Sumulong helped Marcos in the 1969 election while Dante supported his opponent, Sen. Sergio Osmeña, Jr.

In late 1968 Sison approached Dante, perhaps because of his romanticized image and their similar ages, suggesting he participate in the rebirth of the Philippine Communist movement. The appeal of the alliance to both Sison and Dante can be easily imagined: Sison, the urban intellectual, playing the role of Evangelista, and Dante, a Pampangueno peasant, the new Taruc.

On December 26, 1968, student radicals and Dante met in Manga, barrio Talimundok (Capas), Pangasinan Province, for a "Congress of Reestablishment." During meetings that went on until January 7, a party constitution was drafted to replace that of the 1938 merger of the PKP and the Socialist party. The new document declared that, "under the supreme guidance of Mao Tse-tung, the acme of Marxism and Leninism in the present era," a new party was formed. Sison became chairman, and Dante, commander in chief of the New People's Army, the NPA, which was officially created on March 29, 1969.[50]

The NPA became one of several rival armed groups operating in central Luzon in late 1969. The American embassy estimated that overall the groups comprised some four hundred regular armed men, five hundred armed combat support personnel, and three to four thousand unarmed general support personnel, all undergirded by a mass base of thirty to eighty thousand people.[51] When in September 1970 Sumulong was captured and in October another Huk leader, Pedro Taruc, was killed, the way was open for Dante to combine forces in Pampanga and Tarlac. The NPA's organization was aided by the defection of Lt. Victor Corpus, a Philippine Military Academy graduate, in 1971. He remained at large until 1976, and his specialized training must have been useful.

Little is known about the CPP's early years, although they surely must have been marked by internal struggles and intense psychological pressures, given among other things Sison's reputation as a difficult person. The divisions were so intense that in 1970 Eduardo Lachica reported, inaccurately, that the Dante-Sison alliance had broken up. Moreover, one of Sison's key compatriots, Arthur Garcia, was murdered by his own men and others were betrayed.[52]

Indications of the party's early difficulties surfaced in a 1972 document by the group's Central Committee entitled "Summing Up our Experience after Three Years." In it the party's leaders noted the danger of "sectarianism"—that is, a "small group mentality" whereby some cadres were unwilling to expand their numbers. At the same time they warned against "adventurism," or expanding too quickly, especially militarily, without effective "consolidation work" among the masses. Insufficient preparation entailed the danger of a "purely military viewpoint, ultrademocracy, disregard of organizational discipline, absolute equalitarianism, subjectivism, individualism or putschism" arising. The leaders stressed the importance of building both an ideological base and an organizational framework at the same time.

The party claimed to have at this point 2,000 members and candidate members with a mass base of 400,000 in eighteen provinces. Although the leaders conceded that many were of "cadre quality," they expressed concern over their members' differing approaches to revolution. Three perspectives were noted: (1) "subjective trends" among "petty-bourgeois" members with "ideological weaknesses"; (2) "dogmatists" who were too "smugly satisfied," acting without "learning from the masses"; and (3) "empiricists" who "disdain[ed] . . . book learning" but did not relate "limited experience to the general principles." Also criticized was in-fighting: some cadres called others "opportunists" without "concrete facts"; others monopolized decisions "creating the danger of 'bureaucraticism' " which could stymie the party's growth.[53]

"The problem is no longer how to start a revolution. It is how to extend and intensify it," Sison had said in December 1971.[54] At that moment, his remark showed either great foresight or sublime hope, for the CPP and the NPA were on the run. They had been pushed back into the mountainous jungles of northern Luzon after they had failed to develop a base in the traditional Huk region in the lowlands of Tarlac and Pampanga. The NPA had been "hemmed in" in Tarlac, according to the party's leaders, by the "Taruc-Sumulong gangster clique" and the "Eduardo Cojuangco clique." (Cojuangco, a wealthy political ally of Marcos and first cousin to Corazon Aquino, controlled Tarlac.) Their failure to establish a base in the region was instructive, however. It forced the leaders to rethink their strategy and gradually develop a base far out of reach of military forces. Perhaps they were heeding Mao's advice, "Fight, fail, fight again . . . till their victory; that is the logic of the people."[55]

Other setbacks dogged the group: the CPP was having financial and recruitment problems; the NPA suffered a major blow in the Bicol region in the mid-1970s when a key commander defected to the government, revealing the names of his troops;[56] and cadres in other provinces were captured or killed.

Nevertheless, conditions were improving for the revolution, although neither the Philippine nor the American governments perceived it. A classified American embassy cable reported in November 1974, for example, that the NPA had decreased in strength and that martial law had "dealt a severe blow to CPP/ML [Communist Party of the Philippines–Marxist-Leninist] and NPA efforts at expansion." The embassy cabled the next year that the Philippine military had been "able to effectively neutralize the CPP/ML–NPA at a limited cost to itself." And yet another cable noted in 1981 that "on balance, the martial law government probably did more to impede NPA growth than it did to unwittingly promote it."[57] But all the appraisals were wrong, for a factor was encouraging the insurgency: social and historical conditions. Once the movement had put down roots, there was fertile ground for it to spread. The movement's leaders, although they made some serious mistakes, were intelligent and capable of rectifying their errors. The Philippine government and the Americans were too complacent, mistaking errors in tactics for errors in strategy.

The CPP's strategy, in fact, was long-term organization performed slowly and systematically under the government's shadow. Some American observers by 1981 recognized that the CPP's most significant impact would come from its "building of political awareness among farmers whose traditionally restricted outlook . . . led them to expect little from their national government."[58]

The group's organizational work was aided by the increasing alienation of all social strata from the Marcos government. The United States made a critical mistake when it misread Marcos's character and the nature of his regime. His objective was not to reform but to exploit, and his greed undermined both the government's and the economy's stability. Corruption and the plundering of resources destroyed what remained of the government's legitimacy, especially in the rural areas, leaving a vacuum to be filled by the CPP's infrastructure.

The elites too grew disillusioned with the government, particularly after 1980 when the economy began a downward spiral. In that decade President Marcos's rule came full circle. The "New Society" he had heralded in declaring martial law had become much like the old. Philippine economic and political disintegration worsened, replicating, but more strongly, the problems of the 1960s that Marcos had used to justify imposing martial law. In the face of declining economic growth rates, there was renewed talk about returning to pretechnocratic policies of import substitution, whereby new domestic industries were protected from foreign competition by high tariff barriers. "Crony capitalism," in which a few Marcos cohorts exploited the work of the many, weakened the Manila business community's support for the regime. The political crisis brought on by Senator Aquino's assassination in August 1983 further encouraged a return to the pre–martial law politics of factionalism. The government's loss of credibility helped broaden the CPP's recruitment pool among the middle class and the poor. And most important, the Catholic church was becoming radicalized.

The Role of the Catholic Church

Radicalization of elements of the Catholic church provided an institutional basis through which the CPP could legitimately broaden its organizational activities and gain external support. Its 1978 directive, entitled "Nature of the Church Sector, Organization of Our Political Work and Tasks of Comrades within the Sector," called on party members to "penetrate" church institutions. Another directive, issued in 1982, "General Orientation of Our Work within the Sector," described "ways to use Church leaders" and develop international support.[59] Although the church's political involvement predated the CPP's formation, it gave a degree of legitimacy to the "godless" CPP's organizing work among the poor.

The church's role in rebellion was part of the Philippine revolutionary tradition. In 1872 the Spanish had garroted three native priests —Jose Burgos, Mariano Gomez, and Jacinto Zamora—for their alleged involvement in a native uprising at the Cavite arsenal. The priests had been active in efforts to replace the Spanish friars with native priests.[60] These men were immortalized in the Filipino nationalist liturgy as the first martyrs in the Philippine revolution. Rizal dedicated his novel *El Filibusterismo* to them, and "Gomburzo" (an acronym derived from their names) became the Katipunan's war cry. As Usha Mahajani observed, "The uniformly severe punishment meted out to the Filipinos, Mestizos and Creoles [the priests were Creoles] bridged the gulf that had separated these communities and tended to unite them in common suffering."[61] The priests' martyrdom thus represented the mingling of two traditions in Philippine culture, secular nationalism and religious idealism, and explains in part the CPP's working with those in the church who were mobilizing the poor in the 1960s.

Inspired by liberation theology borrowed from Latin America, church activists challenged the power of the Philippine elite, the military, and foreign businessmen, blaming them for preventing "true Christian egalitarianism."[62] A Philippine Jesuit, Antonio Lambino, promoted this role for the church in these terms: "Effective Christian love is manifested in solidarity with the poor and the oppressed, in sharing their struggle to liberate themselves from the unjust structures of society."[63] The new "church of the poor" struck responsive chords among peasants already conditioned by their liturgical history.

The church's involvement in social welfare has a mixed history in the Philippines. During the Spanish period, there was little to distinguish the church and state; friars owned vast tracts of land on which peasants toiled. And in modern times the church still controls considerable real estate, and the majority of its hierarchy is politically moderate or conservative.[64]

But there has also been a powerful tradition of social activism on behalf of the poor. Some friars, under the Spanish, says Scott, "by their courage and endurance, their affection and gifts . . . often attracted followings with deep personal loyalty; and by their prevention of military excesses and defence of the local people against soldiers' abuses . . . projected an image of a just and benevolent conquest."[65] In this century Jesuits founded the Institute for Social Order (ISO) in 1947, followed by the Federation of Free Workers (FFW), a labor organization, in 1950, and the Federation of Free Farmers (FFF) in 1953. Although these groups were created partly to help the government's counterinsurgency campaign against the Huks, they were distrusted by elites, who are usually suspicious of any effort to organize the poor. Relatively inactive during the late 1950s and early 1960s, the FFW and FFF provided an institutional basis for militancy in the late 1960s.[66]

The philosophical basis for an increasing role for the church in political action was laid down in Vatican II in 1965, when Pope John XXIII called for a dialogue between the church and the left and encouraged the church to focus especially on issues of social justice in the third world. Vatican II's moral impact is almost impossible to overestimate, particularly in the Philippines where it coincided with the beginning of the Marcos era.

By 1966 the Catholic Bishops Conference of the Philippines (CBCP) had organized the National Secretariat of Social Action (NASSA) to establish social action centers in every diocese. In 1969 these centers were given the additional responsibility of focusing on justice and peace. Some of these groups, according to one observer, were later "manipulated by the CPP through supporters of the National Democratic Front."[67] But the centers remained largely peripheral to the needs of the poor prior to the imposition of martial law; their programs benefited mostly the middle class.

The centers' early ineffectiveness radicalized some priests, who felt that "unjust structures were left largely intact and the dependency of the poor remained unchanged." Some of them turned to more moderate mass-based organizations such as the FFF and FFW. Others, however, took more drastic steps. An organization of diocesan priests, Philippine Priests Incorporated (PPI), formed in 1968, was taken over by radical clergymen, including Father Edicio de la Torre and Father Luis Jalandoni. In 1972 the PPI announced its intention to "organize our people in a . . . struggle for liberation." With Jalandoni's help, the National Federation of Sugarcane Workers in Negros was established as a radical offshoot of the FFF. And in February 1972, Father de la Torre founded Christians for National Liberation, a PPI offshoot, which later helped establish the CPP's National Democratic Front in April 1975. In 1973 students, radical Catholics from Christians for National Liberation, reportedly reopened the NPA's front in Negros.[68] Father Jalandoni, who later left the church to marry a former nun, became the European spokesman for the National Democratic Front and a member of the CPP's Central Committee.

Foreign missionaries were part of the ferment. In 1970 Maryknoll Fathers initiated a development concept in Davao del Norte which became the foundation for the first Basic Christian Communities (BCC).[69] The BCCs, which spread throughout the country, but most widely in the South, were important instruments for organizing and educating the poor. Rush has explained that "BCC formation often focuses on understanding political power, on becoming aware that people are poor and powerless for a reason, and that this reason is to be found in the structure —the 'sinful' structure—of the economy and the government."[70]

Of course, church activism at the grass roots put the church in conflict with the Marcos regime. When Marcos declared martial law, he arrested many priests and nuns, drove others underground into the CPP's arms, and gradually politicized more conservative church leaders. In response to these arrests, the Association of Major Religious Superiors of the Philippines, representing priests and nuns, established the Task Force for Detainees in January 1974 to monitor the government's human rights abuses; its documentation helped discredit Marcos's government.[71] Church activism had forced the government to choose between reform and repression. Marcos had chosen repression.

The church, of course, was not monolithic in its response to social conditions. Only a small percentage of priests and nuns were reformers; of them, twelve priests reportedly joined the NPA as rebel commanders.[72] Nor was the politically active minority necessarily pro-Communist. This could be seen in the critical role the church played in overthrowing Marcos in February 1986, in Corazon Aquino's use of the church to monitor a sixty-day cease-fire agreement with the NPA in December 1986, and in the part the church played in negotiating regional peace pacts with the CPP in 1987.[73] Thus church radicalism was a two-edged sword: it could be wielded for or against the CPP.

One progressive bishop, Francisco Claver, said the Communists admitted that their revolution could not succeed unless they had the support of the church.[74] Out of the fertile mixture of traditional religious idealism and liberation theology, the CPP derived an affirmation of their own objectives and legitimacy.

The Revolutionary Mystique

Revolution and rebellion have flourished in the Philippines despite the lack of an ideological bias on the part of the peasants. Sison wrote that if there had been "genuine land reform," the CPP would not have "found the ground so fertile for armed revolution."[75] The issue, however, has not been land reform alone but a whole set of social disputes with the elite-controlled government. No single explanation is sufficient. Rather, it has been the way in which the system functions and the way in which Filipinos perceive their world that have provided the conditions that have led to turmoil.[76]

As Robert Redfield has noted, "It is the contact and conflict of differing traditions that brings about the sudden alterations in society and, among other consequences, the change from a mythology that is retrospective to one that is prospective."[77] And Philippine society has been rife with conflict. Conflict has been endemic partly because elites have never supported fundamental structural reforms. They never wished to integrate the peasants into society nor share their wealth and power. Manila, under the Spanish, had ignored the provinces and their problems, and the United States retained the policy, concentrating administrative power in Manila after a brief effort at decentralization.[78] When independence came, the Filipino elites continued the practice. At the end of a long administrative chain, local governments lacked authority and the means to effect change. Thus they would simply make their separate peace. When places like Samar again became centers for rebellion, insurgent leaders found both a ready-made mass base among the discontented peasants and local officials with little ability or desire to resist them.[79]

The elite's response of repression had been successful in containing movements like the Sakdals and the Huks, but it helped perpetuate future rebellions. The government's counterinsurgency approach guaranteed insurgencies to come, a pattern that could be seen at work during the Philippine-American War, the Huk rebellion, and the flourishing of the CPP under Marcos. The danger still exists under the Aquino government.

An editorial in an American newspaper at the turn of the century noted that the solution to the Philippine-American War was "not altogether a military one," observing that "there is something required besides the rifle."[80] Unfortunately, the rifle was the only response. A native militia and police force under American officers became convenient substitutes for regular American troops eager to return home, but these men were equally unversed in winning the hearts and minds of the peasants. By identifying the Moros or Katipunans as bandits, any measure of harshness could be justified.[81] The United States even fashioned "zones of protection," forcing villagers to relocate in Luzon, Samar, and Cebu in an effort to reduce the revolutionaries' mass base.[82]

Ultimately superior force won out. The country's geography permitted the government to isolate and wear down resistance. Effective military action, coupled with exhaustion and disillusionment, produced relative peace in the countryside after 1911, but with no improvement in the conditions of peasant life.[83] Because the conflict had not really been resolved, the peasants surrendered only a portion of their weapons and wrapped the rest in oilskin rags and buried them for the future. Weapons were their only insurance against the repression they knew would come from Manila landlords and local warlords. The peasants' certainty that oppression was inevitable partly explains their reluctance to forgo conflict. The repeated resurgence of rebellion was a form of "passive dissidence," as Lachica labeled it, a force that grew or diminished according to the "felt need for it."[84] The most successful revolutionary leaders were the ones who appealed most effectively to the strong nativistic tradition of demanding change, a transformation of the peasant way of life.

The CPP, too, was born out of conflict—the leadership conflicts common in Philippine politics: Sison's clashes with Nemenzo and with the Lava family, Dante's dispute with Sumulong. Similar personality conflicts characterized the Katipunan's and the PKP's history. In fact, the least successful rebellions were those marked by the fewest leadership conflicts. Lachica observed that it is unclear how much of Sison's "Maoism was professed for its own sake or used as the spearpoint of his relentless struggle to preempt power in the nationalist councils."[85] But that is precisely the point: the struggle for power meant everything to the ilustrado elites. Rhetoric or ideology, for these men, was only a means to power, although for their followers it evoked a larger promise of paradise.

The successful rebellion, however, required struggles not over ideology as such but over a specific program of equitable reform. An unscientific study of the Huks in the 1950s found that over half had become party members with no ideological convictions. And another study in 1969 found that the NPA cadres and their leaders similarly were not ideologically motivated.[86] What made peasants willing to risk their lives had little to do with grand ideological issues such as imperialism but rather with fundamental ideas about social justice and equality. As the French scholar Gerard Chaliand has observed, "From Mustapha Kemal to the Iranian revolution by Ayatollah Khomeiny and the mollahs, the main explanation of the causes of insurgencies and revolutionary movements in the Third World has been and still is *identity*, the revendication of one's own identity which has been humiliated and a need for dignity and freedom and/or justice born from frustration."[87] These are the reasons peasants have been willing to follow intellectuals who descend into their jungle and participate in their suffering in order to lead them out to the Promised Land. As a priest in Mindanao sermonized:

What can we be thankful for today? We can be thankful for those individuals who stand up against oppressive conditions, who speak out and who respond to the people's needs and who, in doing so, preserve our dignity as a people. They are helping to cure us. They too may break the law. But those who stand by quietly in deference to Marcos's laws are hypocrites like the Pharisees.[88]

The spirit driving the Manila intellectuals to rebel was much the same spirit that catalyzed the peasantry, although it was couched in the more secular terminology of nationalism. But nationalism became a potent force for change only when it was linked to the peasantry's need for a new social contract and to an organization capable of containing the politics of personality while at the same time drawing vigor from the periodic reexaminations of tactics imposed by leadership disputes. This was Aquinaldo's mistake in the Philippine-American War: he became so preoccupied with the form of "nationhood" that he failed to mobilize the "striking laborers and restless peasants."[89] The PKP mistakenly believed that the people would join them simply because of the political and economic situation, that they could spread the cause by osmosis, so to speak.[90] As Sison later argued, Jose Lava mistook a "revolutionary mood" for a "revolutionary situation"; leadership was needed as a catalyst. Moreover, the CPP's ideologues were able to form a much more effective alliance with its implementors, the militia, so that over time the two became almost indistinguishable and were able to create a self-perpetuating organizational structure.

The strategy the CPP ultimately adopted was (as I argue in the next chapter) ideally suited to take advantage of the country's underlying revolutionary condition. Ironically, Sison and others arrived at it through a series of failures, although they were aided by Marcos's declaration of martial law and his extreme hubris. But this empirical process was the CPP's strength, as it had been for other successful Maoist revolutions in Asia. In terms of history, the CPP's development represents a qualitative and quantitative improvement over previous rebellions.

3 Strategy and Tactics of the People's Revolutionary Forces

There are "no more yellows, only reds," a former Rotary governor in Mindanao's Davao City, said in late 1985, yellow being the color of moderate democratic opponents to the Marcos government.[1] Davao was famous in the international press as the "murder capital" of the Philippines, partly as a result of the NPA's assassination team attacks; by mid-1984, killings took place almost daily.[2] "This is a very peaceful place till your time comes. The only rule is not to be at the right place at the wrong time," explained a local journalist.[3] Mindanao was called "the Bleeding Land," and Davao was the CPP's laboratory for testing insurgency tactics.

So successful were they that in 1983, a CPP cadre proposed that a "clear insurrectional direction be defined for the mass movement in major urban centers" and argued that the strategy of gradually building a base for a strategic offensive should be changed in favor of devising a "fast track" to victory through insurrection.[4]

Yet by 1986 the NPA's fortunes in Mindanao apparently had dramatically changed. The group had pulled out of Davao and was replaced by a local self-defense force, the Alsa-Masa (Up-from-the-Masses), consisting of some former NPA cadres. The Alsa-Masa claimed they had rid Davao of the NPA with the support of the local military chief and private businessmen. Their success was heralded as a model for similar anti-Communist vigilante groups elsewhere in the country.

Having pulled back to the mountains, the NPA was caught up in internal disputes about party strategy following Corazon Aquino's ascension to power in the 1986 presidential election. The party had advocated an unsuccessful boycott of the election and this had reopened the old debate: which was more effective—the "armed struggle," emphasizing the NPA, or the "political struggle," emphasizing electoral and cause-oriented politics? At the same time, revelations that government agents had penetrated the party's infrastructure led to a self-destructive witch-hunt within the Mindanao branch, resulting in the execution of many cadres. In addition, the NPA's bloody tactics of daily assassinations in Davao weakened its mass support.

Even as the party retreated to Mindanao, however, it was spreading further elsewhere in the archipelago. Despite the evident popularity of the new president, NPA units increased their attacks and opened up a new front in Manila, executing in 1987 Aquino's local government secretary and three American servicemen from the giant facility at Clark Air Base in central Luzon. The NPA also initiated with mixed results a new economic strategy, blowing up railway lines, bridges, and oil pipelines. Political organizing continued apace, especially in the region surrounding Manila, and efforts were begun to solicit international support. In response the military accelerated its efforts to develop vigilante groups, or "civilian volunteers" as they were euphemistically called. Among the casualties were several prominent human rights lawyers.

In previous chapters we have seen why the terrain was suited for rebellion in the Philippines and why it remains fertile ground. In order to comprehend how the rebellion has survived and grown even after the country's political structure changed from authoritarian rule to democracy, we need to consider the rebels' organization and strategy. Here, the NPA's growth in Mindanao is illustrative.

The NPA expansion into Mindanao did not occur rapidly, although its activity increased markedly in the 1980s. The CPP claims it established its first front in Mindanao at the end of 1972 and its first military unit in 1973.[5] By early 1982 the NPA in Region Eleven, the government reported, had 1,400 regular members, 1,800 active supporters, and a mass base of 18,400. Ambush units operating against the Philippine armed forces comprised 50 to 60 men each. By 1985 the CPP claimed 9,000 full- or part-time guerrillas were operating on 19 fronts in Mindanao, covering 2,700 barrios and influencing 150 factories or plantations and 80 schools. The Philippine military reported 876 NPA-initiated activities that year as compared to 478 in 1983.[6]

A similar pattern of slow early growth followed by rapid expansion occurred throughout the country. For example, the first NPA squad of ten men was established on Panay Island in 1971. In 1977 American embassy officials in Manila reported that NPA strength in Panay was "minuscule," and that they were "primarily engaged in recruitment and propaganda activities, avoiding contact with PC patrols as much as possible." But in 1985 their strength was placed at four thousand, and a Provisional Regional Council of the National Democratic Front (NDF) was formed there in late July. Another example is Negros where the first propaganda team was reported in 1969, the first guerrilla front in 1981, and three fronts in 1984.[7]

The CPP-NPA expanded steadily, first southward and then westward after defeats in the late 1960s forced them into mountainous Isabela Province. (Ironically, the guerrilla movement remained the least developed in Isabela where units until 1984 still operated as undersized platoons.) In the five years following its formation, the CPP formed twenty fronts in seven regions outside of the Manila-Rizal area: northern, central, and southern Luzon, Mindanao, and the eastern and western Visayas.[8] By the mid-1980s, more than forty fronts had been opened.

The general evolution of the CPP-NPA took place in five phases, which, it is important to note, were responsive to revolutionary conditions in the country. Each phase has been marked by shifts in the movement's direction as a consequence of tactical errors and leadership struggles and has entailed a new approach to its grand strategy of winning power. No other movement in Philippine history has demonstrated such adaptability.

The first phase, between 1968 and 1972, occurred shortly after the CPP's founding and was marked by defeat. Failing to develop a base in the traditional terrain of rebellion in the rice-growing plains of Pampanga and Tarlac in central Luzon, the party retreated into the mountains of northern Luzon, which are covered in triple-canopy rain forests and infrequently bisected by dirt roads. There the party could nurse its wounds, rethinking its strategy and training new cadres with little fear of military attack. The second phase lasted from the early to the late 1970s, during which time a small group of cadres began to expand southward, emboldened by the new recruits who flocked to the underground in great numbers after the declaration of martial law in September 1972. Although the party had anticipated the need for an underground railroad and a training program for the bourgeois children from Manila's upper classes once Marcos began his roundups of the opposition, it had not been prepared for the number or the enthusiasm of the new supporters.

Thus the third phase was a period of consolidation beginning around

1976 and ending in 1980. The party concentrated on solidifying its rear base, organizing the native tribes of the Cordilleras (on whose protection the early cadres from central Luzon had depended), and instituting political and military organizations in such areas as Mindanao, Samar, Negros, and Bicol, all of which were distant from Manila and the government's firm control. These preparations also laid the foundation for an expanded NPA, which initiated a series of tactical offensives during the fourth phase in the early 1980s. Military actions were concentrated in northern and eastern Mindanao and political activities in the central and western Visayas, forming broad political fronts with social sectors to prepare for a "national uprising."[9] Aided by Marcos's declining public popularity, the growth of opposition groups among the moderate Manila upper classes, and the deteriorating economic situation that weakened the government's effectiveness even further in the rural areas, the NPA assumed a Robin Hood–like image as "Nice People Around."

Their popularity seemed to peak at the beginning of the fifth phase in 1986 when Marcos was forced into exile. Not having anticipated Aquino's defeat of Marcos, however, the party advocated a boycott of the February 1986 presidential election. The people deserted them, turning out in droves to vote for "Cory." Beginning in mid-1986, following Aquino's orders to release from detention several CPP leaders, including Sison, the party reassessed its basic strategy of armed conflict as it faced its greatest challenge: the highly popular Corazon Aquino. Rent internally by leadership struggles and a decline in party support and threatened externally by rejuvenated Philippine military forces and vigilante groups, the party now confronted its most critical phase. For the first time since the Chinese had cut off aid in the mid-1970s, the CPP began seriously seeking external financial and military support, reaching out even to the Soviets in an effort to make up for the decline in domestic support.

These phases, lasting more than twenty years, have demonstrated the group's organizational cohesiveness and strategic direction, which although rooted in Philippine social development are nevertheless unique in the country's politics.

The NPA's gradual spread is indicated by changes in the estimates of its armed troop strength (see table 3.1). These numbers, although probably highly inaccurate, show a persistent upward trend. Equally im-

TABLE 3.1
Estimates of NPA Strength and Influence, 1972–1988

A. American or Filipino Estimates

Date of Estimate	Troop Strength	Percentage of Barrios under NPA Influence
September 1972	1,000–2,000	
Early 1976	1,800	
Early 1979	2,000–3,000	
October 1980	3,500	
August 1981	3,600	
October 1982	6,000	2–3%
June 1983	7,500	
February 1984	10,000	
September 1984	8,000[a]	
March 1985	10,000–12,000	4%
August 1985	20,000	28%
October 1985	16,500	20%
November 1985	16,500	20%
February 1986	20,000	4–5%[a]
March 1986	20,000	
May 1986	22,000	
June 1986	22,000	20%
March 1988	24,000–26,000[a]	20%[a]

B. NPA Estimates

Year	Strength	Number of Fronts	Number of Provinces/Barrios
1968–69	35	– 2	2 provinces
1972	350	10	9 provinces
1976	1,500	21	31 provinces
1977	1,500		40 provinces
1980	8,000	25	43 provinces
1981		30	
1982	10,000	36	60 provinces
1983–85	30,000	45–53	10,000 barrios
1987	7,600 (with rifles)	70	

a. Government of Philippines' estimate.
Sources: Larry A. Niksch, *Insurgency and Counterinsurgency in the Philippines* (Washington, D.C.: Library of Congress, July 1, 1985), 36; testimony of U.S. government officials before Congress in the months cited; issues of *Liberation* and *Ang Bayan*.

portant, if not more so, were estimates of the CPP's influence. In September 1982 the Philippine military said that 3 percent of the nation's barangays (or barrios, the smallest administrative unit, of which there are 41,400) were "Communist-influenced" (that is, 50 percent of the residents were sympathetic), 5 percent were "infiltrated" (30 percent were sympathetic), and 10 percent were "targeted" (10 percent were sympathetic). In 1984 American embassy officials were still reporting about the same figures.[10] By 1985, CPP influence nationally was estimated at 33 percent, with the NPA in control of at least 12 percent of the barangays. In 1987, CPP influence had increased to 37 percent with cadres in all seventy-three provinces.[11]

The CPP's Theoretical Framework

The CPP's policy of expanding its influence gradually was based on a strategy formulated in the early years of the party's founding by "Amado Guerrero" and subjected to repeated reformulations as the tactical situation required. The CPP based its organization on three theoretical works by Guerrero, which drew heavily on Mao Tse-tung. Besides *Philippine Society and Revolution* (July 1970), alluded to in the previous chapter, he wrote *Rectify Errors and Rebuild the Party* (1968) and *Specific Characteristics of Our People's War* (December 1, 1974). *Rectify* justified the need to form a new Communist party and provided a general strategic outline. *Philippine Society*, the party's Bible, was a workbook for party organizers that could, he said, "be studied in three consecutive or separate days." *Specific Characteristics* readjusted the party's strategy after the declaration of martial law in 1972.

The strength of Guerrero's analysis was its practical emphasis on organizing and implementing political change in the Philippines. He astutely interpreted the weaknesses of the Huk movement and perceived how to turn them into strengths. His own weakness was his emphasis on class struggle. His effort to place the Philippines in the historical mainstream of Marxism-Leninism may have contributed to the CPP's ignoring the political force of the coalition of lower, middle, and upper classes that made Aquino's 1986 victory possible.

Guerrero's analysis offered three lessons important to the success of the movement. In the first, he stressed the necessity of applying a process of self-criticism to the party's structure and tactics. In *Rectify* he explained that he had first tried to "rectify" the Philippine Communist Party (PKP) from within, but that the process had become "antagonistic as the entrenched leadership—a tight nepotistic clique of Lava kinsmen and close friends—systematically tried to kill democratic discussion of its shortcomings."[12] Although couching his analysis in Marxist jargon (the "fundamental cause" of the PKP's errors was the "subjectivist, non-materialist and non-dialectical philosophical outlook of the unremolded petty-bourgeois cadres"), Guerrero clearly saw that one of the PKP's weaknesses was its "dogmatism," its rigid application of communist doctrines without "specifying them to concrete conditions."[13] In so doing Guerrero established a standard for applying the strategy that helps account for the CPP's success. As he correctly observed, a major failing of the PKP was what he called its "subjective empiricism": its "tendency to separate political practice from theoretical guidance." Learning through self-criticism and adapting tactics to a changing political environment while remaining within a strategic design was one of *Rectify*'s (and Marxism's) best lessons. That lesson was applied to the implementation of the party's three strategic tasks as prescribed in *Rectify*: building a party, initiating the armed struggle, and forging a national united front.

Guerrero's second important lesson which contributed to the party's success was his understanding finally of how the Philippines' fragmented island geography could be turned to the party's advantage.[14] This assessment came only after the armed struggle suffered its defeats in central Luzon which forced it into the mountains of northern Luzon during the party's first phase of growth. The CPP's ability to make a critical analysis of this initial failure turned the defeat into victory, establishing a pattern for future tactical reversals and making possible the transition into the second phase in which political organization was emphasized. As Guerrero noted in *Philippine Society*, "the countryside offers the widest area possible for maneuver for the revolutionaries because the counter-revolutionaries have no choice but to concentrate their forces for the defense of their urban centers of economic and political power and also for guarding their main lines of communication and transport."[15]

Guerrero began taking these geographical factors to heart only in the period following the imposition of martial law. He was aided by the encouraging influx of refugees from martial law detention and the realization that his earlier vision of the armed struggle "advancing in a series of waves"[16] could not be successful if they were directly confronting government forces. He noted, however, that "waging a people's war in an archipelagic country like ours is definitely an exceedingly difficult and complex problem." Moreover, Guerrero observed:

There are three outstanding characteristics of the Philippines in being an archipelago. First, our countryside is shredded into so many islands. Second, our two biggest islands, Luzon and Mindanao, are separated by such a clutter of islands as the Visayas. Third, our small country is separated by seas from other countries. From such characteristics arise problems that are very peculiar to our people's war.[17]

But events forced a change in outlook. Although it had taken Guerrero many years to make a virtue out of necessity, he perceived now that geography could help the CPP by providing a cover for the spread of cadres in the second and third phases of development while dispersing their opponent's military strength. This tactic was central to the CPP's success during the fourth phase of offensives much as it had been for the Vietminh in South Vietnam. Guerrero saw that mountain ranges could broaden the insurgency's effective operational area, allowing it to operate in several provinces at once while making it more difficult for the army to find them.

Guerrero adapted Mao's vision of a "protracted people's war" progressing through three successive stages of warfare: (1) the "strategic defensive" in which the NPA would retain a tactical offense and the initiative against their opponent's military superiority; (2) the "strategic stalemate" during which the forces would be equal; and (3) the "strategic offensive" in which regular forces would confront each other in the main-force warfare. The party's lack of military experience may have contributed during its disastrous first period to its early preoccupation with Mao's strategy of forming armed units and advancing on Manila from rural bases with regular forces. The realities of warfare, however, made necessary a change in strategy if the party were to survive. Guerrero's and the party's flexibility in this respect was impressive.[18] By 1984, the CPP declared it was already in the advance phase of the strategic defensive.

The third important lesson was the need to deemphasize the military struggle until a base had been prepared and to emphasize the political struggle instead. As is often the case with lessons, this one was learned only through experience and out of necessity. Its seeds had been present in *Rectify*, but military setbacks and the sudden increase in cadres following the imposition of martial law forced the party to refocus on this early principle of coalition building. Armed struggle as such was not resumed until 1980.[19]

In *Rectify* Guerrero noted that constraining the revolution's development was American imperialism coupled with the semifeudal control of the landlord class. To counter the two, Guerrero proposed creating a "broad national alliance" of all classes and strata: "because of the semi-colonial and semi-feudal nature of Philippine society, the present stage of the Philippine Revolution cannot but take a national-democratic character." Before the "proletarian-socialist revolution" could take place, the party had to "wage a national-democratic revolution of a new type, a people's democratic revolution."[20] Thus, emphasizing political efforts over military action, strengthening coalitions with other politically sympathetic groups, establishing fronts with which sympathizers could be identified while cloaking the CPP's interests, and organizing the peasants as the party's power base became the third key to the CPP's success over the next decade.[21]

The implementation of these lessons fell largely to another generation of CPP leaders. Sison (Guerrero) was captured on November 10, 1977, Dante on August 26, 1976, and Victor Corpus and Satur Ocampo, leader of the National Democratic Front, along with four other members of the Central Committee, in 1976. Lori Barros, secretary-general of the Laguna-Quezon subregion was killed in 1976, and Renato Casipe, regional NPA chairman of Mindanao, surrendered to authorities the same year. The change in command these losses necessitated may have made it easier for the new leaders to adapt strategy to the changing tactical situation and for a more aggressive group to ascend to leadership positions, opening the third phase in the party's evolution.

Strategy and Change in the CPP

The CPP's strategy was in many ways a response to the Huks' failures, one of which had been its recruitment program. The

Huks had hoped that people would enlist when social conditions deteriorated; thus the movement would spread through sheer weight of numbers, as had happened in previous peasant uprisings. In contrast, the CPP recognized that people would join the rebellion if it offered something the government did not: hope, justice, medical services, a sense of identity, and so forth. "Bad people" had been recruited into the Huk movement, causing many of the atrocities that weakened its support.[22] The CPP recognized that a slow recruitment process and strict standards for party membership would reduce the possibility of such people joining the group. This would also minimize the infiltration of government agents, which would enhance security.

Huk cadres had been reluctant to leave their home areas, whereas the CPP dispersed their men, testing them and obscuring the party's apparatus in such a way that it was difficult for the government to assess the movement's strength. Legal cadres, for example, who were exposed by the government were sent to the NPA. The Huks had sent their worst cadres into the field;[23] the CPP sent their best. The Huks had directed their activities from essentially two central commands: Politburo-In, located in Manila, which was captured in 1950 and Politburo-Out, located in central Luzon. The Huks had further divided their forces into ten regional commands and military squadrons, but because its only support base was in central Luzon, the command structure remained centralized.[24] Early on, the CPP encouraged the decentralization of power, dispersing its cadres who formed regional party committees and NPA units. The Huks had had trouble maintaining control since many of its members were also full-time farmers.[25] The CPP again made a virtue out of necessity by developing a variety of membership categories, ensuring that their main-force units were full-time combatants who were also trained in propaganda and organization.

Another major constraint on the Huks had been their lack of funding and logistical support, which forced some of them to become bandits.[26] The CPP relied for support on a variety of sources: raids on the Armed Forces of the Philippines (AFP), overseas financial assistance, extortion from wealthy businessmen, local taxes, membership dues. Guerrero stressed the importance of having a self-sufficient apparatus—a policy, ironically, the AFP tried to replicate for different reasons but without success.

Guerrero also recognized the need to maintain a balance between restricting units to a limited area so their efforts could be concentrated and their support base developed and spreading them out enough so they could easily maneuver. He wanted each regional party organization to develop one to three fronts with its executive committee based on the main NPA front. The latter was located at mountainous provincial borders where they could operate easily in several areas from relatively inaccessible bases. Fronts were not to be active where the opposition's military was strongest, especially in Luzon.[27] If attacked by large enemy concentrations, forces could fade away, giving the impression of defeat.

The CPP's strategy was implemented through trial and error. Never perfect, it was subject to internal dissent and frequent change. But it was in essence Mao's strategy as further defined in Vietnam and then refined for the Philippines.

The party's most difficult years came between 1973 and 1975 when it was trying to train, organize, and field the cadres acquired after the martial law proclamation. Because of inexperience, the suddenly increased size, and logistical problems, "ill-armed guerrillas confronted, often inopportunely, AFP formations." The problems forced the CPP to promote members of its student front group in Manila to "candidate member status" and deploy them to regional organizations in August 1974. The Central Committee's staff was reduced in size and also sent to the field. What was called "commandism"—that is, relying on committees "dominated by unreliable but prestigious personalities"— was attacked.[28]

Thus, in December 1975, the CPP altered its command structure, adopting Guerrero's new "archipelagic struggle" concept, decentralizing the party organization into regional committees, and expanding recruitment, all of which signaled the beginning of the third phase in the party's evolution.[29] The decentralization was in part a response to an assessment that the party had grown too slowly since 1973 because of "sectarianism, poor tasking and check-ups, irregular and ponderous study courses, and lack of recruitment planning." The group had failed to build mass organizations.[30]

In 1976 the CPP stated that the new regional organizations were now financially independent and that the party would begin sabotage activities. In March of the next year, it announced the formation of secret cells, of new guerrilla units, of armed and unarmed propaganda units, and of party liaison teams for overt contacts. The establishment of the new groups again indicated that the party was moving into a more aggressive phase.[31]

The guerrillas in Isabela Province decided at this time to switch from fighting in "uninhabited forest regions" to engaging in "mobile guerrilla warfare" in Cagayan Valley and penetrating and forming alliances with tribal groups. Following Sison's arrest in November 1977, the CPP again loosened some restraints on party membership, permitting "instant" memberships in 1978. The Central Committee also ordered stepped-up party recruitment, particularly in Mindanao in mid-1980. This policy, however, exposed the party to infiltration by the government's deep penetration agents (DPA), causing major problems for the Mindanao Central Committee in late 1985.[32]

The fourth period in 1981 brought consolidation and still more aggressive tactics as the party put its new recruits to work. The CPP began "recentralizing," partly to gain greater control over its expanding military forces and partly to reduce the danger of government infiltration.[33] In the same year the CPP reported operating on thirty fronts,[34] and in the next, the NPA began deploying in platoon- and company-size formations. These "under-sized battalions" by 1984 were using stolen vehicles as transportation, which greatly increased their mobility.[35] And, finally, in 1985, the party turned its focus to urban areas and electoral politics.

All the changes in strategy over the four stages were accompanied by much internal dissent. Indeed, in many ways the evolution was a consequence of this dissent. But *Ang Bayan* in 1984 found it necessary to admonish members to focus intraparty struggles on ideas, not comrades. Some struggles, it observed, had become "personal," echoing the problem noted in the movement's first three years when "comrades" called each other "opportunists" without "concrete facts."[36] The paper said that "inner-party struggles take the form of intense discussions which sometimes last the whole night" and noted that "some members have not been contributing . . . just listening . . . taking a neutral stand." Foreign journalists visiting CPP units during annual committee meetings have observed the intensity of the debate during these week-long sessions over how to implement the coming year's program.[37] The extensive debate is partly a reflection of the CPP's decentralized structure, which permits local leaders considerable latitude in implementing central directives, and partly a reflection of differences in tactical approaches among leaders of the constituent groups.

PARTY BUILDING AND ORGANIZATION

The CPP is governed by a Politburo of some fifteen people, with a larger Central Committee (CC) and an Executive Committee (EC), or "troika," which essentially directs the party and is composed of three permanent members and two alternatives, including the CPP's chairman and secretary-general, and the chairman of the National Democratic Front (NDF). The EC is "empowered to decide major policies and plans in the event the Central Committee is unable to convene."[38] The CC is elected by a national congress of party members held every five years: "The Central Committee is responsible for central leadership, ideological and political; for concentration of personnel and resources at the most strategic points in the country; for coordination of all regional forces; and for seeing to it that the nationwide revolutionary struggle rises from one level to another."[39]

Under the CC are four national commissions: the National Commission for Mass Movements, responsible for infiltrating student, youth, labor, and peasant groups; the National Propaganda Commission; the United Front Commission which controls the NDF; and the National Military Commission, which controls the NPA. Also falling under the purview of the CC are the party's six territorial commissions for north, south, and central Luzon, the Visayas, Mindanao, and a special one for Negros. Organized in turn under the territorial commissions are sixteen regional and island party committees which plan tactics and supervise fronts. "Democratic centralism" is the party's basic organizational principle, reflecting the need for security and redundancy in a clandestine organization as well as the need to build support for policies while maintaining operational control. The party's founders recognized the danger that bureaucratic centralism would inhibit the party's growth and thus emphasized the importance of the commissions. When the NPA's National Operational Command is unable to operate, the CC's Military Commission is given command authority.[40]

Decentralization was built into the party's structure in part because of the infrequent meetings of the national congresses; regional party

TABLE 3.2
CPP/NPA Table of Organization

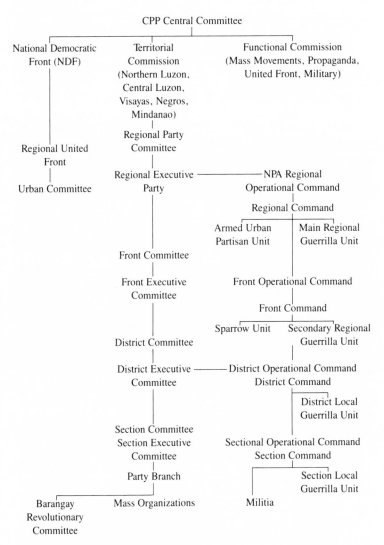

Source: Larry A. Niksch, *Insurgency and Counterinsurgency in the Philippines* (Washington, D.C.: Library of Congress, 1985), 27.

conferences were to be held every three years and provincial conferences every two years.[41] Infrequent meetings probably originally reflected the party leaders' low expectations of building a large mass base and sizable numbers of cadres quickly. The approach also gave more weight to the Executive Committee's pronouncements in the interim between regional or national congresses. The structure of the CPP is illustrated in table 3.2, which demonstrates how the CC maintains control over both the NDF and the NPA down to the local level and makes clear that the NDF and the NPA are set up as parallel structures, reinforcing each other's activities.

Another manifestation of decentralization was the creation of regional newspapers. For example, *Himagsik* (Revolution) serves central Luzon; *Silyab* (Start a Fire), Bicol; *Pakig-bisog* (Struggle), Cebu; *Daba-Daba* (Flame), Panay; and *Paghimakas* (Struggle), Negros. The NPA has *Pulang Bandila* (Red Flag), which began publication in 1985, and the party as a whole, *Ang Bayan*.[42] In 1976 a short-lived theoretical journal called *Revolution* was begun for distribution to party members only, because of the "paucity of exchange of worthwhile experiences" between regional organizations. Befitting the scholarly background of the party's principal founder was the great stress placed on having a "definite educational plan" in the belief that without "ideological building . . . there can be no organizational building."[43]

The party's "organizational building" is divided into three sectors: political cadres in the Central Committees direct political, social, and economic activities; the regular armed units of the NPA control military actions; and the NDF supervises the illegal and quasi-legal front activities. The degree to which the activities of these units in the field overlap depends on the size of the party membership and mass base. In small locales, they may be indistinguishable.

Communist penetration into an area usually occurs in several stages. A party member returns to his home village or is introduced into a village through a member's family. Once in the barrio the member conducts an assessment, or social investigation, of local problems and identifies potential sympathizers and troublesome officials or landlords: "In essence, what we are after is the local balance of forces, the capabilities, strengths, and weaknesses of the revolutionary forces, as well as those of the enemy."[44] Following the assessment, Semi-legal Teams, composed of small bands of youths as young as fourteen, enter a village to propagandize. Children later become an integral part of the party's network once a village is organized, providing an alert system against intruders and acting as guides and couriers.[45] Armed Propaganda Units or Teams, also known as Expansion Groups (Sandataang Yunit Pan Propaganda, or SYP; also spelled Samahang Yunit Pampropaganda), both proselytize and carry out assassinations, establishing the initial Organizing Group, which becomes the basis for the Party Branch.

For example, CPP cadres may begin by asking the barangay chief's permission to hold a meeting, at which they will address two issues: security (what villagers should do if soldiers come and they are interrogated or harassed) and education (identifying the people's problems). Propaganda focuses on three main issues: the U.S.-Marcos dictatorship (now the "Aquino clique"), bureaucratic feudalism (such as that practiced by multinational corporations), and fascism (the militarization of Philippine society and human rights abuses). They do not teach communism as such but, rather, oppose the government, according to one Philippine military officer. The CPP tells villagers that the AFP appears strong but is "rotten to the core" with "fatal weaknesses" because "it is an antipeople organization." In this way, a U.S. embassy official reported in 1981, the CPP has had a significant long-term impact in building "political awareness among farmers whose traditionally restricted outlook has led them to expect little from their national government."[46]

In the next stage a Barrio Liaison Group (BLG), or Contact Group (Grupong Tagapaguguay), is formed of initial sympathizers with whom the Semi-legal Teams can conduct teach-ins. After enough sympathizers have been acquired, the BLG is broken down into the Organizing Groups (OGs) representing various sectors of the community. The OGs recruit new members and educate them through formal and informal seminars. As these groups become effective, People's Organizing Committees, or Barrio Organizing Committees, are established for the entire barrio but again are divided according to sectors. At this stage, party members are recruited and party branches formed, leading to the creation of a Barrio Revolutionary Committee (BRC), which usually has nine members equally divided among the barangay council, party branches, and mass organizations. The BRC becomes a shadow government, with its own tax collection system and People's Court. At this point a local militia is created and members are recruited for the NPA's regular units.[47] To ensure "solid organizing," cadres try to involve the peasants in "gradually more demanding tests of their loyalty" such as protest marches, boycotts, and raids. As had the Huks, the CPP found that military action was effective only when "combined with measures to improve public support."[48]

During the party's first historical phase of development, Central Committee members were used as organizing cadres. This permitted the rapid development of new fronts, and the decentralized structure, under Guerrero's policy of "centralized leadership, decentralized operation," gave the leaders of these fronts considerable latitude to operate. The radical, well-educated Manila youths who became the CPP's peasant organizers did their job well—but with one drawback. Although they benefited from the traditional respect usually afforded educated individuals by the peasants, this deference made it difficult for the organizers to develop leaders among them. During the party's second phase, the "petit bourgeois background of some cadres, with more "book learning than experience," resulted in their taking a dogmatic approach to building mass support.[49]

The CPP, however, wished to rebuild the barrio's social structure (as had the Vietnamese Communist movement), which led in part to the emphasis in the late 1970s on recruiting tribal groups and local peasant leaders.[50] At every level—the regional committees, the front committee, the district and section committees, and finally the party branches—the form and function of the Central Committees were replicated. Although this approach suited the CPP's objective of transforming society, it became more difficult, as the party's size increased, to ensure quality control. The Semi-legal Teams, for example, the critical building blocks, began to consist of less experienced cadres. One knowledgeable Filipino observer has argued that Maoism "ceased to be a positive force" because of the decentralization. And a defector complained that he could not travel anywhere without the district committee's authorization.[51] "Now that our struggle has grown by leaps and bounds, our needs have grown multifarious; they have become bigger, heavier and more extensive, and they have to be met," noted the October 1975 issue of *Ang Bayan*.

The party's rapid spread in Mindanao in the late 1970s created tensions within the Central Committee. Mindanao regional committee members thought that some other regions, especially Metro Manila, were too slow, that their "purist standards" for membership were impeding the establishment of a mass base in Manila.[52] In retrospect it can be seen that both sides were partly correct. On the one hand, the rapid expansion in Mindanao provided easier access for government agents and their counterinsurgency efforts, especially in Davao. In that city, public support for the NPA weakened as a result of indiscriminate assassinations by undisciplined militia—so much so that the NPA was forced to withdraw in 1986. On the other hand, the failure to develop a broad enough mass base in Manila made it easier for the Yellows to capture the government in the February 1986 revolution.

Guerrero, in *Philippine Society*, had recommended that the central leadership constantly shift its organizational arrangements; he also observed that the SYPs (the Propaganda Units) and the first guerrilla units were extremely vulnerable because the country's geography forced them to operate along narrow fronts.[53] Unfortunately these strictures were not remembered during the fifth stage in the CPP's evolution. Tension within the party, partly caused by its apparatus, contributed to divergences among the NPA, the NDF, and the CPP in some ways similar to that between the Huks and the PKP.

Rodolfo Salas, a former university lecturer who was also known as Ka Bilog (Ka is an abbreviated form of Kasama, taken by the movement to mean comrade), became party chairman after Sison's arrest in 1977. He reportedly assassinated three American naval officers in Subic Bay, the American naval facility, on April 13, 1974. The party's secretary-general now was Rafael Baylosis, graduate of and former lecturer at the University of the Philippines. Baylosis served concurrently as chairman of the Mindanao Commission. It was he who was responsible for the rapid expansion of the party in Mindanao, along with Benjamin de Vera (reputed to have organized Davao in 1971 and later appointed chairman of the Mindanao Commission) and Romulo "Rolly" Kintanar (who arrived in Mindanao in the mid-1970s to organize the NPA).[54]

Salas wanted priority given to the armed struggle. A split developed between the older generation of Central Committee members based in Luzon who had a Maoist heritage and the younger members in Mindanao who were attracted by Nicaragua's Sandanistas. Some traveled to that country and some Sandinistas visited the Philippines.[55] Their success confirmed for these new CPP leaders that armed struggle was the correct strategy. Nevertheless, an older group, mainly within the NDF, represented by Satur Ocampo, Edgar Jopson, Tony Zumel, and Horacio "Boy" Morales, remained strong advocates of the political approach. After the successful Sandinista revolution, an attempt was made to adjust the party's strategy to account for (1) the higher level of urbanization in the Philippines, (2) the larger urban middle class, and (3) the bourgeois-democratic tradition in Philippine politics which provided an "increased role for the urban struggle and the people's war." As Villalobos, a party cadre, observed, "The military struggle, countryside work, and the domestic front would still play the principal role, but the political struggle, urban work, and the international front would not be too far behind."

The tension between these two approaches to revolution dominated the party's debates during the 1980s. *Ang Bayan* in December 1984, said that "legal and unarmed struggles are part of the revolution's arsenal . . . [but] social conditions dictate that our revolution should, in the main, take the path of armed struggle." The success of that approach, during the party's third phase, on Mindanao, the second largest island in the archipelago and the most mountainous and least developed, distorted the Central Committee's and Salas's assessment of the revolution's strategy. What worked on Mindanao, they thought, would work elsewhere. Guerrero, though, had viewed the value of a Mindanao front primarily in terms of its weakening the enemy's forces in Luzon.[56]

Although Guerrero had stated that "political power grows out of the barrel of a gun" and that the NPA's principal task was "seizing political power and consolidating it," he looked upon armed struggle as secondary to political struggle.[57] He stressed the need for the NPA to win the peasants' hearts and minds, repeating two sets of Mao's dictums from the *Little Red Book*. The first, the "Three Main Rules of Discipline," were:

1. Obey orders in all your actions.
2. Do not take a single needle or thread from the masses.
3. Turn in everything captured.

The second, the "Eight Points of Attention," instructed the cadres:

1. Speak politely.
2. Pay fairly for what you buy.
3. Return everything you borrow.
4. Pay for anything you damage.
5. Do not hit or swear at people.
6. Do not damage crops.
7. Do not take liberties with women.
8. Do not ill-treat captives.[58]

Guerrero closely adhered to the Maoist strategic concept of a "people's war"; it would require a long-term struggle, but victory was inevitable.

Guerrero emphasized the NPA's value in compelling "the enemy to disperse its forces at great costs across the archipelago" so that they could be destroyed "piece by piece."[59] But he also recognized that the Huks had misjudged the stage their armed struggle had arrived at. They had become overextended, politically isolated, and abusive. The NPAS were to become active only after a popular base had been established. Progress would be defined by the struggle's impact on "popular consciousness."[60] This had been Guerrero's rationale, before his arrest, for building a mass base and forming political cadres during the party's second stage of development. He had wanted to avoid precisely the problems that arose when Salas began expanding forces in the late 1970s. And, indeed, as the movement grew, the NPAS became a force in some ways independent of the party.

CONDUCTING THE ARMED STRUGGLE

The NPA began with nine squads of approximately seven men each.[61] Their strength lay in the fact that they were difficult for the enemy to isolate and destroy, and they remained the basic military formation of the NPA even as larger units were formed.

The regular forces of the NPA were organized into Main Regional Guerrilla Units (MRGUS) of 80 to 150 fighters, Secondary Regional

Guerrilla Units (SRGUS) of 30 to 60 men, and Armed City Partisan Units/Sparrow Units (ACPU/SUS) of 1 to 4 persons. As urban operations expanded, ACPUS in 1987 were further divided into Regular Partisan Operations (RPOS) and Special Partisan Operations (SPOS). The RPOS attacked small targets, such as lower-ranking AFD soldiers and civilian officials, whereas SDOS targeted higher-level officials in more complicated operations. Logistics and other support activities were provided by the Barrio Revolutionary Committees (BRCS), the Semi-legal Teams, the Propaganda Units, or local militia forces of the BRCS. The MRGUS and SRGUS were not necessarily separate units. In larger engagements, SRGUS formed to become MRGUS just as squads grouped to become SRGUS. These regular forces were directed by the regional and front committees. Each unit was under the command of a troika consisting of a commander, vice-commander, and political officer, each of whom had to have two to three years' service.[62] The organization resembled the Huks who were organized in battalion-sized field commands (one hundred to seven hundred men) with a headquarters detachment and several squadrons. There were four types of personnel: the hard-core, or "twenty-four-hour Huk" regulars; the combat support provided by "twelve-hour Huks"; the service group, or legal cadres; and the mass base.[63] Unlike the Huks, however, the NPA maximized mobility and camouflage by operating in smaller units. In this manner the NPA could implement Guerrero's tactical advice of "concentration . . . or dispersion" according to circumstances. Units concentrated to attack and dispersed to propagandize or organize.[64] This, of course, put a premium on communication and discipline.

Discipline was maintained by demanding obedience to Mao's "Three Main Rules of Discipline" and "Eight Points of Attention." These standards were embroidered upon in an elaborate social system that was almost monastic. People were to practice "simple living, thrift," said *Ang Bayan* in October 1985. Drinking was frowned upon; drug use, including marijuana, was grounds for a court-martial; casual sex was forbidden as was homosexuality; troops lived on root crops with little meat or rice. Many were or became ill with such diseases as tuberculosis or schistosomiasis. That discipline could be maintained under such conditions was impressive, for the majority of NPA cadres were peasants under thirty. One rebel observed, "If you want to court a girl, you must submit her name, and she will be investigated." The party could force marriages and break up relationships. As one NPA member put it, "The NPA is my family now and the movement is my religion."[65]

Although very little is known about this NPA subculture, one report on their marriage practices suggests that the NPA has blended Catholic and Communist ritual. A couple may begin courting after two years' service in the NPA but only after receiving the collective's permission. After a year's courtship, an engagement may be announced during which the couple's collectives meet to evaluate their "discipline and honor of marriage" and their "love for the masses." A "marriage collective," formed of the couple's sponsors and "solemnizer," acts as a "marriage encounter therapy group scrutinizing the merits and demerits of the couple." The ceremony itself begins with a "reading on the theme of marriage," followed by the sponsors' speeches "on the importance of proletarian love, how the couple's love for each other must be contextualized in their love for the people." The two give their reasons for marrying, a marriage pledge to serve the people is made with their hands placed on crossed M-16s, the CPP's flag is draped over their shoulders, and the "Internationale" is sung.[66] "Sex love," according to the party's "Rules of Marriage within the Party," codified in 1970, is subordinate to "class love": "The revolutionary youth in the countryside avoid early marriages so they can be relatively free from family responsibilities for a longer time." Women have been given equal status as NPA fighters, although this has been more difficult to enforce as they are treated at times as sex objects or given safer positions as medical aides or file clerks.[67]

The group's tactics are based mostly on American military field manuals and the study of other successful revolutions, although in 1987 the NPA General Staff published a three-volume military manual on NPA organization, military hardware, and combat training. A new recruit receives some basic training before being sent out in a squad, but his training is limited, especially by a lack of live ammunition. The party, according to one report, was said to have "systematized the political and military training of its personnel" after 1980. Troop participation in annual retraining courses was sufficiently successful that they were ahead of schedule in reaching their three-year target of transforming the majority into regular forces.[68] Full-fledged platoons were formed owing to increases in arms, trained commanders and cadres, and combat support units. There were even sufficient personnel, it was said, to form reserve units. But in 1985, another NPA cadre disputed this view, saying, "We are not yet well trained. . . . We are trying to raise the quality of our curriculum in tactics and techniques. We have enemy manuals. We study them and try to adapt the methods. We learn as we go."[69]

Not much is known about the process and standards by which justice is meted out within the NPA ranks. Some cadres who surrendered were reported to have been court-martialed for bad behavior, especially for displaying a lack of military initiative and courage.[70] Court-martial is one of the more benign punishments. Criminal penalties include a reprimand, reprimand and reassignment, demotion, suspension, expulsion, and expulsion and execution.[71] There appears to be little concern about individuals defecting nor is a concerted effort made to eliminate them later—unless they inform in which case they may be assassinated. Government informers (demonyos), or deep penetration agents, discovered within the NPA's ranks are liquidated after trial and torture.[72] Discipline is critical both for control and security within the NPA's ranks and for the movement's financing.

Funding for the CPP's activities comes from four sources: theft (more kindly known as confiscation), foreign contributions, extortion of businesses including multinational corporations, and taxes in areas under their control. The party's constitution initially stipulated that financing was to be from "members' entrance fees and dues, by productive undertakings of the Party, and by unconditional contributions."[73] Dues were initially set at fifty centavos a month with the Central Committee receiving 80 percent of the income. Each front and commission operates on an annual budget, and the CPP ensures control over regional operations partly through its design of budgetary targets and its allocation of political and military objectives. The average NPA soldier costs about two to ten pesos a day for food and receives an allowance of ten to fifteen pesos a month.[74] But, though troop cost is low, the party's growth is restrained by its parasitical relationship with the society it lives on, which in turn affects the party's strategy. Thus, it cannot implement a radical land reform program, giving land to the landless, without destroying the wealthier landowning or tenant-farming peasants on whom it depends for taxes and support.

The CPP's financial policy was "adopted in desperation" in the mid-1970s after the People's Republic of China cut off funding. A new program of "total financial self-reliance" resulted in a complex taxation/extortion plan, commercial business ventures, and rural development plans, such as farmers' cooperatives. In 1981, for example, the American embassy reported that the CPP had achieved "moderate success" in forming a marketing cooperative in Banaue.[75] This financial situation may have been another reason the party changed its focus in the late 1970s, expanding its activities and giving greater independence to the regional commissions.

The group levies two types of taxation, those on individuals and those on businesses. Individuals or families under NPA control must pay a weekly progressive tax. Peasant families are expected to give two to ten pesos and two cups of rice per month; although in some cases they give it freely, coercive pressure is always present. Some tenant farmers pay a portion of their harvest—between 2 and 50 percent—by underdeclaring production levels to their landlord.

Businesses are charged a monthly tax rate and/or "licensing fee" on their equipment. For example, a logging firm might be charged a licensing fee of $2,273 per truck, or its tax might be levied by the board-foot produced. Tax assessments are conducted with some sophistication by NPA "auditors"—college students with an accounting background.[76] The local party tax section usually sends a preliminary letter to the business being taxed, outlining procedures and establishing code names to authenticate tax collectors. The amount of taxes is determined through a negotiation process with the CPP, which includes at times auditors evaluating the business's profitability. If a business fails to pay up, it might encounter labor problems or sabotage, or its equipment might be destroyed or its operations otherwise disrupted; its executives might even be murdered.[77] Since enterprises, especially logging or mining concerns, often are already paying protection money to local military officials, there is little incentive for them not to pay the CPP; they simply tack it on to business costs.[78] In 1987 the Philippine government estimated that 300 million pesos (not including Metro Manila) had been raised annually and that regional contributions ranged from 5 million to as high as 80 million pesos.[79]

The party functions like a piecework factory in which every unit is evaluated on how effectively it meets its military objectives. Production targets for numbers of captured areas, ambushes, typewriters, teach-ins, new recruits, and so on are established at the Central Committee's annual meeting. They are then portioned out down the chain of command to the squad and the BRC. The way in which these targets are met is established within each collective. Businesses might be taxed in kind rather than in cash, for example, and be forced to provide vehicles, personal computers, ink, paper—whatever the party needs.

Weapons are obtained from the Philippine military either through *agaw armas* raids ("arms-grabbing") or by purchasing them from soldiers.[80] There are no indications that they receive weapons from abroad, although they did so during the party's early years and could do so again. The group began to develop a primitive weapons-building capacity in the early 1980s, which enabled them to fabricate M-16 bullets and remote-controlled primitive land mines. They also are reported to have obtained—perhaps through purchase—weapons from such illegal gun-making businesses as those controlled by Marcos crony and warlord Ramon Durano in Cebu. These weapons were shipped across the Tanon Strait into Negros.[81] Some unsubstantiated reports have also suggested that the NPA has cultivated marijuana to exchange for weapons.[82]

The NPA's growth forced the group to focus attention on organizational matters in the mid-1980s. It instituted "strong and centralized commands for overall planning, [for] systematic launching of coordinated military campaigns, and for sharing resources and personnel to expedite army-building."[83] Because its organization is decentralized, the NPA must rely on a sophisticated command-and-control system both within its areas of operation and intraregionally. Its primary communication system consists of couriers and telephones or telegrams, to which long-range radios were added in the mid-1980s. Fishermen and seamen were targeted for political work in order to develop communication routes, an effort that met with some success.[84] Interisland commercial airlines provide another mode of courier transport—one that the Philippine military has found extremely difficult to intercept.[85]

Another example of NPA organizational strength is its ability to obtain professional medical attention for wounded soldiers. In Luzon, seriously injured personnel are driven by private vehicle into Manila where in the past they have received attention in church-affiliated hospitals. Father Balweg, a rebel leader in northern Luzon, reportedly spent several weeks in a Manila hospital. Rodolfo Salas had been treated at a Manila hospital when he was captured with his wife and driver in

1986. The less seriously wounded are sent to Manila via public transport. Private physicians may treat rebels in their offices, and the NDF established a front, the National Association of Health Workers (MASAPA) to recruit nurses and doctors.[86] The NPA field medics' training is limited mainly to acupuncture and herbal treatments, a restriction that has become a serious constraint on their operations.

A final NPA strength lies in its ability to carry out carefully chosen assassinations, which, until 1985, won it considerable support. As a U.S. Senate report noted, "The NPA uses violence selectively."[87] In Mindanao, Sparrow Units perfected an intelligence system that permitted them to move into cities without attracting notice in order to carry out a hit, usually against an unpopular government official or policeman. This required surveillance of the target, selection of the best ambush position, and development of a cover to blend into the site, such as posing as a local vendor on a busy street corner. Given the densely populated and integrated city communities, the operation required considerable finesse and local support. Sparrow Units are noted for their quick kills carried out with a minimum of ammunition (sometimes only one shot to the head) and their rapid escape. The technique developed in Mindanao, especially Davao, in the early 1980s during the period of tactical offensives was later applied elsewhere. For example, a Sparrow Unit killed Gen. Tomas Karingal at a Quezon City beer hall in May 1984 in the first operation of a Manila-based Armed City Partisan Unit known as the Alex Boncayao Brigade.[88] Aquino's local government secretary and the architect of a civilian defense force, Jaimé Ferrer, was murdered in July 1987—the first Philippine cabinet official ever to be assassinated.

Over time, however, the NPA has become more indiscriminate in the killings. A military officer based in Davao observed that the Partisan Units changed their strategy in 1984. Originally, they attacked policemen, then soldiers, then informers, and then "noncooperative civilians," until their attacks had become random. A member of the Philippine military reform group charges that in Manila NPA soldiers allied themselves with local criminals and employed paid assassins.[89] (The Vietminh also employed these types of "social marginals," assigning them the most dangerous tasks.) As one NPA cadre said, "Most of the Sparrow killings are by young boys who have had no training. It's sort of an 'on-the-job training.' We select young unknowns for Sparrow duty because they can move about easily without being noticed."[90]

An American human rights group has reported that NPA cadres have murdered villagers who refused to pay their taxes and others, including journalists, who made anti-Communist statements. There are "very few people that brave to witness that NPA actually did [murder someone]," observed a nun active in Mindanao's human rights movement. In an attack by NPA regulars in Cagayan they reportedly executed wounded AFP troops after battle, a departure from their policy of helping the enemy's wounded in order to gain their support.[91]

Their more customary practice is to win over people by administering rough justice against the people's oppressors. In Misamis Oriental, for example, NPA cadres killed the provincial governor's sister for "being abusive and using barangay funds for personal use" and executed a Civilian House Defense Force military man in eastern Samar for rape and election fraud.[92] Magno Yabut, the son of a former Makati mayor, was killed in July 1987 for allegedly raping two women, stabbing a man, and terrorizing residents of a small town. The letters NPA came to stand for "Nice People Around," the "Nice People's Association," or "No Permanent Address," the latter reflecting a popular perception of the group as a band of young Robin Hoods.

Their popularity was helped along by the fact that many Filipino families, including the elites, had friends or relatives who were members of the CPP-NPA. Rolly Kintanar, the principal strategist behind the ACPUS in Davao, had a brother who was a colonel. Antonio Zumel, chairman of the NDF, was a former editor of the *Manila Bulletin* and president of the National Press Club. Zumel's brother, Brig. Gen. Jose Maria Carlos Zumel, was commandant of the Philippine Military Academy and a leading supporter of Marcos even after Marcos was exiled. Horacio "Boy" Morales, who defected to the NDF in 1977, was one of the rising stars of the Development Academy of the Philippines. The Philippine elite and middle class had difficulty imagining these people as blood-thirsty protégés of the Khmer Rouge.

The NPA was helped militarily by the AFP's weakness, which came as a surprise to the group. But initial successes in the early 1980s exaggerated the NPA's capabilities. Its commanders were promoted ahead of political cadres, helping to institutionalize further the emphasis on armed struggle. Only in 1985—after a reassessment of the party's failure to gain popular support for its boycott of the 1984 elections, a dramatic increase in mass protest movements after Senator Aquino's assassination, and rising public concern over the Philippines' becoming a "killing field" with the NPA cast as the Khmer Rouge —did the party shift its emphasis substantially toward parliamentary struggle and the third element of Guerrero's strategy, the united fronts, completing a process begun in 1981. Said *Ang Bayan* in April 1985, "It would have been impossible to achieve major advances in the open mass movement in the past few years if the Party had not given it the necessary special attention and corresponding organizational adjustments needed in its advance."

FORGING A UNITED FRONT

The third "magic weapon" of the revolution, according to Guerrero, was to be a national united front, which would provide the means of creating an alliance of the working class, peasantry, and intellectuals. The legal struggle of the national front would, through mass protests, teachings, strikes, and similar tactics, help mobilize these groups, who though uncommitted were "extremely receptive to revolutionary propaganda." Guerrero observed that the "bourgeoisie" were "verbally abusive" of imperialists but doubted the effectiveness of a revolutionary mass movement. They did not oppose the revolution, but they had a "strong tendency to stay 'neutral.' " They had to be won over in order to shift the balance of power in the society.[93]

Coalition construction was an inherent part of the Philippine political process. The legal parties were themselves loose coalitions or alliances of various political fiefdoms.[94] The Huks had failed to construct a mass base to support their own revolution. Their United Front never became fully organized as an adjunct to the PKP, and because the PKP's own roots were weak, it could not provide the coalition-building function needed to acquire power.[95] The brilliance of Guerrero's analysis lay in his perception of this error and his attempt to rectify it. With the Communist party outlawed and the NPA beyond the law, quasi-legal groups were needed to reach out to segments of society, such as the church, health workers, and teachers, in order to mobilize them; thus was born the National Democratic Front. The CPP directed the formation of the NDF as early as 1971, but not until late 1972 was there sufficient support to organize it. In October of that year, following the declaration of martial law, the CPP, called for mass mobilization through the creation of "revolutionary trade unions," appeals for peasant support, the formation of "mutual aid societies," the cultivation of student underground groups, the encouragement of petit bourgeoisie and intelligentsia, and the solicitation of financial support from the middle class. Alliances were to be founded with the military, expatriates, the church, and political leaders.[96] A united front would build support for the armed struggle and its national democratic revolution.

If martial law had not been declared, the CPP might not have formed the NDF despite the amount of planning that preceded it. The CPP had prepared for martial law with contingency plans for many cadres to disappear underground (although it was unprepared to absorb the large numbers of new recruits who joined the party when the law was declared). Others could remain in the open, maintaining a legal cover while operating through newly formed mass organizations.[97] The culture helped facilitate this behavior. From historical times, it had been common practice for elites to disguise their influence by manipulating others.

On April 24, 1973, the NDF was founded allegedly at the instigation of several groups: the Revolutionary Peasant Association, Christians for National Liberation, Nationalist Youth, League of Filipino Students, Youth for Nationalism and Democracy, Patriotic Health Association, and Association of Nationalist Teachers. Its ten-point manifesto focused on "U.S. imperialism as the mastermind behind the setting up of the fascist dictatorship":

1. Unite all anti-imperialist and democratic forces to overthrow the U.S.-Marcos dictatorship and work for the establishment of a coalition government based on a truly democratic system of representation.
2. Expose and oppose U.S. imperialism as the mastermind behind the setting up of the fascist dictatorship, struggle for the nullification of all unequal treaties and arrangements with this imperialist power, and call for the nationalization of all its properties in the country.
3. Fight for the reestablishment of all democratic rights of the people, such as freedom of speech, the press, assembly, association, movement, religious belief, and the right to due process.

4. Gather all possible political and material support for the armed revolution and the underground against the U.S.-Marcos dictatorship.

5. Support a genuine land reform program that can liberate the peasant masses from feudal and semifeudal exploitation and raise agricultural production through cooperation.

6. Improve the people's livelihood, guarantee the right to work, and protect national capital against foreign monopoly capital.

7. Promote a national, scientific, and mass culture and combat imperialist, feudal, and fascist culture.

8. Support the national minorities, especially those in Mindanao and the mountain provinces, in their struggle for self-determination and democracy.

9. Punish, after public trial, the ringleaders of the Marcos fascist gang for their crimes against the people and confiscate all their ill-gotten wealth.

10. Unite with all peoples fighting imperialism and all reaction, and seek their support for the Philippine revolutionary struggle.[98]

It was not until 1975 that the national democratic movement began to take on substance, aided by the public's growing realization that martial law was permanent. In 1977 the NDF's ten-point program was altered slightly, and in 1982, "a year after the national democratic revolution entered the advanced substage of the strategic defensive," the program was further "revised to lay down a more detailed program of government and to explain the process by which victory is to be achieved."[99]

The need to change the tone, if not the direction, of the front's activities reflected the growth in non-CPP-backed movements and the gradual return to some form of constituent government. The CPP was inactive during the 1976 referendum amending the constitution but with the elections to an Interim National Assembly in 1978, local elections in 1980, and the lifting of martial law in 1981, the political process, however slightly, was opening up. In the 1980 elections, the party formed a coalition with the Benigno Aquino–backed Laban (Fight) party in Manila. In the June 1981 presidential elections, the NDF backed a boycott coalition as it did in the 1984 National Assembly elections and in the 1986 presidential election.

The shift toward the political struggle which began in 1981 also reflected the success of the armed struggle. A turning point had been reached in 1981, according to the CPP, as the party moved into its fourth historical period. By the end of 1980, the party was active in 50 percent of the nation's provinces. The party emphasized "politicization and recruitment," using military force only on a selective basis as a means of demonstrating its might. On Samar, the NPA had moved beyond the strategic defensive phase. The party started preparing for a national uprising in 1984 and 1985.[100]

The increasing success of the CPP's strategy of armed struggle in the rural areas at the expense of urban activities and work on the political front may have been another reason the party believed it could afford to shift toward more political activities. As part of its preparation, the party started strengthening the NDF in 1981, emphasizing political organization by front groups. Marxist ideology was subordinated to nationalist themes, and the NDF began publication of *Liberation*, which also stressed traditional nationalist issues, such as American imperialism and oppressive foreign investors.[101]

From prison, Sison preached the new policy, saying in a 1981 interview, "the CPP alone cannot dislodge Marcos from power now. But a united front for armed struggle can, within the near future, not exceeding a decade. For maximum effort, the united front can include the direct components and associates of the National Democratic Front, the Moro National Liberation Front and the conservative opposition and middle forces in general."[102]

Surprisingly, Aquino's assassination in August 1983, which mobilized the middle class and elites to create a cornucopia of new protest groups, caught the NDF unprepared. With the failure of the boycott the next year, the NDF went back to its drawing board and produced a revised twelve-point program in January 1985. The program comprised three parts. The first, the "People's War and the National Democratic Front," was a preamble to a general program of long-term tasks and a specific program of immediate tasks. As it had before, the NDF attacked American imperialism, stressing, although in greater detail, foreign policy issues:

> The United States must leave its military bases in the Philippines and cease to provide military assistance to local reactionaries.

The military bases shall be used for military and civilian purposes by the democratic republic. No foreign power shall be allowed to set up military bases on Philippine soil, nor to carry by any means of transport, nuclear weapons into Philippine territory.[103]

The specifics of the new program included immediate political, military, economic, social welfare, cultural, educational, and foreign affairs tasks to be carried out. There was little that was new; rather, it emphasized creating mass organizations, establishing links with the landed gentry and the bourgeoisie, encouraging sabotage, and attacking the enemy. Mirroring Guerrero's earlier view of a people's democratic coalition government as being more socialist than communist, it called for partial cancelation of foreign debt and land rents, higher payments for pensioners, and free medical services. The intent of the program was to focus people's attention on the failures of the Marcos regime and attract broad support for what was essentially a liberal reform agenda.[104] The twelve-point general program differed little from the original NDF platform:

1. Unite the Filipino people to overthrow the tyrannical rule of U.S. imperialism and the local reactionaries.
2. Wage a people's war to win total, nationwide victory.
3. Establish a democratic coalition government and a people's democratic republic.
4. Integrate the revolutionary armed forces into a single national revolutionary army.
5. Uphold and promote the free exercise of the people's basic democratic rights.
6. Terminate all unequal relations with the United States and other foreign entities.
7. Complete the process of genuine land reform, raise rural production through cooperation, and modernize agriculture.
8. Carry out national industrialization as the leading factor in economic development.
9. Guarantee the right to employment, raise the people's living standards, and expand social services the soonest after establishing democratic state power.
10. Promote a patriotic, scientific, and popular culture and ensure free public education.

11. Respect and foster the self-determination of the Moro and Cordillera people and all ethnic minorities.

12. Adopt and practice a revolutionary, independent, and peace-loving foreign policy.

The NDF increasingly was being viewed as ineffective and tarred with the communist brush. Its early leaders, such as Boy Morales, Tony Zumel, and Satur Ocampo, had been arrested in the 1970s when front activities were sacrificed to the exigencies of the armed struggle. Among Filipinos, the military's propaganda efforts to equate the NDF with the NPA were having some effect as concern about the NPA's violence increased.

The twelve-point program was an attempt to rehabilitate the NDF both within the party and within the larger anti-Marcos protest movement. The NDF leadership was trying to justify its views to the Salas-dominated military tacticians. Thus, the 1985 program acknowledged that the "armed struggle is the primary form of struggle that we must wage. This is starkly clear, especially in the face of the fascist dictatorship." Nevertheless, the "armed struggle must be combined with various effective forms of legal struggle."[105] As part of this effort, the NDF engaged in an outreach program abroad, beginning in 1985 the publication of an international edition of its domestic periodical *Liberation* from offices located in Holland. The NDF also shifted its front tactics, trying to distance itself from the new mass organizations being formed in the post–Aquino assassination period. The party had to act as the "force at the core" in order to direct the open mass movements. Cadres had become too involved in the minutiae of "day-to-day legal work" and should instead "delegate to the broad ranks of mass activists the bulk of responsibilities." Rather than directing daily operations, cadres were to become less visible while still providing the general thematic direction of the various mass movements in sectors such as labor, education, health, the arts, and so forth. Also needed were "extra precautions to insulate the specially sensitive lines of Party connections by building surveillance-proof structures between the key Party machineries and exposed legal organizations and personalities," said *Ang Bayan* in April 1985.

The party's need to go more deeply underground was driven by the discreditation of mass groups associated with the NDF, such as two student groups, Nationalist Youth (KM) and the League of Filipino Students (LFS), and the organization of a new front group known as the New Nationalist Alliance, or Bayan (Bagong Alyansang Makabayan). Bayan was a front for a front. Like the NDF it was a coalition composed of organizations from across the political spectrum brought together in conference on May 5, 1985. Its institutional predecessor was the Coalition for the Restoration of Democracy, which in turn had been formed on the base of Justice for Aquino, Justice for All (JAJA), created in response to the senator's murder. Its titular chairman and president were, respectively, the aging nationalist senators Lorenzo Tanada and Ambrosio Padilla. Its secretary-general was Lean Alejandro, a much younger radical who later was assassinated in 1987. Alejandro along with other members of the National Council's Executive Committee, such as Behn Cervantes, a member of Bayan's Popular Struggles Commission, and Etta Rosales, director of Popular Struggles and People's Welfare, had closer ties to the radical left. Cervantes, for example, chaired Concerned Artists of the Philippines and Rosales was active in the Alliance of Concerned Teachers.

Individuals such as Tanada and Padilla were statesmen, not Communists, and their names gave Bayan credibility. Alejandro, Cervantes, Rosales, and others were mass activists doing the party's work, either wittingly or unwittingly, without being members of the party. A typical example of mass activist work was Cervantes's organizing a group of artists to mourn the death of French actress and leftist Simone Sigourney. Cervantes used Sigourney's life to raise people's consciousness about the struggle and their commitment to it. Behind the mass activists was the "force at the core" (the CPP) directing strategy, although the activists themselves were not necessarily party members or even sympathizers.

The organization of the Manila Bayan was replicated in the provinces. Bayan organizers involved prominent local ilustrados who were already active in such groups as the Free Legal Assistance Group (FLAG), Task Force Detainees (a human rights group under the Catholic church's Association of Major Religious Superiors), JAJA, political parties such as former Liberals and Nacionalistas, and even the Rotary Club. Given the small provincial leadership base, individuals active in the Marcos opposition usually wore many hats. The question, of course, was who was using whom. "In the country today there is no organization that is not subject to infiltration," observed a Philippine political leader in 1985. Bayan represented the quintessence of Philippine politics in action: it was a Moro-Moro play, a traditional popular drama about political struggles. Everyone knew what the other's agenda was and the issue was how to manipulate that agenda to serve one's own. It was because of such maneuvering, however, that Bayan suffered an early defeat.

In its 1985 organizing meeting, the CPP tried to pack the organization's Executive Committee with its sectoral representatives, especially those from the rural areas, but the moderates, such as Jaimé Ongpin (chairman of one of the Philippine's largest and most successful corporations, Benguet, and later finance secretary in the Aquino government), objected, in part because they feared that these representatives would be CPP-controlled. Alejandro tried to manipulate the voting by substituting names on the ballot, which outraged the moderates, including Agapito "Butz" Aquino and Sen. Jose Diokno, who walked out. This incident seriously weakened the perception of Bayan as a broad-based mass organization.[106]

Bayan's inspiration was the people's strikes (*welga ng bayan's*) that began in late 1984 in Davao and spread rapidly, focusing especially on the transport system, factories, and the educational sector. The welgas were "a general and coordinated multisectoral form of struggle in the cities" that "may also encompass part of the countryside," said *Ang Bayan* in December 1984. The welgas' aims, it went on, were to paralyze the society, "shake the foundations of the fascist state." They were a means of preparing the people politically for revolution. Representing a preliminary step toward the strategic offensive's popular uprising, welgas were the first sign of an economic strategy which in 1987 evolved into tentative efforts to sabotage the country's economic infrastructure. *Ang Bayan* described the process:

> People's strikes shall be launched repeatedly, in a series, gaining breadth and intensity at every occasion. It shall advance step by step, its integral parts developing in the process—from partial to complete paralyzation [*sic*]; from short to sustained strikes; from simply protesting to wresting substantial concessions from the enemy; from participation of the organized sections to the mobilization of entire sectors; from some major cities and regions to-

wards a nationwide people's strike; from mainly economic towards distinctly political struggles; from coordinated strikes of some factories towards general industrial strikes; from purely political people's strikes towards people's strikes with a distinct military element.

The key to the general strike was a transportation strike. Shutting down transport prevented anyone from getting to work or anything getting to market. The NPA usually helped enforce road blockades and other actions like stonings, which would keep vehicles from moving. In the first welgas such enforcement was unnecessary, but as the strikes became increasingly politicized by the CPP and as people tired, more brutal measures were needed.[107] In Davao by the end of 1985 support for welgas was only lukewarm, contributing to the loss of NPA support in that city in 1986 and the rise of the Alsa-Masa.

Welgas were similar to the mass protests and demonstrations in the United States in the 1960s. An almost fiesta atmosphere prevailed at the rallies and marches. Sectoral groups—peasants, students, fishermen, transport workers, and so forth—were represented, each marching under its own banner. Protest songs, played on guitars and sung, were broadcast through portable loudspeakers on into the night. Skits were performed, sometimes featuring a mock-up of Uncle Sam as a symbol of imperialism. Nuns and other church figures were active in organizing the meetings, partly to defuse confrontations between the people and the police and military. Bayan became the umbrella organization for many of these mass actions in the provinces, where many of the participating groups lacked sufficient support to organize demonstrations individually. But the degree of leadership Bayan or the CPP exercised depended on the province. The extent of popular participation in the 1986 election, for example, despite Bayan's call for a boycott, suggests the limits of its support.

The CPP's failure to manipulate mass organizations through the new front was apparent in other major sectors where the party had enjoyed initial successes: the church, Muslims, labor, and students. Although Guerrero had attacked the Catholic church as the "defender of the landlord class," the NDF by 1981 was claiming that the religious sector was in the forefront of national mass campaigns.[108] The church's radicalization reflected the changes in society as a whole that martial law had wrought—the deterioration of the economy and the pervasive abuse of human rights. The church and its leadership had had to become radicalized in order to protect its flock and maintain the allegiance of priests and nuns in the barrios.

The most prominent example of the church's radicalization was a Society of Divine Word priest, Father Conrado Balweg, who joined the NPA as a guerrilla in June 1979. Balweg said that he first met with the NPA in 1976 while in Davao but that he did not read *Philippine Society* until late in 1978. Active in organizing the mountain tribes in the Cordilleras, Balweg went underground after being alerted by his bishop of his impending arrest by the Philippine Constabulary.[109] Balweg justified his military activities by maintaining that "the Church has always defended the principle of the just war; and it was Jesus himself who used violence against the money lenders in the temple. The Church's stand against revolutionary, moral, and just violence today is not based on Christian teaching."[110]

A group called Christians for National Liberation (CNL) was formed on February 17, 1972, and cooperated with the CPP in organizing the NDF in 1973.[111] After being outlawed, the CNL went underground when martial law was imposed, and its present relationship to the CPP and its effectiveness are unclear. The NDF claims that the CNL grew from its original seventy-two members to thousands of priests, pastors, nuns, seminarians, and lay workers in 1985.[112]

In the early stages of militancy after the declaration of martial law, the party had an advantage in organization, but as militancy spread, especially after Aquino's murder, and more moderate elements joined the protests, the party had difficulty controlling it. A case in point was the Mindanao-Sulu Pastoral Conference (MSDC) established in 1971. Targeted for infiltration by the CPP early on, the MSDC lost the confidence of the bishops who gradually became concerned about its orientation. They finally withdrew in 1981 because its secretariat had fallen under the NDF's control.

The party also attempted to form an alliance with the estimated 2.5 million Muslim Filipinos living in the Sulu-Mindanao region. Some reports indicated that by March 1974, the NPA had infiltrated 10 percent of the Muslim Moro National Liberation Front (MNLF), and a Philippine general claimed that the MNLF and NPA joined forces in 1983.[113] These reports were questionable, however. Although the party gave the MNLF assurances of its "unswerving support" in 1977, the most prominent MNLF leader, Nur Misuari (one of the university intellectuals who with Sison had helped found the Nationalist Youth), broke with the NPA because of disagreements over his attitude toward Muslims.[114] As NPA activity began to expand into Muslim areas in Mindanao, tension between the two groups increased. The NDF held a secret press conference in the Zamboanga Peninsula in May 1985 ostensibly to proclaim the new Mindanao Provisional Council. The conference, however, also appeared aimed at the Muslims, announcing in effect that the two groups were friendly.[115] It was tacit acknowledgment that an alliance did not exist. Once Aquino became president, peace talks were reopened by Misuari with the new government.

Although "self-determination of the Moro and Cordillera people and all ethnic minorities" is one of the NDF's general principles and was a focus of organizing activity in the 1970s, its inclusion in the list of party principles has not gained great support for the CPP among minorities. Even Father Balweg broke with the party in 1986, announcing the formation of a Cordillera People's Liberation Army and signing a separate peace pact with the Aquino government, although one of his brothers remained with the NPA.[116]

The party has had greater success with students and labor groups. The Nationalist Youth organization all but died during the years of martial law. But it held its fourth national congress in November 1984—the first in fourteen years.[117] The attempt to rejuvenate the group was part of a strategy shift that year aimed at moving into urban areas. A base had to be prepared for both the armed and the parliamentary struggles, but the timing may have been too late.

In 1977 the League of Filipino Students (LFS) was formed with a three-part program: restore democracy on campus, end the imperialist control of education, and dismantle the U.S.-Marcos dictatorship. On September 18, 1982, a Student Day of Protest was declared with simultaneous boycotts of classes in Manila, Baguio, Cebu, and Davao. The LFS was an immediate beneficiary of the radicalization of the "martial law baby generation," but, as happened in the church, initial successes were blunted by the politicization of the moderate middle class. At the University of the Philippines, for example, the LFS and another student group linked to Bayan, the National Student Council (Sandigan ng mga Magaaral at Sambayanan, or SAMASA), were defeated in student elections by a moderate group, United Response (Nagkaisang Tugon, or TUGON).[118]

The party came late to organizing labor unions which may account for some of its continued success as late as 1987. (The PKP, too, had been criticized for its slowness to organize trade unions.)[119] Early party attention focused on peasant organizations, as had the Huks, with the formation of the Association of Workers (KASAMA). The NDF began issuing a worker's paper, *Proletaryo*, in September 1979, and at an organizing meeting in May 1980 at Manila's Araneta Coliseum, the group founded the May First Movement (Kilusang Mayo Uno, or KMU) to forge "the worker's open struggles into a solid and strong machinery."[120] The KMU, founded by Felix Olalia and subsequently chaired by his son, Rolando, until his brutal torture and murder by still unidentified assassins in November 1986, claimed that year to have about six hundred members. It took the lead in labor issues and organization, especially during Aquino's first two years in power. The KMU cooperated secretly with the CPP following the party's 1976 decision to emphasize working among laborers. Said an article in *Revolution*, "The party secretly links and coordinates all our trade unions. Our 'independent' unions can retain more income from membership dues and are somewhat saved from control by the reactionary trade union leaders."[121]

After the KMU's formation, other militant labor groups were established. Among them were the Central Luzon Farmers Alliance (CLFA) in 1981; the National Coalition of Workers against Poverty (Pambansang Koalisyon ng Mangaggawa Laban sa Kahirapan, or PKMP) in 1984; the Peasant Movement of the Philippines (Kilusan ng Magbubukid sa Pilipinas, or KMP) in 1985; and the Association of Nationalist Teachers (Katipunan ng mgu Gurong Makabayan, or KAGUMA) in the early 1980s. The KMU boycotted the 1986 election but quickly recognized the Aquino government. It opposed her new constitution in the 1987 plebescite, however.

The KMU's activities were countered by the Trade Unions Congress of the Philippines (TUCP), the largest of the unions with 1.2 million members, which was established with government support in December 1975 and later received aid from the American AFL-CIO. Members of the TUCP included the Associated Labor Unions (ALU), the Federation of Free Farmers (FFF), and the Philippine Transport and

General Workers Organization (PTGWO). The TUCP's general secretary, Ernesto Herrera, who led the ALU, was elected to the Senate on the Aquino slate in the 1987 congressional elections.[122]

Union personalities have always been more important than organization, mirroring the political situation. The importance of personality is one reason the KMU, despite its early association with the CPP, could develop a status independent of the party and continue to grow after Aquino became president. For although the KMU was tarred as a CPP front, its leader, Rolando Olalia, was not identified as a party member, according to independent observers. The NDF could not ensure its control over its affiliates because their semilegal, overt position meant that some leaders and probably most members did not belong to the CPP.

THE IDEOLOGICAL STRUGGLE INTENSIFIES

Even as social conditions in the Philippines appeared to favor the party's two-pronged strategy of armed and political struggles following Senator Aquino's assassination and the country's economic collapse, ideological schisms in the CPP intensified. The party argued in 1984 that the "people's war" had "entered the advanced substage of the strategic defensive" and predicted that the final "strategic offensive" would begin soon. The underpinnings of Guerrero's successful strategy were even attacked for making "empiricism" the NPA's "dominant ideological trend" rather than the ideas of Marx, Engels, Lenin, Stalin, and Mao.[123] *Ang Bayan* in December declared there could not be a "peaceful revolution" or a "revolution without tears," only an "armed revolution." The NDF struck back with Zumel arguing that the "military struggle is a very important form of struggle. But there is also the political struggle. The enemy continues to hold a big edge in the balance of forces militarily."[124] By 1984, party leaders had begun assuming what were called "dogmatic positions." The independence of the NDF had been "overstretched," it was charged, and the Central Committee began to tighten its control.

Party ideologues suggested that the failure to translate the works of Marx, Engels, Lenin, Stalin, and Mao into Philippine dialects had resulted in the wrong strategic approach. They complained again about the lack of cadres who could "lead without getting frequent guidance from the national leadership" and at the same time worried that peasants and the tribal minorities depended too much on leaders from the petit bourgeoisie. Party leaders, said one member in 1986, were too rigid, closed-minded, dogmatic, arrogant, and overbearing.[125]

The PKP had said much the same in its time, complaining that only the top leadership studied communism and not the lower party cadres. The Huks did not understand the difference between being a member of the party and a member of any other organization, and they ignored their leaders' instructions. The PKP cadres had also noted that discipline and commitment suffered because the expansion of revolutionary activities into other organizations and fronts meant membership was no longer homogeneous. People were being made members of the party before they had been sufficiently indoctrinated.[126]

Similar problems within the NPA and the failure to resolve the strategic debate between armed and parliamentary struggles had begun to weaken the movement by 1984, when Metro Manila and other urban areas such as Cebu City, previously off-limits as a NPA rest-and-recreation site, were targeted for actions. In December of that year, Rolly Kintanar was transferred to Metro Manila to establish an Armed City Partisan Unit (ACPU). His transfer was partly related to personality differences with the de Vera brothers, Jose and Benjamin, in Mindanao. (Benjamin de Vera chaired the Mindanao Commission and was national operational commander.) Kintanar's presence in Manila also signaled a decision that experimentation in Davao had reached the point where it was felt that the armed struggle could be expanded into other urban areas. Instead the party suffered setbacks: ACPUs in Cebu were infiltrated and captured, and an NPA safehouse was discovered in Manila in May 1985. The heralded "urban offensive" fizzled as political events overtook the party's strategy.[127]

Corazon Aquino's victory over Marcos in 1986 intensified the factionalism over strategy within the party's ranks. The CPP had decided to boycott the presidential election on February 7, 1986, saying the "U.S.-Supported Election Serves to Prolong the Marcos Dictatorship and Enables It to Escalate War against the Filipino People." That Aquino might win was "a fairy tale," the party said, and insisted that the only way to bring about Marcos's downfall was not by elections but by the "total mobilization of the Filipino people using all the various forms of military struggle." When Aquino won, the party had to backpedal quickly. Now it announced "A People's Victory over the U.S.-Backed

Marcos Regime; A People's Continuing Fight to Advance Democratic and Patriotic Gains!'' ''The Marcos fascist regime has been overthrown,'' it declared, ''his fall hastened by direct popular struggle of the Filipino people.''[128] No mention was made of the election or the failure of the CPP boycott.

Thus the movement and its strategy had suffered a grievous blow. The failure to develop the parliamentary struggle had contributed to a discrediting of the CPP's political fronts when put to the test by moderate forces. As one cadre observed in 1986, alliances with liberal democrats were ''growing smaller and smaller,'' setting the stage for the fifth phase in the party's development.[129]

The CPP's Future in the Post-Marcos Era

The presidential election boycott was a ''major tactical blunder,'' concluded the Central Committee's Political Bureau in May 1986, acknowledging the ''searing impact of this error'' because a ''large, if not the larger, part of our own mass base did not heed the boycott call and voted for the opposition.'' To save face, the Political Bureau claimed that just before the election, the party had decided to ''shift away from the active boycott stance . . . to position our forces for the intensified struggles'' but that the policy shift was ignored.[130]

The Political Bureau criticized the Executive Committee for failing to understand U.S. policy and overestimating the American capacity to ''impose its subjective will on local politics.'' Closer to home, the Executive Committee was accused of ''a serious violation of democratic centralism'' for failing to discuss the boycott decision with the Political Bureau. The committee was ordered to conduct ''self-criticism,'' and every party organ had to analyze the effect of the boycott decision on its functions.[131]

Now occurred a purge of the party's leadership, including its chairman, Rodolfo Salas. Subsequently, in September 1986, Salas, his wife, and his bodyguard were arrested in Manila after leaving a hospital where he had been treated for goiter. Juanito Rivera, the head of the NPA, was replaced by Romulo ''Rolly'' Kintanar. The military seized Rivera in November 1987 at his home in Capas where he was ill with tuberculosis. Rafael Baylosis y Guzman also resigned as the party's secretary-general, and he was captured along with Benjamin de Vera and Romulo Kintanar on March 29, 1988. The new acting Central Committee chairman, Benito Tiamzon, escaped the roundup. The changes in personnel, however, did not resolve differences in tactics and strategy.

Their first problem was to understand the new government which, in one of its first acts, released all political prisoners, including Jose Maria Sison. The military was also ordered into a defensive position and an effort was made to improve civil-military relations. Finally Aquino offered to hold cease-fire talks in an effort to achieve "national reconciliation." The NDF appeared conciliatory toward this proposal, and Satur Ocampo was named the CPP's chief negotiator for the truce talks. Ocampo stated that "we are now looking for a settlement to the problem without the full revolutionary method and program we advance."[132] He added, "As a democratic front, the NDF is *not* a Communist organization. Although the Communist party is part of it, the NDF is not a total Communist organization, nor its program, Communist."

The party also acknowledged this new role for the NDF, stating in *Ang Bayan*'s July 1986 issue that the "unarmed means of struggle . . . assume greater importance," although members were reminded that the "armed struggle remains central." An article, "An Urgent Task: Consolidate the National United Front," in the same issue stressed the need "to build the national revolutionary united front" by consolidating the NDF and building NDF committees from the barrio level up. The NDF, however, was also conciliatory to its more militant members. An apocryphal story was recounted in September's *Liberation* of an NDF front group meeting in which a "plump girl" asked "Is armed struggle necessary?" Many "eager hands" were raised, and a member responded, "Yes, it is still important because armed struggle is still the most decisive means for fighting for the people's rights and freedom."

As the date for the cease-fire talks neared, differences within the party about how to exploit the new political climate were not dampened. Not only was participation in the cease-fire talks an issue but also the party's position on the new constitution then being drafted. July's *Ang Bayan* predicted that the "masses" would eventually reject a constitution that served their "exploiters and oppressors," and in September it attacked the "peaceful processes" of "parliamentarism" as a means by which the "ruling classes" could "deceive the people and divert them from the revolutionary path." The Central Committee further asserted its control over regional cease-fire talks such as those held in Davao del Norte in August, stating that they were "authorized by the national leadership" and observing that the talks' failure illustrated that "any agreement for cease-fire can only be forged at the national level."

Ocampo and Zumel, representing the NDF, were the principal negotiators in the talks that began in December 1986 and collapsed in late January 1987. Both the government and the NDF negotiators were constrained by their respective military establishments, and partly as a result, failure was a foregone conclusion. The armed struggle by both sides was destined to recommence.

The end could have been predicted when Rolando Olalia of the May First Movement (KMU) was brutally murdered on November 13, 1986. He had advocated electoral participation, stating in October that the KMU and the leftist People's party, which he had formed in 1986 with Sison's help (his wife was a member of the Executive Board) and which he led, would "pursue ratification of the constitution even if cease-fire talks fail because there still was democratic space." He noted that the "choice was between a liberal tendency and a fascist tendency"; Aquino represented the liberal tendency which ought to be supported.[133]

The failure of the cease-fire talks also cost the party the opportunity to participate in the February 7, 1987, constitutional plebiscite. The CPP called again for a boycott as did most of its front groups, as hardliners within the party asserted their control. The voices for a more moderate approach were lost in gunfire at Mendiola Bridge in Manila on January 22, 1987, when some farmers demonstrating for land reform under the leadership of the KMP's Jaimé Tadeo were killed in a confrontation with military forces guarding access to Malacañang Palace.

The increase in violence, the failure of the cease-fire talks, and the voters' overwhelming approval of the constitution, even in CPP strongholds, suggested that the rectification review begun by the party in 1986 had been inadequate. Internal debates and violent conflict would intensify and another leadership purge was likely. The PKP may have been correct when it criticized the CPP earlier for its focus on Marcos's tyranny as a justification for revolution because it "sacrificed long-term progress in the interest of short-term popularity."[134] The party's leaders found it difficult not to have Marcos to oppose. He had been the perfect foil, but Aquino projected a different image. So now the CPP tried to paint her as a well-meaning but inexperienced housewife, easily manipulated by her advisers and the military.

The January-April 1986 edition of *International Liberation*, while acknowledging Marcos's defeat, observed that the "structures of repression are firmly rooted and institutionalized." *Ang Bayan* in July 1986 predicted that "anti-Fascism will play a key role once again when Fascist rule is restored." Even earlier, a special issue of *Liberation* on March 6, 1984, saw as a possible post-Marcos scenario the "reversion to a bourgeois republic . . . which, while still subservient to U.S. imperialism, retains token representative government and formal processes of democracy." In a special release, dated September 12, 1986, on the occasion of President Aquino's visit to the United States, *Ang Bayan* observed that "the Rightist nature of government interest and policies is becoming more and more pronounced."

But the image of a queen captive in her palace was difficult to sustain as Aquino began to take a more active political role, campaigning first for the constitution's approval, then for her slate in the May 1987 congressional elections, and later in the January 18, 1988, local elections. At the same time "proletarian revolutionaries" were seen by NDF leaders as having "reaped smaller gains and bigger losses."[135] The congressional elections were a case in point. The party avoided taking an overt position. Instead, the leftist People's party fielded candidates (with limited success—its candidates from Samar's Second District and Cotabato's Second District were elected), and in some areas candidates under other political banners received CPP support. Many candidates were "assessed" fees in exchange for not disrupting their campaigns. But the overall result was deeply disappointing. Aquino's candidates won 22 out of 24 Senate seats and 151 out of 200 congressional seats. The People's party had mustered only seven candidates for the Senate. Still, a quantitative study of Filipino voting behavior found that although the People's party's share of the national vote was small, "it had pockets of relatively strong support in all parts of the Philippines: the north, the center and the south."[136]

The failure of the People's party mocked Sison's prediction to the party's Preparatory Commission that it could "build its own strength on a nationwide scale and win political victories on its own account."

The failure of front groups to make inroads into the political system only reinforced the proponents of the armed struggle who now argued in *Ang Bayan* in April 1987 that such a struggle was "not an option one can take depending on the form of rule U.S. imperialism and its local allies employ one time or another. . . . It is a form of struggle waged by the people to challenge the monopoly of power by the ruling big comprador [merchant] and big landlord classes under the aegis of U.S. imperialism."

The failure of the front strategy to win ground domestically and, following the elections, the reappearance of traditional political elites who opposed such radical social programs as land reform vindicated arguments in favor of the "armed struggle." Philippine society was becoming increasingly polarized. President Aquino captured the mood herself when interviewed by the BBC in December 1987:

> I think what saddens me so much is that we are being forced to choose between the NPA on the one hand and the vigilantes, the Alsa-Masa, on the other, and surely we didn't fight the dictatorship just to end up with these two choices. I mean, we've always believed the essence of democracy is choice, but the way it goes now, since I oppose the vigilantes, for example, then I have been called a Communist, that I endorse the NPA.[137]

Confronting Aquino with this contradiction was the political goal of her opponents on both the left and the right who saw greater conflict as their only means to power. The right wing—primarily the Philippine military and its allies among the oligarchy—repeatedly pushed Aquino with threats of coups to adopt a harder line against the insurgents, which limited her ability to pass social reform legislation. Anti-Communist vigilante groups under the direction of local political warlords and military commanders proliferated, which limited the power of local officials. These tactics abetted CPP efforts to recruit new members and to paint the Aquino government, at best, an ineffectual tool of a conservative landowning elite. Correspondingly, the NPA increased its main-force and Sparrow Unit attacks partly to provoke more violent reaction from the military. The more the Aquino government adopted conservative policies, such as restraining wage increases and breaking labor strikes, to placate its right-wing foes, the more the CPP benefited. The party's problem of whom to oppose was resolved.

The tactical problem was also resolved by the increasingly conservative complexion of the government. First, the party adopted more aggressive military tactics. Their attacks were on multiple fronts: against regular military units, using main-force units, and against isolated targets, using Sparrow Units. Manila, in 1987, became for the first time a major center of urban terrorism with the police and military officers the principal victims. Americans, who had not been attacked since 1974, were targeted when two active-duty airmen from Clark Air Base and a retired serviceman were killed on October 28, 1987. Then the cpp began a deliberate program of economic sabotage, increasing illegal labor strikes and destroying bridges, railway lines, and oil pipelines. These tactics had a cost, however. Sabotage of railway lines and bridges in Bicol irritated the peasants, and killings in Manila terrified the middle class.

The cpp announced in February 1987 that any foreigner "directly involved in the planning, coordination, supply and operations of the U.S. counter-insurgency program" would be treated as "combatants." Following the October 28 attack, Satur Ocampo announced on November 8 that Americans were now "targets for attack" because of U.S. government support for the Philippine counterinsurgency effort. Ocampo claimed credit for the American killings, stating that their deaths resulted from a decision taken in June because of "increasingly blatant intervention" by the United States.[138]

The decision to attack Americans was taken in the context of a second decision to expand international support for the insurgents. The increasing vigilante movements and a less tolerant military led to a rise in the incidence of human rights abuses, following a year-long lull in 1986. The party had thereby regained an important international propaganda tool, claiming in *Ang Bayan* in April that "the government and its U.S. backers have been laying the ground for the formation of terror squads nationwide." It charged that the vigilante movement was part of "the larger picture of U.S. global counter-insurgency . . . part and parcel of the imperialists' war strategy to defeat national liberation movements and preserve their interests especially in the Third World."

Amnesty International and the Lawyers Committee for Human Rights provided independent assessments in reports issued in 1988 about the growing human rights abuses by vigilante groups and the military. "A key pattern in the development of vigilante forces in many of the provinces . . . is the encouragement of such groups by local military officials over the objections of local civilian officials," noted the Lawyers Committee. Furthermore, "this pattern has entailed a substantial erosion of civilian government authority during a period when the national government was working to strengthen local government institutions." Amnesty International observed that "since mid-1987 political killings carried out by government and government-backed forces in violation of the law have become the most serious human rights problem in the Philippines."[139] The growing violence, while initially undercutting CPP support, may serve in the long term to bring it more recruits.

This was the first time the CPP explicitly sought external verbal, financial, and military support. The decision to do so had come after considerable internal debate, for the party had long been opposed to any direct support except through "international solidarity work" (this despite the history of Soviet and Chinese contacts by PKP and CPP leaders in their parties' formative years).[140]

The CPP had initially rejected Soviet offers of support. A 1969 CPP document called for the "firmest relations" with China and Albania but did not mention the Soviet Union, and Guerrero in his early work attacked "U.S. imperialism, Japanese militarism and Soviet social-imperialism."[141] Even after Imelda Marcos visited Peking in 1974, the party continued to attack the Soviets, claiming that "it is wrong to put on par a socialist country like China with a social-imperialist country like the Soviet Union which would constitute (were Soviet-Philippine relations to develop) not only one more exploiter of the Filipino people but also a grave threat to the center of the world revolution and the entire world revolution, including the Philippine revolution."[142] The CPP continued to insist in 1976 that "Soviet social-imperialism even as [an] enemy of U.S. imperialism cannot be our friend in any way."[143] The Soviets were vilified and lumped together with the Lavaites until the early 1980s.

The subsequent shift to a more neutral position on ties to the Soviet Union was related to the NPA's need for outside aid. During the group's early years the Chinese had provided some arms but at a price; the supply dried up when money ran short.[144] A classified American embassy study in 1975 reported that the CPP was "heavily dependent on outside financial support," mainly from China, and that there was evidence that the Chinese had "passed up to $200,000 to CPP/ML couriers from mid-1974 to early 1975." Two Chinese shipments of weapons to the CPP were intercepted on Philippine shores by the military in 1972 and 1974; no further shipments were made, although an alleged Chinese courier, taking $77,000 from the Chinese embassy in Ottawa to the CPP via the United States, was arrested in early 1975.[145] Guerrero acknowledged that the movement received foreign support in general terms of "fighting in common" against the superpowers and in unspecified direct aid. But Philippine diplomatic overtures to the Chinese appear to have ended Chinese aid to the CPP by mid-1975.[146]

By the early 1980s, however, the needs of the CPP had outgrown its ability to rely on the homespun methods of *agaw armas* for weapons and material, although *Ang Bayan* claimed in October 1983 that the party had seized one thousand rifles each year in 1981 and 1982. Munro argued that Salas decided to smuggle Soviet arms in as early as 1981 and said that the NDF adopted a pro-Soviet position in January 1982. The arms, AK-47 assault rifles and Makharov pistols, allegedly came from Palestine Liberation Organization stocks and were shipped to the Philippines via South Yemen. A Filipino leather dealer claimed to have smuggled the weapons in fifteen crates hidden aboard a shipment of hides financed by Morales.[147] There was, however, no other hard evidence of foreign-supplied weapons, according to both American and Philippine intelligence officers.[148] As an American report noted in 1982, "CPP leadership continues to affirm the principle of self-reliance, an indication that foreign support remains a negligible factor in the insurgency equation."[149] Instead the party relied on its increasingly onerous tax system imposed on the mass base of poor peasants, who, when squeezed, became hostile toward the movement, and on extortion from businesses, who were suffering too from the economic decline. These pressures forced the party to seek support abroad.

Zumel, the NDF spokesman, confirmed that they were seeking "material and political support from abroad," but he denied that the CPP received Soviet aid.[150] *Ang Bayan* said in its July 1986 issue, "We must expand and intensify our international solidarity work and link it directly with our national revolutionary struggle. This requires us to make a strong international projection of the NDF and to establish firm revolutionary linkages and diplomatic relations with various governments." In an interview during that period, Satur Ocampo acknowledged that "in the past, our lack of ties to foreign governments was a kind of moral point with us. . . . We are now reviewing this party line, the international line. . . . We are not actively seeking aid from the Soviets, but we would accept all forms of aid if there were no strings attached." Ocampo's wife, Carolina, also with the NDF, admitted in January 1987 that the CPP received aid from foreign governments and would welcome "high-powered arms, all kinds of arms," but she too denied receiving Soviet assistance.[151]

The shift in party attitudes toward the Soviets was very clear in 1984. Sison observed, "Even the Soviet theorists have been uneasy and disturbed about the Lavaites' conceding that the U.S. and the Marcos regime are carrying out industrialization in the country as this preempts a Soviet offer of 'noncapitalist development' to the regime." Sison further criticized the Lavaites for having "unwittingly cast away the Soviet theory of noncapitalist development," noting that "the only thing that the Soviet Union can be happy about the Lavaites is their trying to obscure the third world demand for a new international economic order."[152]

The reasons for the moderating attitude toward the Soviets was, first, a much more aggressive Soviet presence in the Philippines through its embassy and, second, the expansion of NDF activities abroad. The World Peace Council, for example, held a meeting in Manila in November 1984 at which time Soviet agents reportedly met with CPP members using PKP contacts as cover, and two Tass correspondents visited Davao for the first time in early December 1984, ostensibly to compare educational systems.[153] Philippine government officials were becoming concerned about Soviet ships present in areas around the islands, fearing that they were being mapped for later infiltration. American intelligence officers noted an increase in the Soviet embassy's staff and activities, including contacts with front groups.[154] In early 1985 the Soviets reportedly offered to provide substantial military aid to the CPP, although it was rejected by the party because of the difficulty of smuggling in weapons. The arms offer was allegedly made through the NDF in Western Europe.[155] Ocampo acknowledged in 1986 that "there have been indications before that they [Soviets] were interested in political relations with us, but nothing has come of it yet."[156]

The expansion of front activities outside the Philippines was another factor in the CPP's moving closer to the Soviets and their surrogate groups. Jalandoni, the former priest and member of the Central Committee, served as the NDF's representative abroad while based in Holland. Munro maintains that Jalandoni's main function was to raise funds, partly through solidarity groups established in Sweden, Norway, West Germany, Belgium, Holland, and Ireland.[157] Bayan leaders admitted in 1985 that they had relations with groups abroad who supported their programs, stating further that "foreign support for organizations should be encouraged."[158]

Activities of the NDF also extended into the United States. Five American-based organizations supporting the "revolutionary struggle" were mentioned by *Ang Bayan* in early 1977, although it is unclear what was meant by "support": the International Association of Patriotic Filipinos (Pandaigdigang Samahan ng Makabayang Pilipino, or PSMP); the Anti-Martial Law Coalition (AMLC); the Katipunan ng mga Demokratikong Pilipino (KDP) based in California; the Chicago-based Pagkakaisa para sa Pambansang Demokrasya; and the Friends of the Filipino People, described as "an association of progressive and anti-imperialist American intellectuals." And *Liberation* said in 1984 that Filipino nurses working in the Washington, D.C., area were forming an NDF underground that year. Despite these activities, however, the United States did not appear to be a major center of fund-raising activity.

The NDF's closeness to the Soviets was made conspicuous by *Liberation*'s failure in its first issue following Aquino's victory to mention that the Soviet Union was the only country that officially recognized Marcos as the victor in the February election. Explained *Ang Katipunan*, an American-based publication on the Philippines, "Though Soviet relations with Marcos were warm, they were entirely superficial. . . . Soviet-Philippine relations during the Marcos years thus can be characterized as pragmatic at best."[159]

Signs of a developing relationship between the CPP and the Soviet Union and its surrogates were evident by 1987, although the relationship's exact nature was still unclear. The underlying assumption of the Soviets had always been that the United States would never permit its vital strategic interests in the Philippines to be jeopardized. And it was clearly not in the Soviet interest to provoke the Americans during the period of détente or to risk possible exposure of links to the CPP by providing traceable weapons. Guerrero, too, expected the United States ultimately would commit its own troops in any struggle because the "stakes are bigger than the Philippines."[160]

The decision of the CPP to expand external support also reflected its need to establish external legitimacy as it tried to overthrow the popular government of Corazon Aquino. Solidarity with other third world movements—such as the African National Congress in South Africa, SWAPO in Namibia, and Fretlin, the Front for the Liberation of East Timor—was a means of establishing such legitimacy. As the Philippine military became more brutal in its repression of the insurgency and the United States was drawn further into the conflict by its rearmament of the military and its need to safeguard Clark Air Base and Subic Naval Base, the party would be able to justify to its international and domestic supporters its own more violent tactics.

Thus, by the end of Aquino's second year in office, the insurgency was taking on some of the characteristics of previous peasant rebellions, such as its resiliency and the government's response to the rebellion. But there were important differences as well. Most prominent was the insurgents' organizational strength. The CPP had demonstrated the discipline needed for any outnumbered underground group to survive. While maintaining an apparently decentralized command structure that permitted a large degree of latitude for regional and local commanders, the party was able to hold on to overall control of strategic objectives and general tactics. Although some units occasionally engaged in renegade maneuvers (which may have been the case in Angeles City when the three Americans were killed in 1987), the party was generally capable of reasserting control. Indeed, despite internal personality disputes and betrayals, the CPP demonstrated greater internal cohesion than did the Philippine military. The latter was so rife with factionalism within both its officer and enlisted ranks that the general staff was unable to provide strategic and tactical control in daily operations.

That organizational effectiveness was clear in the party's personnel practices. Leaders advanced within the hierarchy and were promoted on the basis of performance standards, in contrast to the Philippine military with its personalized and politicized promotion process. In addition, the party showed remarkable resilience in its ability to change key commanders at the very highest levels with no apparent weakening of the organization. It had grown beyond the politics of personality that so clearly afflicted the elite's political structures and the military's chain of command. Even after many of the Central Committee members were arrested, the party and its army continued to function. Against its forces, the Philippine government was able to muster superior firepower but little else, an imbalance the CPP apparently tried to redress by seeking foreign aid and more sophisticated arms supplies. At the end of two decades of struggle, then, the party had evolved into a political organization unlike any previously known in Philippine history.

4

The Role of the Military in Philippine Society

To measure accurately the potential for a successful Communist insurgency in the Philippines, one must examine the Armed Forces of the Philippines (AFP), the NPA's chief military adversary. The role of the AFP in Philippine society is at least as important as an estimate of its strengths and capabilities, for the government has traditionally employed the AFP to protect elite interests, not to ensure the national defense. Thus it has functioned as the primary tool to frustrate social reform. Indeed, the government's failure to acknowledge and resolve the preconditions of rebellion has unintentionally aided the formation and execution of the insurgency. The future stability of the Philippines, therefore, is as dependent on the evolving character of the military as it is on the strategy of the insurgents.

Ironically, too, both the NPA and the military draw their strength from Philippine culture. In many ways Philippine military society is where the traditional culture of patron-client ties bound by *utang na loób* (debt of prime obligation) works best. The importance of culture was brought out clearly when a small group of some two hundred military men revolted against Marcos on February 22, 1986. Holed up at Camp Aguinaldo, the AFP's general headquarters in Quezon City, they were able to turn the entire military against Marcos. One episode in the rebellion illustrates these cultural influences and how they affect Philippine military behavior.

On the morning of February 22, one of the rebel leaders, air force colonel Hector Tarrazona, called upon another air force colonel, Antonio Sotelo, commander of the Fifteenth Strike Wing at Villamor Air Base, for his support. Although Sotelo was not a friend of Tarrazona's group, known as the Reform the AFP Movement (RAM), he agreed to Tarrazona's request because he was loyal to Lt. Gen. Fidel V. Ramos who had joined the rebels. Sotelo did not even know that his deputy and his helicopter squadron commanders had long been secret RAM members. When ordered into the air by loyalist officers, the helicopter squadron under Sotelo's command instead joined the rebels at Aguinaldo.[1]

One can look at this vignette as a good example of how a military long abused and politicized by Marcos found the courage to turn against him. But it also illustrates the weak command structure in the Philippine military, the importance of secret cliques and personal loyalties that overlap and supersede the military chain of command. In moments of crisis—indeed, in the moments in which most military men instinctively obey superior authority—the *informal* command structure controls behavior. In this regard, the NPA's command structure and military culture is superior to that of the AFP. And, again ironically, although the AFP's cultural traits reflect more precisely those of the society as a whole, it is the AFP that is the most isolated from the Filipino people.

Even though the military contributed so dramatically to Corazon Aquino's victory, the public remains deeply suspicious and fearful of it. While strongly embodying Philippine cultural norms, the military reflects as well the rest of the society in that it does not work. Rather than contributing to greater unity and stability, the military, with its many coups and plots of coups, encourages instability and represses the people it is supposed to serve and protect.

The February 1986 military uprising raised important questions about the Philippine military's role in society, and they have continued to be raised during Aquino's tenure, a period punctuated with repeated military coup attempts. Those questions—why didn't the military obey Marcos's commands? why are cultural influences so strong within the military? what is the military's role in Philippine society?—are important, if not among the most critical, determinants of the government's ability to cope with the NPA and to achieve future stability.

The answer to these questions can be found in part in the organizational history of the AFP both before and during the Marcos period. Marcos's almost twenty-year rule in a sense distorted history, giving rise to certain myths about the Philippine military and its role in the society. Three myths characterized the picture of the pre–martial law military: its professionalism, its commitment to civilian supremacy, and its mission of preserving the state. These myths were reinforced by the military's early formative years under American tutelage. Having been created on the American model and trained by American officers and having presumably adopted American values, the military, it has been assumed, behaved like the American military.

Accordingly, the conventional view holds that it was martial law that led to the militarization of Philippine society. The expressions of this view have been numerous: As the military acquired new power, it substituted an authoritarian ethos for a democratic one and institutionalized military control over private and public sectors.[2] Gen. Fabian Ver, formerly Marcos's chauffeur, became "Marcos's major instrument in politicizing the once strictly professional armed forces."[3] Prior to martial law, the military had "little desire, if any, to intervene in politics." An American-modeled constitution of checks and balances kept the military subordinate to civilian rule through control of defense appropriations and promotions beyond the rank of colonel, and through periodic changes in the political party in power.[4] The military lacked "a sense of superiority" or a "militaristic" tradition.[5] The existence of a free press and popular opposition were other reasons offered for the improbability of a military coup.

In fact, however, when martial law was declared, it received both active public support and passive acquiescence. And a free press was unable to check the military despite a year's advance warning of President Marcos's intention to declare martial law. That martial law could be declared and Marcos rule for another thirteen years indicate that the system did not work and had not been working as the conventional view suggests.

Indeed, the quality of Philippine democracy has always been questionable—one of the reasons for periodic rebellion. Marcos's authoritarian rule was rooted in a long history of executive-military control.[6] The military was not traditionally as "docile and politically weak" as supposed.[7] Any checks on its power actually contributed to its politicization. For example, the need for congressional approval for admission to the general ranks meant that officers had to curry favor with key politicians.[8] Arguably, too, the informal political party system in the Philippines in which politicians frequently changed their party allegiances, shifting alliances with provincial political kingpins, encouraged politicization of a military in which a provincial army commander could be a deciding factor in who won an election. Filipino officers, although officers, were nonetheless Filipinos, influenced by

TABLE 4.1
Armed Forces of the Philippines, 1965–1987

	1965	1966	1967	1968	1969	1970
Army	25,000	25,500	17,000	15,500	18,000	18,000
Navy	4,000	5,000	5,000	5,500	5,500	6,000
Air	7,000	7,000	8,000	9,000	9,000	9,000
PC[a]	15,500	15,500	17,000	17,000	17,000	17,000
Total	51,500	53,000	49,000	47,000	49,500	55,000

	1971	1972	1973	1974	1975	1976
Army	17,600	16,000	19,300	35,000	39,000	45,000
Navy	8,000	6,000	12,200	11,000	14,000	17,000
Marines[b]					(3,500)	(7,000)
Air	9,000	9,000	11,200	9,000	14,000	16,000
PC	23,500	23,000	27,180	34,900	34,900	35,000
L.H.D.[c]					(25,500)	(25,000)
Total	58,100	54,100	69,880	89,900	101,900	113,000

	1977	1978	1979	1980	1981	1982
Army	63,000	63,000	65,000	70,000	70,000	70,000
Navy	20,000	20,000	22,000	26,000	26,000	26,000

	1983	1984	1985	1986	1987
Marines	(7,000)	(7,000)	(7,000)	(7,000)	(6,800)
Coast Guard					2,000
Air	16,000	16,000	16,800	16,800	16,800
PC	40,000	40,000	47,000	43,500	43,500
L.H.D.	(25,000)	(25,000)	(35,000)	(35,000)	(65,000)
Total	139,000	139,000	150,000	156,300	158,300

	1983	1984	1985	1986	1987
Army	60,000	60,000	70,000	70,000	62,000
Navy	28,000	28,000	28,000	26,000	26,000
Marines	(9,600)	(6,800)	(9,600)	(9,500)	(9,500)
Coast Guard	2,000	2,000	2,000	2,000	2,000
Air	16,800	16,800	16,800	17,000	17,000
PC	43,500	43,500	40,000	50,000	50,000
L.H.D.	(65,000)	(65,000)	(65,000)	(65,000)	(65,000)
Total	150,300	150,300	156,800	165,000	165,000

a. PC: Philippine Constabulary.

b. Marine figures are included in Navy figures and thus are not added separately into totals.

c. L.H.D.: Local Home Defense Forces. Because these groups are not part of the regular armed forces, the figures shown are not included in the totals.

Source: Institute for International Security Studies, *The Military Balance* (London: IISS, for years cited).

their culture and affected by their history. There are strong continuities in the military's role in Philippine society which predate democratic institutions.

Today, the AFP consists of four principal services: the Philippine Constabulary (PC), the Philippine Army (PA), the Philippine Navy (PN) and the Philippine Air Force (PAF). Subordinate to the navy are marine and coast guard units. Elite troops include marine and Scout Ranger units. In addition to these major branches, there are reserves and paramilitary forces under the Integrated National Police (INP), the Civilian Home Defense Forces (CHDF), and the Office for Manpower and Reserve Affairs (called the Citizen Armed Forces). The substantial increase in the military's size and the apportionment of troops among the various services are shown in table 4.1.

The AFP was originally organized in 1935 by Gen. Douglas MacArthur. The bulk of its troops were recruited from the PC, the oldest service, established in 1901. The PAF was formed in 1937 from the PC's air corps and the PN in 1939 from the PC's naval units. In 1939 a Department of National Defense was created. The AFP's original anniversary date was December 21, coinciding with the signing of Commonwealth Act No. 1, the National Defense Act, of 1935. In 1983, in an effort to establish greater legitimacy for the armed forces, Marcos designated March 22 as the anniversary commemorating the establishment in 1897 of the Katipunan's first armed unit. The search for more nationalist roots than those associated with American colonialism is difficult because the AFP's heritage is one of collaboration with foreign occupiers to repress the Philippine people, as the constabulary's and army's histories show.

The Military's Role before Marcos

Historically the Philippine military has lacked legitimacy. Prior to martial law it was viewed by peasants and the poor as an instrument of elite repression, the pawn of the landlords.[9] With the imposition of martial law, the military became the instrument of everyone's repression, regardless of class, providing the means for a few to suppress the demands of the many. The search for greater legitimacy has in many ways been the dominant mission of the military before, during, and after martial law.

The historical roots of the military's lack of legitimacy date principally to the American colonial period, when it was essentially a collaborationist force. As a chronicler from the 1930s observed, "The Constabulary was a unique and successful application of the principle of employing native infantry, officered by white men, in the subjugation of their own tribesmen."[10] The constabulary was meant to be a police unit, not a military one, but the country was not fully pacified when it was formed.

The Philippine Constabulary (PC) was organized on July 18, 1901, on the remnants of the Spanish Guardia Civil, established in 1868 from local levies to enforce Spanish rule—the Spanish garrisoned few troops in their colonies. The Guardia Civil's mission was to suppress the *tulisanes* (bandits) that frequented the Philippines after 1850, but it was generally hated by Filipinos. The PC's mission was similar; it was to supervise local police forces and suppress guerrilla activity. Initially called the Insular Police Force, it was officered entirely by Americans and other Westerners until 1907. One of the unit's early chroniclers described it as resembling a mercenary force.[11]

Originally officers of the constabulary were titled "inspectors" or "chiefs," and the ranking provincial officer was called a "senior inspector." But one year after the unit's formation, military titles and khaki uniforms were introduced because of army hostility to the new force's paramilitary activities.[12] Several of its Filipino officers later became provincial administrators, ranking as high as deputy governor.

The PC was created at a moment when the United States was trying to fight one of the first guerrilla wars of the twentieth century. (On another continent the British, too, were contending with guerrilla-style attacks in the Boer War of 1899–1902.) Pacifying the islands "required a decade of remorseless police activity" to first identify the supremos and then eliminate them. The elite *provincianos* supported the drive while the common *taos* (peasants) aligned themselves with those independence fighters and religious Robin Hoods seeking an "ill-defined utopia," such as the Babilanes in Negros, the Pulajanes in Samar, and the Santa Iglesia of Central Luzon.[13] The Insular Police Force was "a subrosa body of unofficial American soldiery, created to quell, with discretion and without publicity, a very serious public disorder."[14] The early PC was dominated by Filipinos so mestizo that they were hostile to Filipinos. As Ileto has described them, "Many of the soldiers of the Constabulary rank and file are of the same class of informers, spies, and other former servants of the American military government who have frequently their private vengeance to pay, and do not scruple to do so under the cover of the terror which their uniform inspires."[15]

The constabulary was also part of the American effort to concentrate administrative control. The Americans established the precedent for centralized government in the Philippines, devolving power away from local governments to Manila.[16] This helped contribute to the perception of the constabulary as an occupying force.

The problems continued when the AFP was organized in 1935:

> The discipline of China's elite troops, however, was too much to expect in the Philippines, which had almost no military tradition. Quezon and his military advisors endured a variety of harassments, including difficulty in attracting enough regular army personnel in the ranks; reservists declining active duty; trainee strikes and demonstrations against officers; occasional terrorism by detachments in provincial areas; individuals running amok in uniform; and botched maneuvers. Political difficulties included alleged favoritism in award of Army contracts and continued rivalry between the Scouts and the Constabulary.[17]

The Philippine Army's history is similar to that of the constabulary. The PA's origins can be traced to the Philippine Scouts, a force formed around 1899 as American sepoys during the Philippine-American War. Scout recruits principally came from the Macabebe tribe in Pampanga, a group with a history of mercenary work. The scouts were a "native infantry," part of the regular U.S. Army but about 75 percent cheaper to maintain and a means by which American troops could be withdrawn from fighting the increasingly unpopular war.[18] The scouts assisted in the capture of Emilio Aquinaldo, the leader of the Philippine independence movement. Although the scouts remained a part of U.S. forces until independence and the bulk of the PA was formed from PC members, it is to the scouts that the army owes its heritage.

Before an alternative image of the AFP could coalesce, World War II intervened. Although Filipino troops generally acquitted themselves better than American troops during the Japanese invasion, the Philippine military nevertheless was discredited further during the occupation, with PC units in particular being used against guerrillas. Only two senior generals out of nine in the PA remained loyal to the United States; and as many as 80 percent of the AFP's officers were estimated to have collaborated with the Japanese.[19] The charges of collaboration constituted a major issue in the postwar Philippines and it had a direct impact on the military. One Filipino said that "the Philippine Army is a collaborationist army in its essential make-up. There are, of course, noncollaborators in the upper bracket of the military hierarchy, but it is the politicos who run the show."[20]

The use of the PC to suppress the Huks during the war only aggravated a preexisting hostility that deepened in the immediate postwar period when the PC as the Military Police Command (MPC) continued its abusive behavior. With only limited supplies and pay, the MPC was forced to survive, like parasites, off the people.[21] The new civilian leaders of an independent Philippines did nothing to restrain the military. During the Huk campaign, some PC units were called Nenita, or "skull squadrons," as part of the government's psychological warfare program, and during the late 1960s, PC assassin teams, known as "Monkees," roamed central Luzon.[22]

As the favored force in the Philippine military from the mid-1950s until 1973, the PC was the first choice of graduates from the military's elite school, the Philippine Military Academy, modeled on West Point and Annapolis. The army's size was reduced until the constabulary became the stronger of the two,[23] which extended the American use of the PC as the principal means of enforcing peace and increased popular resentment of the group. With its forces usually dispersed over a wide area and with only limited equipment, the PC fell back on the sentiment expressed in its motto, "To Be Outnumbered, Always; To Be Outfought, Never." The troops thus were often in difficult situations, and their behavior only added to their reputation as principal abusers of human rights.

Involvement in the immediate postwar political maneuvering was a means by which the military could attempt to erase the collaborationist taint and restore its legitimacy. Manuel Roxas, whose collaboration with the Japanese had been only partially absolved by General MacArthur, was running for president. Because his victory would make it unlikely that other collaborators in the armed forces would be purged, the military backed his candidacy in the 1946 election, establishing a pattern for military involvement in future elections.[24]

Besides being active in the 1949 election, the military took charge of the judicial system in October 1950 when habeas corpus was briefly suspended. The next year the military was deputized by the government to secure balloting, and in the 1953 presidential election, American military officers even inspected Philippine units in an attempt to keep them from tampering with results.[25] The military also began taking a more active role in government administration. President Elpidio Quirino put his brother, an army colonel, in charge of a special group of "thugs" within the Military Intelligence Service, and President Ramon Magsaysay appointed officers to government posts, beginning a practice upon which Marcos expanded.[26]

But no other factor contributed as profoundly to the role of the military in Philippine society after 1951 as did the threat of a coup d'etat. Senators Claro Recto and Lorenzo Tanada in February 1953 recommended to Magsaysay, then secretary of defense, that he sponsor a coup in order to prevent the loss of the presidential election. The military also reportedly considered a coup after Magsaysay's sudden and still suspicious death in a plane crash in 1957. Two generals were dismissed in October 1958 after rumors of a coup attempt against President Carlos P. Garcia. The military actively opposed Garcia's more nationalist foreign policy of "Asia for Asians," and in July 1959 a group of retired officers formed their own party, the Grand Alliance. Both Presidents Garcia and Diosdado Macapagal rarely permitted officers to serve beyond their retirement age, and Macapagal, perhaps because of the military's involvement in politics, began promoting ROTC graduates over graduates of the Philippine Military Academy.[27]

In addition to the military's increasing role in civilian affairs, other developments contributed to the breakdown of control over security forces. After the Sakdal uprising in the 1930s, paramilitary forces were formed. Although at first limited to the provincial hacenderos, civilian guards had expanded significantly by the 1940s and 1950s. Politicians used them both for personal protection and for ensuring electoral victories. Repressive actions by these groups may have contributed to the growth of the Huks.[28]

Factionalism also characterized the military before Marcos, although he exacerbated differences. Since independence, the military has been divided along several lines: Philippine Military Academy graduates versus the ROTC reservists (also known as "integrees," which refers to the integration of reserve officers into active duty forces); the Ilocanos versus other tribal groups; generation versus generation; and combat versus noncombat officers.[29] Educational, tribal, and linguistic differences were also important prior to 1972.

Integrating reserve officers into the regular forces after World War II and the Korean War created friction, for it reduced promotion possibilities for academy graduates. This was aggravated by the thirty-year mandatory retirement rule, which for the graduates dated from their first year in the academy but for others depended on their commission date. Thus reservists could serve longer, reducing promotion possibilities for academy men.[30] The academy's Alumni Association promoted the careers of its members to such a degree that a similar group was formed for reservists in 1986. The prestige associated with being an academy alumnus made other officers feel insecure.

Linguistic differences were also strong. Traditionally, Ilocanos produced the most military men, both officers and enlisted. One study of the Military Academy found that 21.8 percent spoke Ilocano and 14.4 percent were actually Ilocanos or came from Mountain Province. The majority spoke Tagalog and were from central or southern Luzon.[31] A 1983 University of the Philippines study of the backgrounds of 104 generals found that 36 were Ilocanos and 35 were Tagalogs, but that the Ilocanos dominated the intelligence service.[32] Although Ilocano representation in the military was breaking down, Marcos's Ilocano preference helped perpetuate such distinctions. Yet a focus on linguistic or educational differences distorts the ultimate cause of factionalism: personal loyalties developed during years of common service.

Thus, prior to the election of Ferdinand Marcos in 1965, several disturbing trends were apparent in the AFP, particularly its growing involvement in the political and social affairs of the country without a commensurate increase in popular (not elite) support for the military's new role. In addition, the military did not even function effectively as a security force, as evidenced by the rise of private armies and the Huks.

The Military's Role under Marcos

Ironically, Marcos, who appeared to favor policies that strengthened the military both before and during martial law, presided instead over the almost complete destruction of the military's legitimacy. It is doubly ironic because the military was the initial basis of his political power.

An Ilocano, as were many in the military, Marcos advanced the interests of Filipino veterans who were eligible for American benefits and tried to develop a political base by claiming leadership of a guerrilla unit, the Ang Maga Maharlika. In 1947 he was one of three members of a Philippine Veterans Mission to the U.S. Congress. After the war, he claimed to have formed an eighteen-hundred-man guerrilla unit in December 1942, most of whose members were related to Marcos or were fellow Ilocanos. Among them, he said, were Narciso Ramos (later his secretary of foreign affairs), Ramos's son Fidel (later Marcos's vice-chief of staff and Corazon Aquino's chief of staff), Fabian Ver, and Marcos's brother, Pacifico E. Marcos. Although his claim for American veterans' benefits was disallowed by U.S. officials who declared his unit had never existed, Marcos produced affidavits from some legitimate guerrilla leaders such as General Peralta. He was the general who later awarded Marcos a number of questionable military decorations shortly before the 1965 presidential election which brought Marcos to power.[33] Having a military pedigree was extremely important not only to Marcos's image of himself but also to his acquiring military support for his election.

Upon becoming president, Marcos undertook the most thorough reorganization of the military's structure since 1950 and placed all four services under the chief of staff's tactical control.[34] During his first thirteen months in power, Marcos also served as secretary of defense (President Magsaysay had done the same for five months) at which time he supervised the largest personnel shake-up in the AFP's history. Both the structural and the personnel changes had one purpose: to impose Marcos's personal control over the military.

Marcos claimed in 1982 that a further reorganization would make the military more effective in combating the NPA. This announcement followed Fabian Ver's appointment in 1981 as chief of staff, the lifting of martial law the same year, and increasing concern over the institu-

FIGURE 4.1.
Military Command Structure: Central Commands prior to 1983.
Source: David Jenkins, "Insurgency, Not External Threat, Is the
Worry," Far Eastern Economic Review, *March 10, 1983, page 18.*

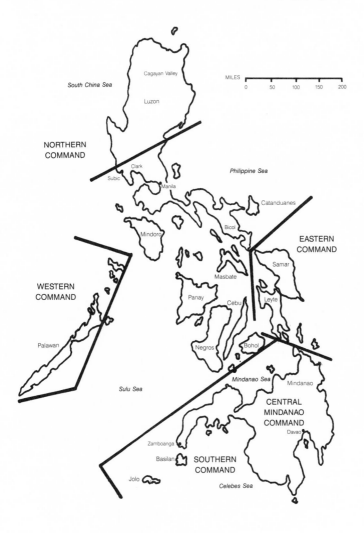

FIGURE 4.2.

Military Command Structure: Regional Unified Commands after 1983. Source: Larry A. Niksch, Insurgency and Counterinsurgency in the Philippines, *Report prepared for the Committee on Foreign Relations, U.S. Senate, by the Congressional Research Service, Library of Congress (Washington, D.C.: U.S. Government Printing Office, 1985), page 17.*

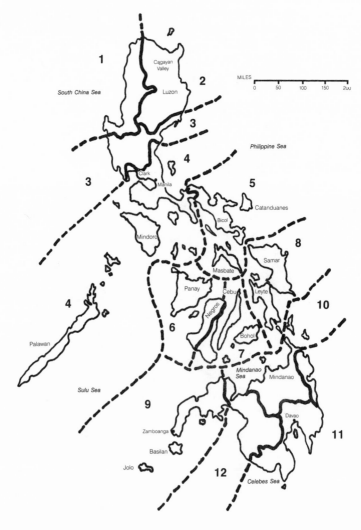

tionalization of a succession process. The General Military Council (GMC) met for the first time in April 1982 and in November 1983 the military began attending cabinet and executive committee meetings. Ver responded by creating Regional Unified Commands (RUC), which put all forces under one commander who reported directly to the chief of staff. Figures 4.1 and 4.2 illustrate the increasing complexity of a command structure designed to ensure centralized control rather than efficient military operations. This effectively concentrated power and bypassed the Ministry of National Defense and the vice-chief of staff, Fidel Ramos, who, although its commander, lost operational control of the Philippine Constabulary.

Marcos thus did not design the military to be an effective counterinsurgency force. As an American embassy official reported in 1982, the government had not "developed a coordinated civilian-political doctrine to combat the insurgency." Although Marcos said that the NPA was a "terrorist problem requiring, in the first instance, a military response," he was more interested in his personal security and power than in real military reform.[35]

Rather than changing the military, then, Marcos promoted his loyalists. The Presidential Security Command (PSC), the Metro Manila police forces (METROCOM), and the two key Manila military units—such as the First Infantry Division at Fort Magsaysay and Scout Ranger companies at Fort Bonifacio—were dominated by Ilocanos. Gen. Victor Natividad, the METROCOM commander, and Gen. Roland Pattugalan, commander of the Second Infantry Division and nephew by marriage to Marcos, were former PSC members as were other RUC commanders appointed by Fabian Ver. Imelda Marcos began developing her own coterie of bright young officers in 1983, perhaps in response to rumors of unhappiness among the junior officer corps because she already had "her" people in the senior ranks. These included General Ramas, the army chief from the Visayas; PC colonel Dionisio Tan-Gatue, who was her bodyguard; General Zumel, commandant of the PMA, her former bodyguard; and the PAF's deputy commander, Carlos Martel, her brother-in-law. The commander of the coast guard (established in 1967), who was later promoted to head the navy, was Brillante Ochoco; his qualification for high command was his earlier service as skipper of the presidential yacht. By retaining officers on active duty past their retirement time, Marcos was able to ensure even more subservience.[36]

A classic example was Fabian Ver, who had been a captain from 1952 until Marcos's election and reached mandatory retirement age in 1974.

Marcos, rather than strengthen the military, permitted the growth of ad hoc paramilitary groups, such as the CHDF. Predecessors of the CHDF were the Barrio Self-Defense Units (BSDUS) in the 1960s and Civilian Guards of the 1940s and early 1950s. Integrated Civilian Home Defense Forces (ICHDF) were first formed in the late 1960s as local counterinsurgency forces. They had American support in the tradition of Brig. Gen. Henry Hill Bandholtz, who in 1903 had armed "the more intelligent natives" with guns to suppress "bandit" activity.[37]

The 1973 constitution, which Marcos adopted after declaring martial law, called for the formation of a citizens' army, the local Self-Defense Forces. In March of that year the military began issuing arms to Christian local defense units in Mindanao because of an increase in Muslim insurgency. In 1976 the Civilian Home Defense Forces of the ICHDF were established with seventy-three thousand authorized members (sixty-three thousand full time and ten thousand part time). There were three categories of CHDF, illustrating their close connection with the military and the elite: (1) active reservists, including planters, which provided an excuse for high officials and prominent businessmen to carry weapons; (2) private security guards employed by prominent businessmen; and (3) the bulk of the CHDF, part-time "soldiers" paid a monthly salary of two hundred pesos with an annual clothing allowance of two hundred pesos and a nine-thousand-peso insurance policy. The CHDFs were a cheap alternative to regular forces. The government spent 136,710 pesos per month for a CHDF battalion compared to 1.1 million pesos for an equivalent army battalion.[38] Under the theoretical control of the constabulary, which was also responsible for training and uniforms, the CHDFs were actually under the army's direction or that of local political figures. In Negros, for example, the CHDFs in eight towns were placed under a Regional Special Action Command (RSAC).[39]

In addition to the CHDFs, other categories of armed civilians were supposed to come under the ICHDF program: special paramilitary forces (former rebels or other individuals under the command of local politicians), local security agencies, provincial guards, civilian firearm holders, and civilian volunteers (Kawal ng Barangay).[40] The distinctions among all these groups became blurred.

A CHDF's mission was "village defense," protecting a local barangay.

But they were ill trained, unequipped, and incapable of performing that function adequately. The NPA even used the CHDF as an adjunct to their supply lines, easily disarming units. Most of the CHDF units were formed in Mindanao, which helped the NPA expand into that region, for in addition to being incompetent, the CHDFs were brutal. More often than not units were made up of "town toughs and petty criminals" who used their weapons and status to terrorize villages; often they were in the employ of local warlords and plantation owners.[41]

Marcos built up the army and paramilitary forces partly as a counterforce to the Philippine Constabulary. Fidel Ramos was commander of the PC during much of the martial law period, and although he was a Marcos relative, his West Point training made him suspect among Marcos loyalists—a suspicion later shown to be justified when his rebellion in 1986 contributed significantly to the Marcos downfall. Army forces were positioned principally around the Metro Manila area to protect the president, and these units received a disproportionate share of supplies (continuing another colonial legacy when the Philippine Scouts had been better equipped than PC units). Resources were also concentrated in the Presidential Security Command (PSC) and the National Intelligence Coordinating Agency (NICA). The PSC, originally a small presidential security force, grew to about fifteen thousand men with responsibilities for both domestic and foreign intelligence. Both were under the control of Ver, whose three sons (Col. Irwin Ver, Lt. Col. Rexor Ver, and Maj. Wyrlo Ver) were all members of the PSC. Civil Security Units (CSU) were also established in every government agency. The NICA and the PSC were Marcos's secret police responsible for ferreting out information not so much on the state's enemies as on Marcos's foes.[42]

The reforms that took place were all designed to enhance his personal security and centralize control. An example was the creation of the Integrated National Police (INP) first called for in the 1973 constitution. The reason for it was twofold: to create a more professional and modern police force and to reduce the political power of local mayors, many of whom did not support Marcos and who, through their control of the local police, had created their own competing political machines. Ostensibly, the formation of the INP would reduce tension between the PC and local police forces, for PC members were involved in such areas as traffic and firearm control.[43] In January

1976 full integration was ordered, transferring police, jail, and fire units to the military under the PC.[44] The PC commander was made director-general of the INP, but the INP was placed under the direct control of the Department of National Defense and thus under Marcos, while the PC remained a branch of the AFP. The gerrymandering was organized in part to avoid the consequences of Section 660 of the U.S. Foreign Assistance Act of 1974, which prohibited any American assistance for police forces.[45] So the PC continued to receive American military aid.

Marcos played to the military's inherent factional weakness under the guise of strengthening it. The periodic claims of reform, reorganization, and personnel reassignments were meant not to improve the military but to lessen American pressure for change and to enhance his control of the military. Marcos feared that a strong, professional military might ultimately overthrow him, and at times he even promoted the idea that the military might take over in order to discourage opponents. Ironically, he was right. But Marcos recognized that retaining control of the military was not simply a matter of centralizing power. He also had to extend rewards. This he began to do in his first year in office when he announced a new role for the military in the nation's development.

Political power was the hidden rationale for Marcos's first-term policy of involving the military in the government's development program. He had three principal objectives in mind: (1) to gain access to American military aid with maximum flexibility as to its use, (2) to gain additional support from the military by demonstrating his ability to acquire more resources for it and to give it a more important position in Philippine politics, and (3) to secure his political base by using the military to deliver this political pork barrel into rural areas. As with all of Marcos's tactics, these objectives were mutually reinforcing, although their long-term consequences were not fully considered.

The basis for the military's role in development was the Socio-Economic Military Program (SEMP) created in 1958 to "employ or otherwise assign military personnel for public works construction, food production, land resettlement and rural development."[46] The program was little more than rhetoric until early 1965 when a proposal jointly written by American and Filipino officers, entitled "Proposal for Civic Action by the AFP," surfaced:

Specifically, the military's civic action proposal was designed to gain rural support for the central government through a six-faceted program. The proposal included military training courses oriented to civic action, community relations programs for unit commanders, an economic development corps, socio-economic military programs, emergency relief projects, small-scale civic engineering projects and civic action centers. . . . As initially proposed, the military's role in civic action was designed to undercut rural support for communist insurgency, was directed at the barrio elite, was to be manned by civic action personnel from other agencies, was self-help oriented and *was* specifically aimed at employing otherwise idle military resources.[47]

The Americans proposed the concept because they wanted to involve the Philippine military in the Vietnam War to demonstrate that the conflict was an allied effort. Marcos embraced the idea because it provided a cover for additional American assistance.[48]

During Marcos's first state visit to the United States in 1966, the Americans offered to fund ten new engineering battalions for the Philippine military in return for a commitment to send a Philippines Civic Action Group (PHILCAG) to Vietnam. Marcos had wanted much more for "political purposes," according to recently declassified American documents, but the Pentagon opposed additional funding because the ten battalions were "not essential to the military security of the Philippines." Marcos got most of what he wanted, however. The United States spent at least $7 million in training and equipping the engineer construction battalions in 1967 and 1968 and at least $39 million for the PHILCAG unit. The funds were never fully accounted for because the monies were delivered to Marcos in such a way as to " 'conceal the receipt of these payments from the Philippine public in its national defense budget,' " according to a U.S. government investigation.[49]

Defense spending for development became enshrined in the government's economic development strategy in September 1966. As a summary of the four-year plan observed, "The Armed Forces of the Philippines, with its manpower, material and equipment resources plus its organizational cohesiveness in such discipline possesses a tremendous potential to participate . . . [and] should be exploited to the maximum."[50] Immediately the military was employed to complete a superhighway outside Manila, this activity becoming the basis for the private Construction and Development Corporation of the Philippines, one of the largest Marcos-crony-owned businesses until it collapsed financially in 1983, owing a total of $650 million.[51]

Thus, on the surface, the Marcos years had provided a new role for the military. But it is important to distinguish form from actual function. Given Marcos's real objectives, national development was secondary, if present at all, among his motivations. The military's role in the Philippine polity was expanded not to enhance development but to sustain Marcos in power, a design that became clear during the pre–martial law elections in 1969 and 1971.

In the 1969 elections, Marcos used the military to coerce voters; this strengthened the military's role in politics in preparation for Marcos's bid to remain in power beyond the expiration of his second term. In the November 1971 midterm elections the entire AFP was deputized for the first time to supervise the elections although this did not prevent losses for Marcos's party.[52] Habeas corpus was briefly suspended again in August 1971 — a first test of Marcos's ability to govern illegally. And in further preparation for martial law, he again reshuffled the military's command.

Marcos, then, could not declare martial law without the military's support and that support had come at a price: the military's increased involvement in the domestic economy. Prior to imposing martial law, Marcos consulted with his "twelve disciples" who included the major military commanders, such as Defense Secretary Juan Ponce Enrile and PC Chief Fidel Ramos, but did not include the AFP's vice-chief of staff, Rafael Ileto, who was shunted abroad as an ambassador after martial law was declared.[53] (Ileto in November 1986 became Aquino's minister of national defense.) The action that provided the excuse for his declaring martial law on September 21, 1972, was a staged attack on Enrile.[54]

The benefits of martial law were immediately apparent to the military: all senior AFP officers were promoted one grade, pay was increased, a military investment company was formed, new benefits were announced for new retirees, dependents, and veterans, and even academic scholarships were established. The military was given subsidized commissaries, insurance, and positions with government corporations. On Loyalty Day 1973 the AFP pledged its loyalty to the commander in chief.[55]

In return for this largesse, the military arrested nearly sixty thousand people. A national curfew was enforced until April 1978, strikes were suppressed, the mass media and all public utilities were taken over. Anyone could be arrested, even upon the simple accusation of rumor-mongering. The new powers and authority soon imbedded the military in the nation's social fabric. Individual petitioners ignored civilian officials and addressed their complaints instead to military authorities. Half of the presidential regional officers for development were military men by 1978. The military even controlled the Ministry of Muslim Affairs.

Martial law, in the eyes of one officer, gave the AFP "a new status and a dignity,"[56] but in fact, it undermined both Philippine society and the military. The absence of the rule of law destroyed the judiciary. The use of preventive detention actions and emergency decrees allowed Marcos to bypass both the administrative and the criminal law systems. Gradually, even these became irrelevant as the system rotted from within: the only basis for decisions became personal ties.

The military learned that it was "permissible to use official positions for personal gain."[57] They became involved in almost every type of business activity—legal and criminal. Officers controlled or extorted payments from the black market for dollars; they controlled car-theft rings, marijuana syndicates, illegal logging, gambling, prostitution, fishing, mining, gunrunning, and robbery. Smaller rackets were principally the province of junior-ranking officers and enlisted men whose basic pay and living conditions had not significantly improved; field grade officers and their superiors controlled larger enterprises such as illegal logging and drug smuggling. Military units even began to attack each other in struggles over the control of rackets.[58]

The military's involvement in criminal activities was only an extension of its involvement in legal business activities. Marcos created two military businesses as part of his redistribution of rewards: the Philippine Expeditionary Forces to Korea–Investment and Development Corporation, a military investment company, and the Philippine Veterans Investment Development Company for retirees. In addition the military took control of the steel industry, sugar trading, and all major utilities. The chief of staff, Romeo Espino, reportedly controlled fifteen expropriated companies. Air force general Ramon Farolan, a cousin of Marcos's, was made commissioner of customs, and Gen. Cesar Kelpan was named president and general manager of a gold-mining company and chief of the National Development Company. In 1981, when martial law was nominally lifted, twenty-three officers and seventy-two enlisted men were recalled from their civilian jobs. But General Ver stated in 1984 that in fact only 5 percent of the military serving in a civilian capacity had been transferred "because the heads of these agencies utilizing their services persisted in requesting the retention of our men whose talents and services they still need."[59] The military both raked in profits themselves from legal businesses (like Gen. Antonio Venades of the Southern Philippine Development Authority who was involved in Zamboanga's legal barter trade) and were used to protect the business interests of Marcos cronies. In 1984, for example, PC/INP forces disrupted a union vote in a sugar mill owned by Fred Elizalde. Imelda Marcos used the military for her pet projects, such as building the Folk Arts Center. The minister of national defense was authorized to issue procurement contracts without public bidding, further helping to institutionalize "legal" corruption.[60]

Corruption of the military's ethics was evident too in the rise of paramilitary groups. Since the days of the Sakdalistas when the hacenderos began organizing private armies, paramilitary groups had been active in the Philippines. Many prominent political families, including Corazon Aquino's family, had private security forces. Under martial law these became institutionalized. Eduardo Cojuangco, a chief Marcos crony and a reserve colonel, had a several-thousand-man private army trained by Israeli mercenaries and equipped with Brazilian-made light tanks. Among the most notorious groups was PC Lt. Col. Carlos Lademora's "Lost Command," also called "Charlie's Angels." Lademora had been the PC provincial commander in Agusan del Sur from 1975 to 1979. Although his international notoriety eventually led to his apparent dismissal, Lademora and his men simply moved to another province, reportedly under the direct control of Fabian Ver, to work as security guards for the Paper Industry Corporation of the Philippines and the British-backed Guthrie plantation.[61] The Lost Command was only one of many such groups operating in Mindanao. In Zamboanga an Active Counter-Terrorist Sector militia was formed of civilian volunteers, and a People's Liberation Organization under a former Moro rebel, Abudakar Kadsulo, was established with AFP support near Davao —precursors of the vigilante groups that proliferated after 1986.[62]

By far the worst were the quasi-Christian groups which the AFP armed to "give the Catholic Church a dose of its own medicine"; this was a reference to the church's alleged pro-NPA bias.[63] Among these were the Tadtad ("hackers" or "chop-chop," so called because of their method of killing with bolo knives) and the Ilagas. The Tadtad was a group of religious fanatics operating in the "golden triangle" of marijuana growing in Cebu, Balamban, and Toledo City and later in Davao; they aided the military who forced farmers to cultivate the drug. The Ilagas were an anticommunist religious cult based in General Santos City; the group had originally formed to help the government fight the Muslims. Besides slicing their victims' bodies apart and disemboweling pregnant women, they would also consume their victims' brains and livers in the belief that this gave them supernatural powers. In many cases members of these cults served as local CHDF guards.[64]

In the cities, especially Manila, Marcos encouraged the formation of death squads, or secret marshals, patterned after counterterrorist assassination squads organized in 1967 and abandoned in 1969. In Manila they were called the El Diablo Crime Busters Association, formed in 1982. Members' fingers were tattooed for identification. Later this group became known as the Guardian Brotherhood, characterizing itself as a military fraternity of enlisted men. The paramilitary groups constituted Marcos's counterinsurgency program, obviating the need to strengthen the AFP.[65]

Realizing that his continued power depended on his retaining the unqualified support of the armed forces, Marcos thought he could accomplish this through his hold on his chief commanders.[66] Thus, most of his general and flag officers were kept in office beyond their retirement dates; they were usually granted only six-month extensions, however, so their loyalty was constantly under review, creating factions of officers competing for palace privileges — much in the manner of Louis XIV. This centralization of power and concentration of favors ultimately proved to be Marcos's undoing (as it had for the Bourbons as well) because it neglected the government's fundamental constituency — the masses and the military's mass base, the junior officer corps.

Some officers by the mid-1970s had become "despondent" over the direction of the "New Society" and the military's corruption. In 1979 the AFP's "lawlessness" was a frequent topic in the press, with official government figures showing that 150 complaints were filed each day.

Young officers pushed for the long overdue retirement of the generals and complained about the "demoralizing effects" of the promotion system.[67] The incidence of crime began rising in 1976 and overtook pre–martial law levels by 1983. Some retired generals suggested that the AFP was losing the war against the NPA.

The final straw, which brought the dissatisfaction within the AFP into the open, was the murder in August 1983 of Senator Aquino by military personnel at the Manila airport. Aquino's execution shocked both the public and elements of the military into a reassessment of their future and that of the Marcos regime.

REFORMING THE AFP

A reform movement now began to take shape within the military. It was initially guided by Defense Minister Enrile as a power bid to position himself in American eyes as the best successor to Marcos and the individual most capable of dealing with the insurgency. Gradually developing into a distinct organization, it later became known as the Reform the AFP Movement (RAM). Its formation had important implications for the country's future political stability.

The RAM represents a reorientation of the Philippine military away from its traditional principle of obedience to civilian rule to one more in keeping with the attitude prevailing among many third world militaries during the independence movements of the 1950s and 1960s. This attitude portrays the military as an idealistic, apolitical force whose duty is to purify the nation of corrupting influences. As Col. Gregorio B. ("Gringo") Honasan, leader of the 1987 attempted coup against President Aquino, declared in an interview justifying his revolt, "We're not doing this anymore for ideology or for politics. We are doing this for survival."[68] Nevertheless, this posture has provided a rationale for more direct military involvement in the country's political and economic structures.

. Reports had circulated as early as 1978 that a group of young Philippine Military Academy graduates had secretly founded a reform movement. In January 1980 some two hundred soldiers, led by retired PAF colonel Jose Reyes, were arrested on attempted coup charges.[69] Opposition became more visible in March 1984 when the academy class of 1969 boycotted the annual alumni parade, protesting an officer's promotion that had been accelerated for political reasons. Later that year, an air force officer said, "We see ourselves as powerless to change the situation. The middle-level officers are not a cohesive group."[70] To counter the appearance of restiveness, a group of senior officers issued a manifesto in October 1984 declaring their "unwavering loyalty and support" to General Ver who was charged in the cover-up of the Aquino assassination. The Pentagon discounted reports of a reform movement even after March 1985 when a group marched at the next alumni parade under a "We Belong" banner, calling for reforms. This was the group that later became known as the RAM, with *We Belong* the title of its official publication. The majority of RAM members, less than a thousand, were from the academy classes of 1969 through 1984, although most of its leaders, such as Honasan, were from the class of 1972. The core leaders, within Enrile's Defense Ministry, were members of a special study group and part of his personal bodyguard. They received specialized training in late 1984 from two British mercenaries retired from the Special Air Services, Britain's elite commando unit. Within the Defense Ministry, the reformists were assured of protection from Marcos as long as Enrile remained in power. In mid-1985 army chief Josephus Ramas reportedly formed a six-hundred man countercoup force, and late that year, Marcos threatened to arrest the "Ramboys."[71]

That a reform movement first began among Military Academy graduates is not surprising. A study of graduates before 1972 found that cadets were more tolerant of political and social diversity, less conservative, and less misanthropic than other students. They even became less authoritarian as they progressed through the academy. Indeed, although cadets were more strongly patriotic as seniors than they had been as freshmen, they were also less committed to a military career.[72] These findings suggest at least one reason the graduates became leaders of the military reform movement: they were more attuned to social development.

Another reason was their cohort experience: they had graduated during the martial law period. Younger officers had combat experience, having entered service when the Muslim and Communist struggles were becoming serious threats. They resented the promotion, especially to the general ranks, of officers who had no combat experience but were the favorites of the president and his wife. They were also the officers who experienced the terror of battle and the frustrations of inadequate supplies and support in the field. These men, from lieutenant to colonel, were well represented in the academy classes from 1961 through 1985. Their common experiences and personal loyalties gave their reform movement an organizational cohesion similar to that of the CPP, although it lacked the party's depth.

Although supported by Enrile, the reform movement began to take on a life of its own as Marcos's power crumbled in late 1985. The Pentagon actively encouraged its growth, praising it in congressional testimony in 1985. By August of that year RAM leaders were plotting Marcos's overthrow, even his murder if necessary, with a target date of mid-1987 after the next scheduled election. But Marcos's decision to call a snap presidential election for February 7, 1986, caught the RAM by surprise, forcing its members to improvise and speed up their plot. In late February 1986, RAM leaders precipitated the revolt by General Ramos and Enrile, leading to the disintegration of military support for Marcos. Fearing for their lives if he remained in power, the RAM leaders had planned to assault the palace. Word of their plans leaked to Marcos who began his own countercoup efforts and attempted to arrest Enrile, Ramos, Aquino, and other leading opponents. Word of Marcos's actions were in turn leaked to Enrile who decided to rebel.[73]

"Marcos is the linchpin of the military, which would fall into quarrelling factions if his monopoly on political power was ended," a Filipino opponent of the regime had argued in 1984.[74] That prophecy almost proved correct during the February 1986 "people power" revolution, when marine tanks approached regular army forces occupying Camps Aquinaldo and Crame. That it did not is partly indicative of the vestigial remnants of the military's belief in its own professional myths. More important, it indicates the enduring strength of personal ties in the military which supersede the chain of command. The event itself, however, ushered in a new era for the military in Philippine society.

The military's role in restoring democracy was seen in a positive light in the immediate aftermath of Marcos's overthrow; it had gained legitimacy in the public's eyes. The AFP, in recognition of this, at first changed its name to the New Armed Forces of the Philippines. But it soon became apparent that there was a dark side to the new image: military officers no longer saw themselves as subordinate to the civilian political elite. Traditional officers had tasted real political power; the younger officers of the RAM believed that they served a higher order than civilian officials—the nation itself. Having eliminated one civilian leader whose policies had encouraged the growth of a Communist insurgency and corrupted the military, they did not want another civilian leader to do the same.

This new perception of the military's role was an unintended consequence of the Marcos period. Marcos had developed a policy rationale to justify a military role in development. This "developmental ideology"[75] encouraged the view among the military that it was the one organized apolitical arm of government at the service of the nation's welfare. The Marcos regime, by corrupting the integrity of the military's ranks, strengthened the conviction among younger officers that they must purify the military and the rest of society of these pernicious influences.

"The Movement does not seek to serve any personality in the AFP but the AFP itself as an institution and the citizenry as the ultimate benefactor," reform officers had declared in a May 1985 statement. They were motivated by the perception "at a very early stage [of] the gradual and insidious isolation of the government and the AFP from the very people it was supposed to serve. There are indications that the military is slowly being destroyed as the whole profession that it used to be. *We must now put a stop to this*."[76]

The Military's Role after Marcos

In President Corazon Aquino's first year in office there were as many as seven attempted or rumored coups. On July 4, 1986, Arturo Tolentino, Marcos's deposed vice president, attempted a counterrevolution by taking control of the Manila Hotel and declaring himself president with the support of several hundred troops, including marines and members of the Guardian Brotherhood. Their action was prompted by reports that Enrile and Ramos supported them, which again indicated the primacy of personal loyalty and lack of support for the government. The troops, however, returned to the fold after extensive negotiations and were ordered by Ramos to perform push-ups as punishment. Aquino in November forced Enrile's resignation as defense minister after reports of plans by his military supporters to depose her had reached such a fever pitch that she could no longer ignore them. This was accomplished by Ramos announcing that a coup was planned, which became the excuse for Enrile's resignation. Gen. Rafael Ileto replaced him.

In return for their support, Ramos and other generals then demanded certain reforms from Aquino; these included the resignation of additional cabinet ministers perceived as corrupt or leftist and the setting of a firm deadline for the conclusion of Aquino's cease-fire talks with the CPP. Talk of coups had weakened both the civilian government and the public's perception of the military, but it strengthened the military's role in governing. Civilian leadership appeared weak and vacillating, intimidated by the AFP, although military factionalism had increased. Now, in March 1987, Ramos announced that the military could no longer be known as the New Armed Forces of the Philippines, and it reverted to its previous nomenclature. The decision symbolized how little had fundamentally changed.

On August 28, 1987, Honasan, previously relegated to a training post at Camp Magsaysay in central Luzon, launched another coup attempt. Striking in the early morning hours at Malacañang Palace, a Manilan television station, and Villamor Air Base before retreating into Camp Aguinaldo, Honasan almost succeeded in overthrowing the government. Coordinated revolts occurred elsewhere in the country, principally in Cebu, Bicol, and the Philippine Military Academy at Baguio. Almost all day the situation remained fluid. Even though Honasan was in essence cornered in Camp Aguinaldo, General Ramos was sufficiently uncertain about the loyalties of his troops that he could not muster an attacking force until late in the day. The Metro Manila police were called upon to retake the television station. Finally, after the rebels killed a marine enlisted man, a marine detachment agreed to attack and the rebel defenders either surrendered or escaped. Honasan remained at large, giving press interviews and moving freely about central Luzon until his capture in December. This time the government felt secure enough to administer real punishment; several officers were court-martialed and sentenced to lengthy prison terms. But the coup had had its effect.[77]

At this point new pay increases and other benefits, including housing, were announced for all ranks. The United States accelerated arms shipments at the government's request. Several retired military officers were given government positions, and, finally, Aquino announced a hard-line approach to the insurgency, in effect implicitly endorsing the military's support for anti-Communist vigilante groups.

Clearly the military's position in Philippine society is in flux. Honasan escaped in early April 1988 from his prison ship in Manila Bay along with his elite navy guard. Other RAM leaders remained in prison or under house arrest. Ramos became defense minister in early 1988 when Ileto resigned after protesting Ramos's inability to implement a military reorganization. President Aquino inherited an inefficient, demoralized, and corrupt military. But though the bulk of the military continued to consist of traditionalists, oriented as in the past to the interests of the elite, the dynamic force was now different, belonging to the younger RAM officers who grew up during martial law.

The attitude of these younger officers was unlike that of the Manila elite their superiors were conditioned to serve. In many ways they were like the NPA whom they fought and whose strategy they studied. In a sense they shared the aspiration among rural folk for kalayaan. In Western terms this is called nationalism but it was best expressed by an officer who said, "We must try hard to promote the idea of oneness."[78]

Both the Communists and the military reformers observed the deterioration of social conditions in their country and worked to develop a solution. They started at the same spot but traveled by different paths to reach a similar destination: "political liberation, economic emancipation and social concord." The military reformers also took longer to make the journey. In so doing, they adopted some of the interpretive processes of the Communists:

> We have taken the first hundred steps. However, we must not dwell on past victories nor should we be impatient for more concrete results. The tests of commitment and determination are still before us. We have started on a complex and difficult undertaking and we must expect obstacles along the way. We must periodically consolidate our gains and constantly check our bearings in order that we can avoid indecisive and inconsequential activities. From there, we can proceed with confidence towards the attainment of our objectives.[79]

The dynamism of the military reform group derived from their ability to assess, act, and reassess the objective situation of Philippine politics. As traditional leaders focused on the shadows, posturing about the need for social reform while doing little about it, the reform group focused on the fundamentals, the indexes of whether or not there was real reform along the lines their nationalist sentiments took them. This approach makes them a potentially dangerous foe in Philippine politics, undermining efforts of the traditional politicians in the Aquino period to restore the political structures dissolved when Marcos declared martial law.

Even among the military traditionalists, there was an unwillingness to return to their barracks after having contributed to Marcos's downfall. They saw themselves more as a coequal partner with the civilians in government affairs and finally as the ultimate guardian of the state. Threat of a military coup did not come only from the "Ramboys." In a general staff meeting on October 22, 1986, a "Statement of Concern" was issued by senior officers, observing that "the constitutional and statutory roles of the AFP are basically to protect the people and maintain the stability and security of the Republic, and that insofar as the NAFP [the New Armed Forces of the Philippines] is concerned, the stability and the security of the nation are considered as the paramount national interest."

The Marcos years took their toll on military self-perception, solidifying a consensus on the need for greater involvement in government. A poll of five hundred officers conducted in April-May 1987 indicated this changed viewpoint: 96 percent believed the military should play a role in national development; 61 percent thought that officers were as capable as civilian officials in civilian positions; 50 percent wanted more military men in public office; 77 percent believed the NPA's growth was due to incompetence and corruption of local officials rather than military abuses; 50 percent thought that government officials included many leftists or Communists; and 43 percent believed that the military might eventually have to assume power to prevent a Communist victory.[80]

The civilian leaders perceive the military in a different light. In their view, the military, as an instrument of the elite's political goals, should obey civilian commands without question. Their approach to controlling the military is to emulate Marcos by encouraging factionalism and politicizing the promotion and assignment process. Splitting the military, however, only increases the threats to the government and gains more support for the reform element within the military.

Aquino's difficulties with the military mirror problems elsewhere in the society. There are two pressures: an elite pressure to return to the political system they manipulated to their economic benefit before the martial law period and a popular pressure for social reform. Within the military the same pressures exist.[81] On the one hand there is the traditional military whose touchstone is the elite; they would advance elite interests at the peasants' cost. Their instinct is to collaborate, and their shifting loyalties reflect the traditional pattern in Philippine politics. Officers frequently stress that their allegiance is to the Office of the President rather than any particular occupant; thus, the military was able to switch its support to Aquino as the "true" victor in the 1986 elections. In effect, the military was continuing its collaboration tradition of aiding the stronger force. Their waiting by the roadside during the August 1987 coup attempt, watching to see who had the superior force, was another sign of traditional behavior. On the other hand there is the younger group of officers and enlisted men whose roots are often more rural than urban and whose families as well as themselves have been exposed to NPA terrorism. Like the NPA whose touchstone is the people, they too feel they are committed to a higher good.

Colonel Sotelo, who figured so prominently in the February 1986 people power revolution, became Aquino's air force chief. During the August 1987 attempted coup, he was besieged in his office by Honasan's rebels, dramatically illustrating the military's own lack of internal legitimacy and organizational integrity.

The military's commitment to civilian authority has always been questionable and has become more so given its profound involvement in government and the economy during the martial law years. That there have been no successful military-led coups is not for want of effort. That a coup has not succeeded is a function of the military's inherent weakness as a professional organization. The danger in reprofessionalizing the military is the danger Marcos saw of making the military lust for greater power.

Insurgency and Counterinsurgency

In April 1987 a member of the United Farmers' Organization was kidnapped by a local vigilante in Cebu City. Her body, with her head and a leg hacked off, was recovered over a week later. In May a thirty-year-old woman, eight months pregnant, and another young woman disappeared. Their bodies were later discovered, headless and stabbed multiple times. The pregnant woman's abdomen had been slashed open and the fetus ripped out. One day in June a farmer, hoeing his field in Negros, was attacked by several vigilantes who accused him of being a Communist rebel. He was decapitated and disemboweled. They took the head to the local military commander who told them the man had been innocent. The head was abandoned in a ditch to be recovered later by the man's wife. And the vigilantes went free in search of more suspects.[1]

Vigilante groups had sprung up all over the country with the tacit or direct support of the military and the government during 1987 after a year of relative calm in the insurgency. In Mindanao were the Alsa-Masa, the Eagles Squad, the Concerned Citizens' Movement, and the United People for Peace; in Negros, the Philippine Constabulary Forward Command; and in Cebu, the Tadtad and the Citizens' Army against Communism; even in Manila the police began giving weapons training to civilians forming neighborhood patrols. The increasing effort to retail the government's counterinsurgency campaign brought more reports of human rights abuses and no significant decline in the insurgency's strength. International groups, such as Amnesty International and the Lawyers Committee for Human Rights, issued reports in 1988 that suggested that the human rights situation was at least as bad as it had been under Marcos. As table 5.1 indicates, human rights violations —always a problem in the Philippines—did not cease with democracy's return. The government appeared powerless to both restore the rule of law and reduce the threat of the insurgency.

TABLE 5.1

Human Rights Violations in the Philippines, 1975–1988

Year	Arrests	Disappearances	Extrajudicial Killings
1975	—	9	3
1976	—	44	12
1977	1,351	17	51
1978	1,620	10	86
1979	1,961	48	196
1980	962	19	218
1981	1,377	53	321
1982	1,911	42	210
1983	2,088	145	368
1984[a]	3,038	137	445
1985	7,253	213	517
1986	1,712	43	197
1987	7,444	50	242
1988[b]	1,726	82	117

a. Figures for 1984 exclude Mindanao during November-December.

b. Preliminary figures, January 1–June 30.

Note: Figures do not include NPA killings.

Source: Task-Force Detainees–Philippines, *Philippine Human Rights Update* (Manila, monthly issues for periods covered).

In 1982 a now declassified American report criticized the Marcos government's failure to develop a "coordinated civilian-political-military doctrine" to fight the insurgency.[2] In 1987 a Pentagon official testified before Congress that "the Aquino government has also regrettably failed to develop a comprehensive counter-insurgency plan that integrates military, political, economic, and social programs."[3] The historical continuities in the government's approach to countering insurgency are striking. "We cannot just issue arms to all and sundry. What is needed is firstly to abide by the guidelines issued by the local governments and National Defense Departments," pleaded President Aquino while endorsing the Alsa-Masa.[4] But these guidelines were ignored and the central government, including the higher military command, lacked the ability or inclination to see that they were carried out. In the absence of effective leadership and new programs the patterns of the past were repeated.

The United States, too, appeared powerless to effect change. Privately, American policymakers expressed concern about the spreading vigilante movement that threatened to undermine efforts to reestablish local government legitimacy in rural areas. Publicly, the United States neither condemned nor condoned the groups, stating that it was in no position to confirm any of the allegations of human rights abuses.[5] Privately, the American officials expressed concern about the government's inability to formulate and implement programs for social reform and the Philippine military's inability to professionalize its forces. Publicly, the United States rushed more economic and military aid into the country.[6]

Almost fifty years before, when facing a similar crisis in the Philippines, President Truman had commissioned an Economic Survey Mission under the direction of Daniel W. Bell, president of the American Security and Trust Company, to study the country's problems. The Bell Mission, as it came to be known, concluded in its October 1950 report that "unless positive measures are taken to deal with the fundamental causes of these difficulties, it must be expected that the economic situation will deteriorate further and political disorder will inevitably result. Whatever is to be done to improve economic conditions in the Philippines must be done promptly, for if the situation is allowed to drift there is no certainty that moderate remedies will suffice."[7] The Bell Mission proposed a set of major internal economic and social reforms and an expansion of American financial aid. These measures had some impact on the Huk insurgency in the medium term, but gradually the traditional political and economic system reasserted itself such that a 1958 assessment by Congress of the American aid program concluded that "attitudes and institutional rigidities inherited from the past . . . prevented more effective use of larger amounts of aid."[8]

When Corazon Aquino became president, American policymakers, rather than announcing more aid or initiating an assessment of the country's problems and needs, settled for expressions of support. Secretary of State George Shultz visited Manila and, with a yellow Cory Aquino doll pinned to his lapel, told the world of America's undiluted support for her new government, saying that the United States would like to provide more aid but was prevented from doing so by domestic budgetary constraints. Only in mid-1988, in response to a congressional initiative, did the Reagan administration announce its intention to propose a multibillion-dollar, multilateral "mini–Marshall Plan" for the Philippines.

In fairness, Americans, like many Filipinos, believed in 1986 as they had in 1950 that the problem was only one of leadership. The mystique that enveloped Magsaysay's handling of the Huks also affected Corazon Aquino: as Magsaysay had replaced the ineffective and corrupt administration of President Quirino and resolved the Huk conflict so would Aquino replace Marcos and resolve the CPP insurgency. But, as the American embassy reported in 1981, "the rise of the NPA is largely independent of the question of martial law and the exercise of authoritarian rule."[9]

Philippine history shows that rebellions can be suppressed but rarely eliminated for long. The people's apparent submission to government authority only masks their continued discontent. Elites happily collaborate with the prevailing forces to preserve their status; the calm is temporary. Movements are fragmented but not destroyed; they continue to percolate below the surface, only to erupt periodically in banditry and rebellion. The colorums, the Sakdalistas, the Huks, and the NPA are all indicators of the society's failure to satisfy the needs of the peasantry. Because the government did not understand, or did not want to understand, the problems of the rural poor, rebellion flourished.

Peasants rebelled, first, because they had no choice. Revolt was in effect a rational response to the government's failure to improve their social condition. But rebellion was also sanctified by their culture and tradition. Revolt was an effort to cleanse society of corrupt elements, to purge it of foreign influences, and to establish a new social contract achieving true independence, kalayaan. Religion not only justified rebellion but sustained it when, under more objective criteria, it should have ceased. The "little tradition" of rebellion remained strong among the peasantry because they were never made a part of the "great tradition" of nationalism that was the province of an elite whose concept of national independence bore little similarity to that of the poor's.

Elites remained isolated from the people.[10] The depth of the chasm only grew in the 1960s and 1970s with rapid population growth and economic failure. The social system that provided the basis for elite domination and maintained some level of income distribution through the extended family structure and periodic elections broke down. Utang na loób no longer guaranteed loyalty, for elites could not provide sufficient rewards. The share of income by the lowest 20 percent of Filipino families showed an almost consistent decline from the 1950s to 1971, and the number of poor increased.[11] Estimates of the percentage of the rural labor force that became landless ranged from 7.5 percent to as high as 50 percent.[12] The urban population swelled with Metro Manila's density estimated at ten thousand per square kilometer with 10 percent living in slums. These conditions provided fecund ground for discontent.

Using violence "indiscriminately and without regard to political consequences," the government reacted characteristically to the unrest.[13] The military, of course, was not trained to act any differently. And, in addition, the further politicization of the military under Marcos, the promotion of officers for personal loyalty rather than competence, and the concentration of resources in the forces around Manila made it highly unlikely that the military would act any other way. The people were treated with disdain; they reacted accordingly. It was, after all, what they expected. Just as in Vietnam, the government viewed the threat as a military one that could be dealt with only by repression.

We have seen how this historical pattern of repression-rebellion-suppression has been repeated for at least the past century and a half in the Philippines. But we need to examine more closely the government's response to the insurgency. It is in part the government's failure to link its counterinsurgency approach to the systemic causes of rebellion that helps perpetuate the conflict and threatens to draw American troops into another Asian guerrilla war.

The Military's Counterinsurgency Strategy

The NPA found the Philippine military a godsend. It was "rotten to the core," they said, an "antipeople organization" with "rampant" corruption and "demoralized troops," unable to "adopt a strategy." Marcos "encouraged abuses and atrocities," replacing "officers with his relatives."[14] Their assessment was an accurate one and widely accepted. So too was the view that once Marcos was gone the military's problems would somehow magically be resolved and that his counterinsurgency strategy would somehow be replaced by another, more effective one. But this was not to be. The present Philippine government's counterinsurgency approach is much the same as the one developed during Marcos's rule. On paper it looks good but in practice it does not work.

Marcos frequently announced new efforts to modernize and strengthen the armed forces while he implemented a "total approach," an "aggressive campaign" with a four-point counterinsurgency program: (1) to develop the AFP into a "well-motivated" and "people-oriented" force, (2) to separate active guerrillas from the mass base, (3) to keep the people on the government's side, and (4) to prevent the insurgency from taking root. Generals with experience fighting the Huks were recalled, but, as in the late 1960s, there was "no sustained effort by the government to win over the masses."[15]

Civic action was emphasized. The military formed an Army Literacy Patrol System of soldier-teachers in 1982 to provide education, free medical services, and "beautification" of communities. A "love campaign" was started under the First Lady's guidance to "show love and care to the people."[16] Many of the civic action projects were implemented under the KKK program (Kilusang Kabuhayan Kaunlaran, or National Livelihood) to promote waste utilization and agricultural, livestock, and light industry enterprises. Soldiers were given courses in civil-military operations. Engineer brigades were brought in to build roads and water supply systems and to electrify communities. Political officers were trained for rural areas. A public relations campaign was begun to improve the military's image in cooperation with the government's Office of Media Affairs. The army's Civil Relations and Information Service produced radio and television programs.[17]

Efforts were made to improve the military's disciplinary problems. Church-Military Liaison Committees were formed and a dialogue begun with the Catholic Bishops Conference of the Philippines. Although the bishops later withdrew because they thought the dialogue was one-sided, the authorities emphasized their interest in continuing. In 1983 the military began to go into the field to engage in "dialogue" with government and civilian leaders.[18]

In response to accusations of human rights abuses Marcos ordered the military to "cleanse their ranks of undesirables"[19] and Ver proposed forming a "superagency" to handle the people's grievances.[20] Probes were ordered of military crimes; several thousand men were reportedly dismissed from service; studies were made of the causes of military abuses; special discipline committees and tribunals were established. In 1976 officers were made responsible for their troops' behavior at all times. In 1978 Ramos ordered that no one could be arrested, searched, or seized by the PC without approval from the president's office. Ver formed a special rehabilitation battalion for training "abusive and undisciplined personnel." In 1984 Ramos announced that four hundred PC soldiers had been dismissed, five hundred suspended or demoted, and 60 percent of the military sent through special courses to improve skills. A military committee was created by Ramos to investigate human rights abuses. In 1985 seven special discipline barracks were ordered to be established around the country and Ramos sought improvements in the police and military promotion boards to weed out undesirables.[21] Reforms emphasized rebuilding public support, boosting troop morale and discipline, and improving combat capabilities.[22]

U.S. officials in early 1986 began praising military reform actions, singling out the increase in the military's willingness to engage in civilian counterinsurgency programs, Ramos's appointment as acting chief of staff, and Marcos's acceptance of the Agrava Commission report concerning the military's involvement in Senator Aquino's assassination.[23] Paul Wolfowitz, the American assistant secretary of state for East Asia and the Pacific, listed signs of military reform in a speech on February 22, 1985: "A new system to police military abuses, . . . some reorganization of military command and deployment to deal with insurgency, and a more realistic set of military procurement priorities focusing on basic mobility and communications items needed against the insurgency."

Marcos tinkered with military organization to make its combat tactics more effective. Earlier, in 1969, when dealing with Huk remnants in central Luzon and the NPA's beginnings, the AFP had established ten-man barrio self-defense units composed of five enlisted men and five civilians. These were precursors of the Civilian Home Defense Forces. Special task forces of regular units had also been set up to sweep the provinces, an approach that forced the NPA to divide their forces. At the time, Lachica reported that the fifty-thousand AFP force was "sufficient to cope with a dissident force of any possible size."[25]

But, by the early 1980s it was apparent that this strategy was not working. Marcos stated that the battalion unit formations, although suitable for central Luzon's plains, were no longer satisfactory and ordered that small-unit, ranger-type tactics be emphasized. The First Scout Ranger Regiment was reactivated in 1983. Composed of five Scout Ranger companies, two ranger battalions, and one mountain battalion, First Scout had been one of the most effective units against the Huks. The marines also shifted their training to small-unit, ranger-type tactics, and the PC/INP formed a Special Field Reaction Force in 1985 under Gen. Jose P. Magno, Jr., for counterinsurgency work. The PC units were divided into 180 battalions and deployed as small units, reinforced by PA companies, and the Scout Rangers were sent on detached duty as long-range patrol squads. In addition new infantry battalions were recruited and personnel reassigned from clerical work to field service. Ramos in late 1984 ordered AFP headquarters' units and all major service commands to "strip themselves to the bone" so more vehicles, men, and communication facilities could be sent to the field. He also ordered all new officers to be assigned first to the field to serve two years with a combat unit. The air force announced that specially trained teams would be sent to each regional command to select and deploy appropriate aircraft for each operation. Marcos declared that his new strategy to defeat the CPP was "to clear, hold, consolidate and develop"; he would no longer rely on conventional warfare.[26]

The AFP's counterinsurgency program on paper appears persuasive — so why did it not succeed? Certainly because, in part, many of the reforms were not begun until late 1985 and then only halfheartedly and under considerable American pressure. Ramos lacked authority to investigate abuses and corruption and to reassign and discipline soldiers. The disciplinary-barrack program existed only on paper, partly because the AFP, it was believed, could not afford to divert troop strength from the field to retraining.

The military's problems were also in part symptomatic of the society's overall political and economic crisis. Marcos's legitimacy was in question. Local government had been eroded. The economy's deterioration fostered a general malaise that provided a breeding ground for insurgents and a shortage of resources that made it more difficult to strengthen the military. Yet the military's own tactics helped spread the insurgency.

When the traditionally contentious Muslim (Moro) minority of eastern Mindanao rose up in the early 1970s against the government under the banner of Nur Misuari's Moro National Liberation Front, the military's tactics to counter them were essentially "slash and burn." Chemical bombs (napalm) were reportedly used; Jolo City was considerably damaged; paramilitary units were formed; people were "strategically relocated," resulting in an estimated 100,000 to 980,000 refugees. Forced evacuations, free-fire zones, the burning of villages and farmland, strafing attacks, rape, torture, murder, illegal arrest, and economic blockades became commonplace. With all of this, a military stalemate with the Muslim insurgents in Mindanao was not reached until the mid-1970s and then only after the AFP had garrisoned there 85 percent of its combat troops.[27] In 1984 50 percent of the AFP had been assigned to the Christian areas of Mindanao where the NPA was active, and many of the same tactics used against the Muslims were employed against the NPA—but still the insurgency grew.[28]

Strategic hamleting was begun in northern Samar in 1969. The military officially inaugurated a "strategic hamlet" program in the Mindanao province of Davao del Norte in 1981. Called "groupings," the program spread to several other provinces. The military strong-armed municipal assemblies into supporting relocation. The program was so notorious (and ineffective as it tended to create NPA support where none had previously existed) that Defense Secretary Juan Ponce Enrile announced its end in March 1982, saying it had never been authorized. Nevertheless hamleting continued.[29] The military also implemented zoning operations in which barrios were cordoned off for house-to-house searches while residents were collected for interrogation. In NPA base areas the army organized food blockades and rationing, confiscating villagers' food stocks and doling out what was considered adequate to live on, in order to prevent the NPA from receiving supplies. Road blockades, often manned by Home Defense units, became a focus of extortion activities.

To publicize the success of their operations, military commanders (especially those seeking to be promoted) would sponsor mass "NPA surrenders," trucking villagers in to sign oaths of loyalty and renounce "support" for the NPA while posing them for photographs. Implied in the signing of such oaths was the acknowledgment that the villagers had indeed supported the NPA, something that could be used against them in future military interrogations. Ironically, the military did not reward or attempt to rehabilitate anyone really surrendering from the NPA.[30]

"Salvaging," or military murder, and torture were widespread. One general stated that 30 percent of the troops had been involved in human rights abuses in Samar and Zamboanga City, attributing this to battle fatigue and knowledge that, if accused of an abuse, they would be replaced and thus could leave the combat zone. Constabulary and army intelligence units and the Home Defense units were the most frequently reported culprits.[31] The Task Force on Detainees–Philippines, which became a reliable source for reports of military (although not NPA) human rights abuses, may have understated the actual number of cases as it reported only those brought directly to its offices. Despite these often well-documented incidents, the military brought few individuals to trial and then did not publicize cases because the accused escaped with little or no punishment owing to strong bonds of personal loyalty.[32]

In early 1984 American officials began to encourage the government to revise its strategy to emphasize basic logistical and communications equipment, but change was slow. Pervasive corruption of military procurement procedures had left the military in an extremely weak position to deal with the insurgency precisely at the moment the insurgents adopted a more aggressive strategy. The American assistant secretary of state for East Asia and the Pacific stated on February 22, 1985, that American aid would be "premised on the fuller expectation that the incipient reforms we have seen will continue and expand." But little substantial improvement occurred before Marcos's downfall. Ramos tried to arrest the decline after being appointed acting chief of staff in 1985, but he had almost no authority to undertake even cosmetic changes. By 1984, it was evident that the AFP would have difficulty in reaching the 10:1 combat ratio considered essential for defeating the NPA.[33]

Yet, even after Marcos was replaced, the military's tactics vis-à-vis the insurgents remained the same, and its own internal weaknesses continued, including even the more mundane problems of procurement. In their eagerness for greater mobility, for example, the Philippine military requested more helicopters from the United States, and in its eagerness to show support for Aquino, the United States supplied them. But the Philippine military's maintenance system was unable to keep them operating. With unskilled pilots trying to fly in bad weather and even in good weather flying into power lines, the helicopters all too often crashed; then the United States was blamed for giving the Philippines defective helicopters. Another example: the military wanted expensive infrared goggles to improve soldiers' night vision and special secure communications equipment at the very time units in the field lacked such basic equipment as uniforms and trucks.[34] A system of accountability enforced by an inspector general existed only on paper in part because cultural sensitivities required that unit commanders be informed in advance about impending snap inspections. The government also continued to politicize military promotions for the same reason Marcos had done so—because of its fear of a military coup. General Ramos, after the August 1987 attempted coup, began systematically to weed out suspect officers. Of course, many of those suspected of disloyalty were the young military reformists with the greater counterinsurgency experience who had spent time studying the NPA and thinking through new approaches to fighting it. The military's overall strategy against the insurgency has remained much the same under Aquino.

Although the army's manual, *The Infantry Battalion*, stresses that the insurgency is "political warfare" and the AFP's response should be both "military and economic," its strategy in practice is only a military one. Because the military treats the people as if they were the foe, the public, out of fear, does not cooperate with them, as a Davao community leader commented in 1985.[35]

The NPA too controlled Davao through fear as well as through exploiting the government's failure to provide basic services, such as justice.[36] Even when the NPA withdrew from Davao in 1986 and was replaced by the Alsa-Masa who claimed to be protecting the people, the issues of justice—extortion, rape, robbery, murder—remained. Government officials confused the absence of the NPA with dealing with the causes of social unrest. Zoning operations, mass surrenders of "NPA" people, bombings by inaccurate, World War II–vintage T-28 propeller-driven planes—all were again the order of the day.

The military, most of whose senior command came from urban areas and had little combat experience, could not identify with peasant concerns or aspirations.[37] A policy of frequently rotating officers to prevent them from establishing a local political base further served to isolate them from the community.[38] With few ties to the people they were supposed to defend, little sympathy for them, and few resources to work with, it was inevitable that the military would be viewed as the enemy, especially with a new government as unwilling as the previous one to understand why peasants rebel.

Reasons for Rebellion

In the past the insurgents had been able to capitalize on the government's mistakes, responding to the peasants' traditional felt need for liberation: "The AFP and the government seem to act from fear and distrust of the people; the NPA appear to act from concern and confidence in the people."[39] The CPP presented peasants with a more persuasive alternative than had previous insurrectionists. It was not just a change in leadership that was needed, the Communist cadres argued, but a change in society—although their view of how this new society would be constructed was as imprecise as the government's. Still, they made a case for structural reform that promised to liberate the peasants from their poverty and give them a new status in a society that had consistently patronized if not abused them.

The imposition of martial law certainly aided the insurgency's growth, providing a source of new recruits and exacerbating existing social tensions. But a rebellion would have taken place in any event for two reasons. First, elite factions were continually engaged in an intense struggle for political power in which the peasants were pawns. Political processes, even when elections were regularly held, had never been especially peaceful, and after elections, the struggles did not end: wealthy clans simply continued the battle by other means.[40] The democratic political process was weak and parties only thinly disguised structures within which the ruling elites could fight while shedding the blood of their poor supporters. These elites had little interest in legitimizing a political process that would have provided other avenues for political change. A pluralistic normative system would have ultimately undermined their own power. When Aquino assumed office, she reestablished the old political system. The 1987 congressional elections and the 1988 local elections were marked by vote-buying and assassination by elites eager to reestablish their personal power base.

Second, open rebellion was a delayed response to a conflict between the common tao and the hacendero elite that had never been resolved; the conflict dated back to Spanish times although it was particularly strong in the 1930s. The Huks as an organization expired, but their appeal did not, because the root causes of rebellion remained —economic deprivation, social injustice, and a need for a national identity. On this residual base the CPP expanded, proceeding carefully to build its mass base which included the intelligentsia, the middle class, and the peasants. The long-standing nationalist movement with its well-established set of precepts about American imperialism and collaborationism translated easily into Marxist-Leninist rhetoric for middle-class revolutionaries, and the poor were responsive to the equally long-term desire to achieve the magic of kalayaan, which would involve both independence and social equality. The Communists in the Philippines, like those in Vietnam, as Jeffrey Race has written, had a "comprehensive view of revolution as a stage-by-stage social process," whereas the "government's one-dimensional conception of a multidimensional process ensured its defeat, regardless of its resources."[41]

President Aquino and her cabinet ministers have spoken often of the need for a "comprehensive counterinsurgency program"—a phrase that has become a cliché—but they have not really wanted or have not known how to develop and implement one. A key example has been the issue of land reform about which much rhetoric has been voiced but little has been done, especially after a Congress dominated by landowners was elected in 1987. As the government has addressed only halfheartedly this central grievance of the peasants, it is unlikely to understand the need to develop other social programs as part of a step-by-step process to reestablish its legitimacy in large areas of the country under CPP control. In effect, Aquino has projected no vision for the country's future beyond the simple one of rewriting the constitution and reestablishing the semblance of democratic institutions with elections.

Nor has the government addressed the basic issue of organization. The CPP established a self-perpetuating system for control through its recruitment, training, and evaluation procedures. When it made tactical mistakes, it attempted to rectify them. Discipline was enforced;

cadres who did not perform were replaced, including the party's highest officials. The Philippine military had the only similar organization in the government, at least on paper, although in practice it was a poor shadow of the NPA. The government lacked such an organizational framework and ability. Its bureaucracy was bloated; its performance criteria ignored. After years of Marcos's one-man rule, everyone, including cabinet secretaries, appeared to have forgotten how to act without guidance from the president. "I have said clearly all that needs to be said. Am I also expected to take up an M-16 and do it?" Aquino plaintively asked in a speech after the abortive August 1987 coup.

Speaking of another war in another place, Vietnam, Race observed that "the fundamental failure of the government had been a conceptual one" (xvi). The same could be said about the Philippines: "The great difference between ruler and ruled in their perception of the rural situation almost guaranteed that the steps the government took would be the wrong ones, because its understanding of the rural situation was so badly flawed. To high officials, the countryside was basically happy, and grievances were ipso facto communist-inspired and thus to be ignored"(39).

The Balance of Forces in a Social Revolution

Understanding how to counter an insurgency is not simply a matter of identifying and addressing peasant grievances. Equally important is understanding how the peasants perceive the government and the insurgents, both of whom are competing for the peasantry's allegiance. The ruler must perceive the situation from the perspective of the ruled if the ruler's strategy is going to be successful. In so doing, the government will come to understand how an unpaid, uneducated, ill-equipped, medically unfit force of barefoot peasants can defeat a paid, educated, and equipped army.

To understand the success of the CPP it is instructive to compare it to the Vietnam War as Race did. The success of Vietnam's "revolutionary movement" was due to "the fact that it represented a social revolution" (xvii). This point is central. Other explanations for the Vietnamese Communist success—the government's insufficient security and propaganda, its corruption, the lack of a national ideology and consciousness, the country's underdevelopment, external support for the insurgents, tactics like terrorism—may all have some validity, but they do not account for the rebels' victory. A military solution is an insufficient response to a social revolution.

In fact, an attempt at a military solution may carry the seeds of democracy's destruction in the Philippines. Reporting in 1981 an American official cabled:

> As more military resources are required to meet the insurgent threat, American security assistance assumes added importance. If, as the insurgency continues, the civilian sector is unwilling to make the necessary sacrifices, the military response will assume an ever larger significance. An enlarged military role could lead to military encroachments into the political area with potentially adverse consequences for long-term governmental stability.[42]

Troop size alone cannot guarantee security, especially in rural areas. As the Philippine military has grown in size so has the NPA. Moreover, military strength is beside the point, as Race said, if the government's "strategic conception of security" was " 'protecting the people' " when the people were not "the objects of attack"(194). As in Vietnam, the military's concept of warfare was to base its troops in urban areas from which occasional forays were launched into the hinterlands in pursuit of an enemy that rarely remained still (although in 1988 the AFP began creating Special Operations Teams, immersing small units in rural life in an effort to counterorganize villagers).

Terrorism or coercion, too, is not sufficient for explaining the CPP's growth. The CPP could not sustain the support of several million people through coercion alone. Although assassination was a tactic, it was used selectively to ensure the cooperation of a recalcitrant few. As in Vietnam, "the government terrorized far more than did the revolutionary movement"(197) through its strategic hamleting, bombings, arrests, and murders. Certainly NPA cadres did their share of killing but nowhere did their random brutality approach the systematic and repeated savagery of the vigilante movements acting at the military's behest.

Infiltration was even less a factor in the Philippines than in Vietnam. Outside of a few foreign sympathizers and some foreign funding and arms, the NPA was entirely home-grown and self-reliant, in contrast to the Philippine military which absorbed hundreds of millions of dollars in American aid. The growth of the CPP was also proof of the thesis that "the people" did not "just want to be left alone"(198). To the contrary, the Filipino peasant was receptive to organizing cadres because they wanted change—so much so that they were willing to die for it.

The government perceived its counterinsurgency approach mainly in propaganda terms. For example, it latched onto Ross Munro's depiction of the NPA as "the new Khmer Rouge," even though few Filipinos accepted that portrait as valid. Rather than confronting social inequities, the government opted for portraying the NPA as brutal murderers and extortionists, in effect implying the government should be supported only as the lesser of two evils. The military envisioned propaganda as effective lies rather than an opportunity to present convincing truths. As in Vietnam, the government lacked a valid message and the means to convey it. Moreover, its people were not as motivated as the party's even if they had had a message to send. But most important, like the Vietnamese, the people knew all too well what the government had to offer. They had, after all, lived on the same land for generations and had seen official promises of reform repeatedly fail while the elites continued to exploit them. Even President Aquino's promise of a restoration of democracy could not match the CPP's offer of land reform, housing, and medical services. The peasants had experienced before the dubious benefits of Philippine "democracy."

Lack of development does not fully explain the CPP's success, either. What peasants wanted was not a larger pie from which elites would take a bigger slice but, rather, radical changes in the distribution of benefits within the society. The pie in the Philippines had been growing larger for forty years with no clear benefits to the poor whose real wage rates declined. The insurgency actually grew in strength during the 1970s, when the Philippines experienced high levels of growth. As in Vietnam, the Philippine government offered the hope of more benefits derived from incremental change. The CPP's offer of independence coupled with social justice might have been vague, but it spoke more to the peasants' human condition than did the government's empty promises of land reform

Prior to Marcos's exile, corruption was often cited as the key variable in explaining the CPP's growth. And after he was gone, the military continued to see it as a more important factor than their own abuses of human rights (only 18 percent of five hundred officers in a survey believed abuses were significant). Certainly corruption was of some importance in the growth of the CPP. The diversion of government resources and the ineffectiveness of corrupt local officials contributed to creating a void in the rural areas into which the CPP could expand. But as in Vietnam, many local officials were honest. It was the system they worked in that was corrupt, for it served the interests of an elite more interested in political power and amassing wealth than in social reform. As Race said of Vietnam, "corruption was not an independent factor which could have been altered at will, but integral to the organization of the system itself and to the views of decision makers" (204). Even after Corazon Aquino came to power, bringing with her many honest officials, corruption persisted, including some cabinet officials and close family advisers.

Ideology also does not explain the CPP's success or the government's failure. Sison, in fact, emphasized empiricism, not ideology, and ideologues were attacked for their failure to adapt tactics to reality. What the CPP offered was a superior strategic vision and the promise of concrete social change built on superior organization. Their overarching vision of a new Philippine society was admittedly vague. It centered on broad themes, such as land reform and social justice, and offered few specifics. Nevertheless, the CPP actually did implement change in areas they controlled.

As in Vietnam, the CPP's strength lay in its "pragmatism and flexibility" (205). The party promised concrete changes in the peasants' reality, while the government's rhetoric—Marcos's "New Society" and Aquino's "people power"—essentially appealed only to the bourgeoisie. What the government needed was what the CPP had, "an integrated conception of social change" (205), and it needed to do what the CPP did, enforce rough justice and reform. Thus, the party would couple its discussion of social justice with the execution of a cattle rustler. The government would promise social justice but let the cattle rustler go free while permitting vigilantes to behead unarmed civilians. Ineffective administration of justice, however, does not sufficiently explain the CPP's success, although certainly such competence was lacking. The government did not address "the basic problem of distributive conflict. . . . what was significant was the content of that activity, not the efficiency with which it was carried out" (205). For example, a more efficient justice system in which the date of trials would be set by lottery, a method easily and often subverted by bribery, would not have prevented abuses of the law by the law enforcers and lawmakers themselves. Replacing the NPA in Davao with the Alsa-Masa was not the same as restoring law and order.

On the other hand, the lack of national consciousness, unlike the situation in Vietnam, did play an important role in the CPP's success. What the party did was to awaken latent nationalism among the peasants as well as some middle-class supporters. The CPP promised to cleanse the national psyche of foreign influences, in a sense to purify the individual's loób, and establish a utopia, a communal brotherhood. In this the CPP was like the Vietminh in that it built a base on communal ties, emphasizing rather than working against kinship relations, in order to establish a better community. Although the party's organizing of the urban poor may have brought only minor improvements in their standard of living, it demonstrated that it could effect some change and promised even more change later.

Economic improvement in itself is not the answer to the insurgency, however, for the CPP's expansion was not due solely to, say, a depressed market for agricultural products. Economic improvements, reported the American embassy in 1982, "would only be one of the many steps necessary to blunt further NPA expansion." It concluded that "development per se is not the solution to the insurgency problem."[43]

The key to defeating the CPP, then, lies in the elite's willingness to sacrifice its welfare for the sake of the nation's. Even should the NPA repeat the mistakes of the Huks, thereby defeating itself, the seeds of revolution will remain to grow once again unless the society can transform itself. The cycle of conflict can be broken only if the rational reasons for peasant discontent are resolved.

The Future

On the eve of the second anniversary of the 1986 people power revolution, the Philippines had become a nation turning upon itself. Jaimé V. Ongpin, a leader of the revolution who had been one of three key advisers to Aquino during her presidential campaign and later secretary of finance in her cabinet, shot himself in his office after being forced to resign in a cabinet shake-up after the August 1987 coup. It was Ongpin, a leader in the Manila business community and an early critic of Marcos, who had coined the derogatory phrase "crony capitalism" to describe Marcos's corruption. Having devoted his life to improving his country, he was reportedly depressed at the turn of events following the euphoria that had greeted Aquino's assumption to power. Thus Ongpin, despite being a devout Catholic, had taken his own life. In death, he had become the first martyr to the so-called bloodless revolution. He was unlikely to be the last.

Disenchantment with Aquino's government was widespread—although disenchantment may be too strong a term. In effect the political system was simply reverting to its pre-Marcos form. The Aquino coalition was coming apart—that coalition of wealthy matrons, middle-class professionals, students, church workers, and urban and rural poor who had banded together against Marcos first in the 1986 presidential campaign and then in a stunning display in the streets of Manila in support of the military coup against him. The wealthy and the middle class, increasingly fearful of the Communist insurgency that was bringing urban terrorism to Manila, were beginning to side with the military and other conservative elements, expressing support for vigilantism and even speaking, albeit hesitantly, about the need to reimpose martial law. The church leadership, for the most part, had returned to its parishes: Pope John Paul II had told Cardinal Sin that political activity was frowned upon. But the military, after several aborted coups, had not returned to its barracks, and it was still beset by factionalism and disgruntlement with the government and its own commanders. Ramos, now defense secretary, was taking a more and more prominent role in politics, visiting the United States in mid-1988 on a thinly disguised campaign trip in preparation for a presidential election in 1992 or sooner. The urban and rural poor experienced no significant change in their lives, even though high growth rates fueled in part by consumer spending made Manila look like a boomtown.

In Washington, policymakers, in a Reagan administration afflicted with its own scandals and with the normal personnel attrition that strikes any administration in its last year in office, were having increasing difficulty in giving priority to Philippine developments. Once Marcos was out of the way, most members of Congress behaved as if the crisis had been settled and moved on to new issues, such as elections in South Korea, which garnered headlines. Budgetary problems made it difficult to allocate aid for the Philippines. The State Department, concerned about the situation but worried that undue publicity would scare off potential foreign investors, downplayed the obvious negatives of civil war and a Philippine government unable to act. As Americans became targets for Communist attacks, Washington prepared plans to draw back nonessential personnel from the Philippines, and armed American soldiers at Clark and Subic began accompanying Philippine troops responsible for the bases' security on their perimeter patrols. At the same time, in early 1988, the United States expanded its support for retraining the Philippine military, recognizing the dangers of its own military being drawn more deeply into the conflict but with little influence over the Aquino government's prosecution of the war. Indeed, the Aquino government had positioned the United States in the same corner as Marcos had: if the United States did not want to jeopardize its access to its bases, it had no choice but to provide the type of aid the Filipinos requested—even if that aid was inappropriate to the problems the country faced. The United States was relegated to the sidelines in a conflict dependent upon American weapons.

The CPP has girded itself for a protracted armed struggle. Earlier disputes within the movement after Aquino became president concerning the advisability of emphasizing the political struggle have for the medium term been resolved in favor of the armed struggle. The party, however, cannot afford a protracted war without outside financial and military support. This is the party's dilemma as long as the popularly elected Aquino is president. The traditional foreign supporters of Communist insurgencies—the Soviet Union, China, and their allies—are wary of assisting the CPP. Unless Aquino is overthrown or her popularity wanes, it is unlikely that the party will receive much more than sympathy from European leftists. Only Greece's Pan-Hellenic Socialist movement has recognized the party's legitimacy. Even the church's National Secretariat for Social Action was revamped by the bishops in 1988 in a move to restrict its use as a channel for foreign aid to the NPA. Thus, the NPA will have to feed off its mass base, limiting its ability to move beyond small-unit guerrilla tactics. The party's hope is that friction within the elite factions will worsen, as Guerrero earlier predicted, and will lead to a military coup d'etat: "as the revolutionary movement intensifies, factions within the counter revolutionary ranks struggle more bitterly and violently, thus forcing whichever faction is in power to retain its crack forces in the city or in reserve camps to defend itself from coup d'etats."[44]

The CPP insurgency is the most serious challenge the Filipino elite has ever faced. The party's leaders have now had twenty years of experience, devising and revising strategies and developing a broad-based national organization. Ultimately the government's superior firepower may be enough to decimate the party's cadres and temporarily beat the peasantry into submission, but the cost in lives and economic deprivation will be horrendous and will only prepare the ground for the next revolution—unless the government itself changes how it governs. As Jeffrey Race wrote about Vietnam, "To gain victory the revolutionary movement did not need to be 'good' or 'effective' by any absolute standard; it needed to be better than the government" (xv). This is equally true today in the Philippines.

Epilogue

"Has it blown up yet?" Maj. Gen. Adna Chaffee, commander of American forces in the Philippine-American War, reportedly asked his orderly each morning at breakfast.

"What, sir?" his orderly would respond.

"The volcano, dammit! . . . The volcano we're standing on!"[1]

That war, which cost 4,234 American lives and at least four times that number in Filipino casualties, was later seen as the historical antecedent for the American involvement in the Vietnam War. Strategic hamleting, blockades, brutal torture, and congressional and public revulsion against the war characterized the Philippine-American conflict as they did the later one.

Both experiences have affected American perceptions of the current struggle in the Philippines. Policymakers are aware of the limitations within which they must work, both domestically in terms of public reaction to involvement in yet another Asian nation's insurgency and internationally in terms of American influence in such a complex society as that of the Philippines. Filipinos under Aquino as under Marcos have not hesitated to remind Americans of their place as observers and occasional helpmates but not participants in Philippine affairs.

For example, in the fall of 1987 Gen. Fidel Ramos engineered the expulsion of an American military attaché for his alleged ties to the "Ramboys," making it clear to the United States who was in charge. Marcos had done much the same thing in the 1960s when he accepted funds for the Philippine units in Vietnam but refused President Johnson's request to extend their tour of duty there. Filipinos may accept American aid, but they insist on their independence.

This restraint and the limitations placed on aid programs have often led to timid American policies in the past. On the surface, the pattern of previous U.S. aid efforts and their failure to effect structural change would argue for a continued cautious approach to current Philippine problems. Yet the failure to address these problems would put at risk U.S. security interests in the islands and, more important, could jeopardize Aquino's efforts to rejuvenate Philippine democracy.

✓   U.S. security interests are enormous. Subic Naval Base covers 62,000 acres and includes an air station, naval magazine, and repair facilities. (In contrast, the U.S. base in Cuba's Guantánamo Bay is about 29,000 acres.) U.S. Air Force facilities at Clark Air Base in Tarlac and Pampanga provinces cover only about 8 percent of the base's enormous 130,300 acres; much of the excess land is used as a bombing and gunnery range. Both bases have approximately 46,000 full-time Filipino employees. Other American facilities in the islands include the San Miguel Naval Communications Station, John Hay Air Station, Wallace Air Station, several smaller communications stations, and an atomic test monitoring station in Mindanao.

American economic interests are also substantial. U.S. trade accounts for almost one-third of the Philippines' total imports, U.S. banks are owed about 60 percent of the Philippines' commercial bank debt, and direct U.S. investment totals $1.2 billion, about 50 percent of all foreign investment in the country.

Fearful of risking harm to these interests, U.S. policymakers in the past publicly ignored the corruption and destruction of democracy under President Marcos. Henry Kissinger wrote, for example, "Whatever else may be said about the Marcos regime, it contributed substantially to American security and had been extolled by American presidents, including President Reagan, for nearly two decades."[2] In the end, however, American policymakers recognized that promoting democracy was a better way to protect American interests—and was more consonant with American values—than helping to prop up a dictator. The problem now is how U.S. policy can encourage the growth of democracy in the Philippines and avoid its past mistakes.

To this end, U.S. aid should be targeted, first, at helping establish a stable environment in which democracy can grow and, second, at supporting institutions essential for the preservation of democracy. A continuing U.S. dialogue with the Philippines on tackling short-term problems and effecting long-term reforms will be an indispensable part of the process. The short-term problems, such as debt management and trade-policy reform, will be the easiest to resolve. Such long-term ventures as stimulating sectoral growth and retraining and equipping the military will require structural reform—an area in which an ongoing policy dialogue would be most useful.

A good but belated start was the concept of a "mini–Marshall Plan" —renamed the Multilateral Aid Initiative—proposed by a bipartisan congressional group in late 1987 (although as of the beginning of 1989, the idea had not been taken up by the administration). The most useful part of the plan was not its promises of large amounts of aid (which quickly became the focus of internal bureaucratic feuding) but its proposal that a "special coordinator or commissioner who will be responsible for coordinating this initiative" be appointed. Given the disparate problems afflicting the Philippines and the low levels of aid available from an America beset by its own budgetary problems, such a coordinator could maximize the benefits to be obtained from limited funds. A commissioner could also coordinate the programs of the various private voluntary organizations (PVOs) now extending aid independently to the Philippines. Funds, which in 1989 total $3.8 billion from all sources, could be funneled through the PVOs directly to local governments and agencies in the Philippines, bypassing the present aid bottleneck.

Key areas in which such a commissioner could allocate limited American aid most effectively are agricultural production, telecommunications, education, and population planning. Although agricultural production is one of the brightest spots in the Philippine economy, its restructuring still resists reform efforts. Early proposals for a radical land reform program were rejected by the new Philippine Congress, and American proponents of more aggressive approaches took their cue from President Aquino's own reluctance to embrace progressive change. Yet agrarian reform—which entails land tenure changes in some areas and plantation-style economies of scale in others—coupled with providing alternative sources of employment for rural laborers is essential to the Philippines' long-term economic growth and to reducing support for the CPP. Telecommunications is also an area in which the United States possesses a useful expertise. Developing a more effective communications system would help bind the island nation together, providing market information for farmers and business people, bringing educational opportunities to rural areas, and ultimately reducing regional disparities.

Because the Philippines' problems are highly interconnected, reform in one area would strengthen reforms in others. A case in point is education. In 1975, for example, a bilingual teaching program was begun which resulted in a significant decline in the number of English speakers, the lingua franca of the region and a major selling point to foreign investors seeking new sites. The Philippine literacy rate has shown only marginal improvement—from 72 percent in 1960 to 75 percent in 1980—because of population growth and a decline in the quality of educational services. In a 1975 achievement study, students scored an average of 48 percent on standardized tests for which 75 percent was a passing grade. The students' weakest subjects were reading, mathematics, and language. Philippine educational needs are of every variety: classrooms, supplies, better curricula, and teachers. Improving the quality and availability of education would strengthen not only the economy but democracy, too.

Another key area for U.S. policy dialogue is that of population planning. As bad as was President Marcos's program in this area, it was actually better than the Aquino government's effort—perhaps as a result of pressure from or an implicit bias of the Catholic church. In 1960 the Philippine population was 27 million; now it is over 55 million. The official growth rate of 2.5 percent underestimates the actual rate, which is probably closer to 3 percent. The average family size is 5.2 with an overall fertility rate of 4.2 children. Although contraceptive use has increased, the least effective methods are used. The high growth rate has changed the Philippine demographic profile; over 40 percent of the population now is fifteen years or younger. High population growth has meant a decline in real wage rates, especially in agriculture, a decline in arable land per capita, and a rapid increase in rural-urban migration, all prescriptions for greater social tensions. Employment must grow at about 4 percent per annum to absorb new labor force entrants over the rest of the century. Population policy is an example of where U.S. aid could be effectively used to confront social issues that Filipinos themselves, for a variety of reasons, may not wish to address.

The United States could help Filipinos understand the nature of their problems and develop solutions by making available badly needed information. A general understanding of the issues is widespread, but government agencies and private-sector groups have lacked the resources to thoroughly investigate their nature. One example is land reform:

there has been no systematic survey of the amount of land and its location that could be made available for allocation to the landless. A set of surveys, highly detailed and geographically specific, would help inform the policy debate in Manila. The United States could thus provide the information Filipinos need to make decisions for themselves about their future. It is no accident that the NPA wins supporters by undertaking—albeit in a more limited and politically defined way— such "social surveys" before penetrating a village. Accurate information is a prerequisite to effective governance.

The United States, also, could further military reform through its military aid programs. In the past much of this aid has been diverted; there is some evidence, for example, that Marcos's cronies sold U.S. military equipment on the international black market. In the meantime, Filipino soldiers went unarmed, unclothed, unfed, unpaid, and untrained. And even now, there continue to be indications that the Philippine military command requisitions or attempts to requisition the wrong items—for example, the infrared goggles for night vision mentioned in an earlier chapter. But for the first time the Philippine military itself seems to understand the need for reform, and the United States and the Aquino government should capitalize on the sentiment. The immediate focus should be not on equipment but on training. U.S. military aid should initially finance the construction of basic training camps, the creation of training programs, and the provision of instructors. And the curriculum should emphasize not only military skills and discipline but education in democracy and respect for human rights. American aid has already rebuilt Camp Magsaysay, a training facility in central Luzon devastated by a typhoon in 1987, but regional training camps still need to be constructed. Moreover, the Philippine people must also be assured that the military establishment will obey civilian authority. This would be a massive effort that would take years to accomplish, but before the United States initiates any major rearmament program, the Philippine military must learn how to use safely and fairly the weapons it now has.

Not all elements within the military will be willing to accept a reoriented American aid program, however. U.S. money is thought of as "compensation" or "rent" in exchange for access to military facilities in the Philippines, and nationalists, on both the left and the right, have argued that those funds should be provided with no strings attached.

The new military compensation agreement of 1988 (covering the two years remaining in the 1947 Military Bases Agreement which expires in 1991) includes an increase to $400 million as opposed to $320 million for the Economic Support Fund and an additional $192 million for development assistance and food aid. Much of the money earmarked for the military is already destined for equipment. And when one reviews the history of the AFP, one becomes wary of the supposition that more military assistance or even a closer working relationship between the U.S. military and that of the Philippines will result in a more competent, less abusive, and less politicized force. Indeed, the history of other American efforts to produce more professional and more democratic military forces elsewhere in the third world reinforces one's pessimism. Foreign militaries tend to nod at American rhetoric and walk away with the weapons to implement coup d'etats.

All these American initiatives in the final analysis would be taken at the margin of Philippine affairs. The United States lacks the financial resources, the will, and even the right to define the Philippine future. America can only help clarify the problems—perhaps simply by not further muddying the waters—and provide the means whereby Filipinos themselves determine their destiny.

Notes

Chapter 1. The Social Context of Philippine Insurgencies

1. See Lewis M. Simons, *Worth Dying For* (New York: Morrow, 1987) for the best description of these events.

2. Amado Guerrero, *Philippine Society and Revolution: Specific Characteristics of Our People's War* (Oakland: International Association of Filipino Patriots, 1979).

3. U.S. Department of State, Airgram (confidential), American Embassy (Manila), "Communist Insurgency in the Philippines" (E.O. 12065, January 23, 1981).

4. Dennis Morrow Roth, "Church Lands in the Agrarian History of the Tagalog Region," in *Philippine Social History: Global Trade and Local Transformations*, ed. Alfred W. McCoy and Ed. C. De Jesus (Quezon City, Metro Manila: Ateneo de Manila University Press, 1982), 27. For further descriptions of the peasant revolts, see also the chapters by Ed. C. De Jesus and Bruce Cruikshank.

5. For a more complete history of this movement and others, see David R. Sturtevant, *Popular Uprisings in the Philippines, 1840–1940* (Ithaca: Cornell University Press, 1976); Reynaldo Clemena Ileto, *Pasyon and Revolution: Popular Movements in the Philippines, 1840–1910* (Quezon City, Metro Manila: Ateneo de Manila University Press, 1979); Teodoro A. Agoncillo, *A Short History of the Philippines* (New York: New America Library, 1975); and Usha Majahani, *Philippine Nationalism: External Challenge and Filipino Response, 1565–1946* (St. Lucia, Queensland: University of Queensland Press, 1971).

6. David Sweet, "A Proto-Political Peasant Movement in the Spanish Philippines: The Cofradia de San Jose and the Tayabas Rebellion of 1841," *Journal of Asian Studies* 7 (April 1970): 96–97, 115, 108, 114.

7. Daniel Doeppers, *Manila, 1900–1941: Social Change in a Late Colonial Metropolis* (Quezon City, Metro Manila: Ateneo de Manila University Press, 1984), 56.

8. Brian Fegan, "The Social History of a Central Luzon Barrio," in *Philippine Social History*, 99.

9. Sturtevant, *Popular Uprisings in the Philippines*, 96–99. See also David R. Sturtevant, "Guardia de Honor: Revitalization within the Revolution," *Journal of Asian Studies* 4 (August 1966): 342–352.

10. Ileto, *Pasyon and Revolution*, 317.

11. Sturtevant, *Popular Uprisings in the Philippines*, 121–125; Alfred W. McCoy, "A Queen Dies Slowly: The Rise and Decline of Iloilo City," in *Philippine Social History*, 324–325.

11. Sturtevant, *Popular Uprisings in the Philippines*, 123.

12. Ileto, *Pasyon and Revolution*, 317.

13. See Agoncillo, *A Short History*, 144–148.

14. As Sturtevant does, who argues that the Sakdal Movement of the 1930s represented a transitional step from Calosa's Tayug movement, which was a blind response against real or imagined sources of frustration, toward rational movements dedicated to purposeful change (the category in which he places Abad Santos's Socialist party). See *Popular Uprisings in the Philippines*, 255. See also Majahani, *Philippine Nationalism*.

15. As cited in Sturtevant, *Popular Uprisings in the Philippines*, 242.

16. Ibid., 195.

17. Marshall S. McLennan, "Changing Human Ecology on the Central Luzon Plain: Nueva Ecija, 1705–1939," in *Philippine Social History*, 73.

18. McCoy, "A Queen Dies Slowly," 325. Fegan, "Central Luzon Barrio," 75.

19. Doeppers, *Manila, 1900–1941*, 59.

20. Sturtevant, *Popular Uprisings in the Philippines*, 195.

21. Ibid., 195–204.

22. Ibid., 208, 213.

23. Ibid., 219. See also David R. Sturtevant, "Sakdalism and Philippine Radicalism," *Journal of Asian Studies* 21 (February 1962).

24. Sturtevant, *Popular Uprisings in the Philippines*, 228.

25. McCoy, "A Queen Dies Slowly," 328–329; Fegan, "Central Luzon Barrio," 108, 107, 111; Doeppers, *Manila, 1900–1941*, 126.

26. Sturtevant, *Popular Uprisings in the Philippines*, 123.

27. Cited in ibid., 174.

28. See Sturtevant, *Popular Uprisings in the Philippines*, 115–119, and Benedict J. Kerkvliet, *The Huk Rebellion: A Study of Peasant Revolt in the Philippines* (Berkeley: University of California Press, 1977), 37–38.

29. Eduardo Lachica, *The Huks: Philippine Agrarian Society in Revolt* (New York: Praeger, 1971), 22.

30. Willem Wolters, *Politics, Patronage and Class Conflict in Central Luzon* (Quezon City: New Day Publishers, 1984), 27–28, 136.

31. World Bank, *The Philippines, Agrarian Reform Issues in the Philippines: An Assessment of the Proposal for an Accelerated Land Reform Program*, (Washington, D.C.: World Bank, Report No. 6776–PH), 10.

32. Thomas Claus Nowak, "Class and Clientelist Systems in the Philippines: The Basis for Instability," (Ph.D. diss., Cornell University, 1974), 102.

33. McCoy and De Jesus, "Introduction," 8.

34. Michael Cullinane, "The Changing Nature of the Cebu Urban Elite in the 19th Century," *Philippine Social History*, 283–284.

35. Nowak, "Class and Clientelist Systems," 23a, 102.

36. See Gary Hawes, *The Philippine State and the Marcos Regime: The Politics of Export* (Ithaca, N.Y.: Cornell University Press, 1987).

37. Doeppers, *Manila, 1900–1941*, 57.

38. World Bank, *The Philippines*, 2–3.

39. Ibid., 7–8.

40. Ed. C. De Jesus, "Conclusion: An Agenda for Philippine Studies," in *Philippine Social History*, 448.

41. Milagros C. Guerrero, "The Provincial and Municipal Elites of Luzon during the Revolution, 1898–1902," in *Philippine Social History*, 155; Nowak, "Class and Clientelist Systems," 145; Fegan, "Central Luzon Barrio," 120.

42. Fegan, "Central Luzon Barrio," 119. Wolters (*Politics, Patronage and Class Conflict*, 139) would agree.

43. Pilar R. Jimenez and Josefa S. Francisco, *The Rural Poor in Leyte: A Social and Institutional Profile* (Manila: De La Salle University, March 1984), 23, 29.

44. See Sturtevant, *Popular Uprisings in the Philippines* 82, for a description of similar attitudes among the Spanish.

45. Quoted in Clayton Jones, "Voices of the Revolution: Filipino Rebels," *Christian Science Monitor*, February 13, 1987.

46. George M. Guthrie, ed., *Six Perspectives on the Philippines* (Manila: Bookmark, 1968); David Joel Steinberg, *The Philippines: A Singular and a Plural Place* (Boulder, Colo., Westview Press, 1982).

47. Charles Kaut, "Utang Na Loob: A System of Contractual Obligation among Tagalogs," *Southwestern Journal of Anthropology* 17 (1961): 269. On the acronym SIR, see Frank Lynch, S.J., *Four Readings on Philippine Values*, IPC Papers no. 2 (Manila: Ateneo de Manila University Press, 1964).

48. Kaut, "Utang Na Loob"; Guthrie, *Six Perspectives*, 79.

49. Robert Lawless, "The Foundation for Culture-and-Personality Research in the Philippines," *Journal of Asian Studies* 5 (April 1967): 118; Mark McDonald Turner, "Interpretations of Class and Status in the Philippines: A Critical Evaluation," *Cultures et développement* 10 (1978): 280; Robert J. Morais, *Social Relations in a Philippine Town* (De Kalb: Northern Illinois University, Center for Southeast Asian Studies, Special Report no. 19, 1981), 5.

50. Ileto, *Pasyon and Revolution*, 19.

51. Guerrero, *Philippine Society and Revolution*, 15, 56.

52. Ibid., iv.

53. Ileto asks: "Is the independence that the ilustrados managed to wrest from the Americans equivalent to the condition called Kalayan? Or is it just the supreme product of the manipulation of appearances?" He later states: "Ilustrados who ostensibly fought for independence through legal means were regarded as inauthentic because of their preoccupation with personal wealth and status rather than Christ-like suffering and the transformation of loos." (*Pasyon and Revolution*, 225, 318. Vice Governor Hayden noted during the Sakdal uprising that " 'caciquism' [economic exploitation by the elite] is linked with the American domination" and leading Filipino politicians such as Quezon, Osmena, and Roxas (all later to be presidents) were viewed as "traitors" (Norman G. Owen, ed., *Compadre Colonialism: Studies on the Philippines under American Rule*, [Ann Arbor: Michigan Papers on South and Southeast Asia no. 3, 1971], p. 209).

54. Richard Hooley, "Economic Growth and Prospects for Democracy in the Philippines," paper presented at the Conference on Development and Democracy in East Asia: Taiwan, South Korea, and the Philippines, American Enterprise Institute for Public Policy Research, Washington, D.C., May 18–19, 1988, 17.

55. Cited in Ileto, *Pasyon and Revolution*, 150.

56. Quoted in Lucy Komisar, *Corazon Aquino: The Story of a Revolution* (New York: George Braziller, 1982), 78.

Chapter 2. Origins of the Communist Party of the Philippines

1. U.S. Congress, House of Representatives, Hearings before the Committee on Foreign Affairs, Subcommittee on Asian and Pacific Affairs, *Recent Events in the Philippines, Fall 1985*, November 12 and 13, 1985 (Washington, D.C.: U.S. Government Printing Office, 1985), 76; Testimony by Richard C. Armitage, assistant secretary of defense for international security affairs, before the

U.S. Senate Committee on Foreign Relations, June 3, 1986.

2. Eduardo Lachica: *The Huks: Philippine Agrarian Society in Revolt* (New York: Praeger, 1971), 11.

3. David A. Rosenberg, "Communism in the Philippines," *Problems of Communism*, September-October 1984, 34.

4. Benedict J. Kerkvliet, in *The Huk Rebellion: A Study of Peasant Revolt in the Philippines* (Berkeley: University of California Press, 1977), argues that the PKP did not control the Huks and their relationship existed as a "precarious alliance" (210, 164). Lachica argues the Huks were directed "behind the wings" during the Japanese occupation and then later openly (*Huks*, 20). The conflict's outcome suggests, however, that the PKP was the dominant partner in the coalition.

5. Norman Lorimer, "Philippine Communism: An Historical Overview," *Journal of Contemporary Asia* 7, no. 4 (1977): 466.

6. Usha Mahajani, *Philippine Nationalism: External Challenge and Filipino Response, 1565–1946,* (St. Lucia: University of Queensland Press, 1971), 41; Renato Constantino, *The Philippines: A Past Revisited* (Quezon City: Tala Publishing, 1975), 156, and Mahajani, *Philippine Nationalism*, 57–62.

7. Justus M. van der Kroef, *Communism in South-East Asia* (Berkeley: University of California Press, 1980), 14, 66, and Lachica, *Huks*, 91.

8. Constantino, *Philippines*, 367–368.

9. Lachica, *Huks*, 83–85; Constantino, *Philippines*, 379.

10. David R. Sturtevant, *Popular Uprisings in the Philippines, 1840–1940* (Ithaca: Cornell University Press, 1976), 255.

11. Van der Kroef attributes the decision to unite to the intervention of an emissary of the American Communist party, Sol Auerback, who had been helpful in winning Evangelista's release from prison on conditional parole in 1913, but this is perhaps simplistic (*Communism*, 23). See also Stanley Karnow, *In Our Image* (New York: Random House, 1989), for a discussion of this period.

12. Lachica, *Huks*, 101. See also Kerkvliet, *Huk Rebellion*, 53.

13. Kerkvliet, *Huk Rebellion*, 67, 139; Rosenberg, "Communism," 30. Lava's "retreat for defense" strategy, modeled after the Chinese "Long March" followed a major Huk defeat by Japanese forces in March 1943. The Japanese then tried a "policy of attraction." Lava's fall from grace thus did not occur until over a year later, suggesting that there were other reasons for his resignation and that the strategy may not have been altogether a failure. See Lachica, *Huks*, 115–116. A similar retreat to the mountains during the CPP's early

years has been labeled the CPP's "Yenan strategy," but Sison denies such a tactic was plotted.

14. See Lachica, *Huks*, 119–120. See also Kerkvliet, *Huk Rebellion*, 141.

15. See David Joel Steinberg's excellent analysis of the collaboration issue in Philippine politics in *Philippine Collaboration in World War II* (Manila: Solidaridad Publishing, 1967), and Hernando Abaya, *Betrayal in the Philippines* (New York: A. A. Wynn, 1946).

16. Kerkvliet, *Huk Rebellion*, 128.

17. Lachica, *Huks*, 120–121; Kerkvliet, *Huk Rebellion*, 157; Lawrence M. Greenberg, *The Hukbalahap Insurrection: A Case Study of a Successful Anti-Insurgency Operation in the Philippines, 1946–1955* (Washington, D.C.: United States Army Center of Military History, 1986), 45.

18. Lachica, *Huks*, 123; Kerkvliet, *Huk Rebellion*, 179.

19. Kerkvliet, *Huk Rebellion*, 141

20. Ibid., 265.

21. Ibid., 180–181. Jose Lava is faulted for several strategic errors, among them deciding in 1949 that a revolutionary situation already existed in the Philippines and thus spurring the armed insurgency on to greater activity before the terrain had been properly prepared, and, second, calling for a "geometric progression" beginning in July 1950 by which each PKP and Huk member was to recruit three new members every three months, an action that opened the party to infiltration and misfits. Lava did call for these actions but the degree to which they were implemented and his ability to influence them are questionable.

22. Greenberg, *Hukbalahap*, 57.

23. Harold Ward Maynard, "A Comparison of Military Elite Role Perceptions in Indonesia and the Philippines" (Ph.D. diss., American University, 1976), 328; Robert Ross Smith, *The Hukbalahap Insurgency: Economic, Political, and Military Factors* (Washington, D.C.: Office of the Chief of Military History, Department of Army, 1963), 121.

24. Alvin H. Scaff, *The Philippine Answer to Communism* (Stanford: Stanford University Press, 1955), 38, 55. Kerkvliet, *Huk Rebellion*, 239; Smith, *Hukbalahap Insurgency*, 107; Donald L. Berlin, "Prelude to Martial Law: An Examination of Pre-1972 Philippine Civil-Military Relations" (Ph.D. diss., University of South Carolina, 1982), 116. Magsaysay secretly paid journalists to promote his program—an effort probably helped by having the three major Manilan dailies owned by Americans and twelve out of forty-one Philippine radio stations operated by VOA. See Greenberg, *Hukbalahap*, 110, 109, 139, 133.

25. Kerkvliet, *Huk Rebellion*, 208, 236; Lachica, *Huks*, 231.

26. Frank Golay, "Economic Collaboration: The Role of American Investment," in Golay, ed., *The United States and the Philippines* (Englewood Cliffs, N.J.: Prentice-Hall, 1966), 106.

27. The tacit historical links deserve some note: Recto once served as the lawyer for Jose Lava and authored legislation to make Rizal's *Nole: Me Tangere* and *El Filibusterismo* compulsory reading in all schools. In the 1920s Recto began a campaign to prevent the deportation of an Indonesian Communist agent, Tan Malaka—a cause célèbre of the era. Sison placed himself directly in the mainstream of the Propaganda movement, calling for a "Second Propaganda Movement . . . to arouse our nation anew to the struggle for the fulfillment of the national-democratic tasks of the Philippine Revolution." See Sison, *Struggle for National Democracy* (Quezon City: Progressive Publications, 1967), 127.

28. Renato Constantino and Letizia R. Constantino, *The Philippines: The Continuing Past* (Quezon City: Foundation For Nationalist Studies, 1978), 223–224.

29. Justus M. van der Kroef, "Philippine Communism and the Chinese," *China Quarterly*, April-June 1967, 142. Tillman Durdin, "Philippine Communism," *Problems of Communism*, May-June 1976, 41, states that Guerrero's works borrowed from the writings of D. N. Aidit, chairman of the Indonesian Communist party.

30. Sison continues to skirt the question of whether or not he was the CPP's founding chairman and author of *Philippine Society*. See "Released CPP Leaders on Detention, Aquino," Philippine News Agency report by George V. Jularbal, March 9, 1986, reprinted in the Foreign Broadcast Information Service, *Daily Report, Asia & Pacific* (hereafter *FBIS*, March 11, 1986, 6–8. A report published in the *FBIS* of March 31, 1986, 10, based on an article printed in *We Forum*, March 18–24, 1986, states, without directly quoting him, that Sison admitted to being the party's chairman.

31. Lachica, *Huks*, 177 and interviews, Manila, November 1985. Sison married Juliet de Lima, later an official in the leftist political party formed in 1986, Partido ng Bayan.

32. Francisco Nemenzo, "Rectification Process in the Philippine Communist Movement," in Lim Joo-Jock, ed., *Armed Communist Movements in Southeast Asia* (New York: St. Martin's Press, 1984).

33. Justus M. van der Kroef, "Communist Fronts in the Philippines," *Problems of Communism*, March-April 1967, 72; see also *Mr and Ms* (Manila),

October 11–17, 1985, 22–25 (the KM has been variously translated as Nationalist Youth and National Youth Movement); Lachica, *Huks*, 178.

34. Lachica, *Huks*, 184; Nemenzo, *Rectification*, charges that all the groups were fronts for the PKP.

35. Nemenzo, *Rectification*, 75, identifies Amado Guerrero, head of the PKP youth section, as author of this study—a fact Rosenberg, *Communism*, 34, repeats. There is some suggestion that Guerrero was really Arthur Garcia (A.G.), a close Sison associate and cofounder of the CPP. See Lachica, *Huks*, 183. More recent reports suggest (as is likely) that *Philippine Society and Revolution* and Guerrero's other works were collaborative ventures of the early collective but that Sison was the primary author. See the *News Herald*, June 10, 1986, 6, cited in *FBIS*, June 13, 1986, 9, which states that Tubianosa wrote a chapter in the book. All these works are highly derivative of Mao's writings.

36. Nemenzo, *Rectification*, 76

37. Rosenberg, *Communism*. Jay Taylor, *China and Southeast Asia: Peking's Relations with Revolutionary Movements* (New York: Praeger, 1976), 325.

38. Guerrero, *Philippine Society*, 161. Lachica, *Huks*, 180, states that Tapales resigned from the KM to form the MPKP but this is inaccurate. Author's interview, source close to Tapales, 1987, who also indicates was never a member of the KM.

39. Taylor, *China*, 328.

40. See, for example, Nemenzo, *Rectification*, 77; Rosenberg, *Communism*, 35, and Leif Rosenberger, "Philippine Communism and the Soviet Union," *Survey* 29 (Spring 1985): 113–145. Taylor, *China*, 253.

41. See van der Kroef, "Philippine Communism," 119. He also states that a branch of the Chinese Communist party was founded in Manila in 1930 (117). See also van der Kroef's *Communism*, 24. Lachica, *Huks*, 109, discounts these reports.

42. See Richard J. Kessler, Jr., "Development Diplomacy: The Making of Philippine Foreign Policy under Ferdinand E. Marcos" (Ph.D diss., Fletcher School of Law and Diplomacy, 1985), chap. 4.

43. van der Kroef, "Philippine Communism," 145, and Taylor, *China*, 324.

44. Nemenzo, *Rectification*, 77–78.

45. See ibid. and van der Kroef, *Philippine Communism*, 137–140. Sison in 1963 became executive director of the Philippine-Indonesia Friendship and

Cultural Association (Taylor, *China*, 321–323). Sison admits to having first studied in Indonesia in 1962 from which he brought back "a mixture of books; these were not all made in Peking and Moscow" (Sison, *Struggle*, 229).

46. U.S. General Accounting Office, *Military Assistance and Commitments in the Philippines*, Report no. B-1333359 (Washington, D.C.: Comptroller General, 1973), 8.

47. Guerrero, *Philippine Society*, 51. Lachica, *Huks*, 193, 29.

48. Ferdinand E. Marcos, "First Address to the Nation under Martial Law," September 23, 1972. Lachica, *Huks*, 17, notes that the increase in Huk violence in 1966 was due to the attacks against them by Marcos for having supported Macapagal's candidacy. Pampanga was the only province Marcos lost in the 1969 election.

49. As quoted in Rosenberg, *Communism*, 35.

50. Lachica, *Huks*, 162, and Guerrero, *Philippine Society*, 192.

51. U.S. Senate, Committee on Foreign Relations, Hearings before the Subcommittee on United States Security Agreements and Commitments Abroad, *The Republic of the Philippines*, Part I, September 30, October 1, 2, 3, 1969 (Washington, D.C.: U.S. Government Printing Office, 1969), 226–227. A declassified secret report of CINCPAC on July 1, 1970, entitled "Military Assistance Plan for the Philippines" reported that these groups were receiving no outside support but that only the "Maoists" had a plan for "violent action."

52. Lachica, *Huks*, 203, 19. A Staff Report of the U.S. Senate Committee on Foreign Relations, *The Situation in the Philippines* (Washington, D.C.: U.S. Government Printing Office, October 1984), 23, also repeats this story.

53. Central Committee, Communist Party of the Philippines, "Summing up Our Experience after Three Years," March 3, 1972 (mimeograph), 3–4, 12–13.

54. Guerrero, *Philippine Society*, ix.

55. "Summing Up," 13. Stuart R. Schram, ed., *Quotations from Chairman Mao Tse-Tung* (New York: Bantam Books, 1967), 37.

56. Alfred W. McCoy, *Priests on Trial* (New York: Penguin Books, 1984), 12–13.

57. U.S. Department of State, Airgram (Secret) from American Embassy, Manila, "NPA Assessment as of Mid-1974," November 5, 1974. U.S. Department of State, Airgram (Secret) from American Embassy, Manila, "NPA Assessment as of Mid-1975," October 1, 1975. U.S. Department of State, Airgram (Confidential) from American Embassy, Manila, "Communist Insurgency in the Philippines," January 23, 1981.

58. Airgram, "Communist."

59. See William Branigan, "Philippine Rebels Targeting Rights Groups, Churches," *Washington Post*, October 18, 1986, A-13, A-18, and Sheilah Ocampo, "Pushed into Purgatory," *Far Eastern Economic Review*, September 10, 1982, 31–32. Branigan refers to the 1978 document as "Sector, Orientation," while Ocampo calls it "Sector, Organization." Ocampo states the document's authenticity is in doubt. Ocampo was married to Satur Ocampo, a leader of the NDF.

60. See Constantino, *A Past Revisited*, 146–148; Teodoro A. Agoncillo, *A Short History of the Philippines* (New York: New American Library, 1975), 68–70.

61. Usha Mahajani, *Philippine Nationalism, External Challenge and Filipino Response, 1565–1946* (St. Lucia, Queensland: University of Queensland Press, 1971), 51.

62. Robert L. Youngblood, "The Protestant Church in the Philippines' New Society," mimeograph, Department of Political Science, Arizona State University, Tempe, n.d., 18.

63. Cited in Robert L. Youngblood, "The Cross and the Sword: Church-Military Relations in the Philippines," paper delivered at the Canadian Council for Southeast Asian Studies, Institute of Asian Research, University of British Columbia, Vancouver, November 9–11, 1979, 6.

64. See Mahajani, *Philippine Nationalism*, 283; Sheilah Ocampo, "A Pope among the Politicos," *Far Eastern Economic Review*, February 13, 1981, 16–17; James R. Rush, "The Philippine Church, Part I: A Faith That Does Justice" (Hanover, N.H.: University Field Service Institute Reports no. 31, 1984), 2–3. Robert L. Youngblood, "Church Opposition to Martial Law in the Philippines," *Asian Survey* 18, no. 5 (May 1978): 506.

65. William Henry Scott, "The Spanish Occupation of the Cordillera in the 19th Century," in Alfred W. McCoy and Ed. C. de Jesus, eds., *Philippine Social History: Global Trade and Local Transformations* (Quezon City, Metro Manila: Ateneo de Manila University Press, 1982), 49.

66. See Rush, "Philippine Church," 3–4; McCoy, *Priests*, 45, 114–115, 118, 134. The FFF's national president, Jeremias Montemayor, supported Marcos during martial law (McCoy, *Priests*, 142). David Howard Bain, *Sitting in Darkness: Americans in the Philippines* (Boston: Houghton Mifflin Co., 1984), 266.

67. Robert L. Youngblood, "Ideology and Christian Liberation in the New Society," paper presented at the Second International Philippine Studies Con-

ference, Honolulu, Hawaii, June 27–30, 1981, 9–10. Robert L. Youngblood, "Basic Christian Communities in the Philippines: A Structure for Subversion or Liberation," paper presented at the Association of Asian Studies
Annual Meeting, Philadelphia, March 22–24, 1985, 21. In 1981 bishops
broke with the Mindanao-Sulu Secretariat of Social Action because of NDF
influence (ibid., 22).

68. Youngblood, "Ideology," 11–12. McCoy, *Priests*, 45, 11, 134–37;
Rosenberg, *Communism*, 43–44; William Chapman, *Inside the Philippine
Revolution* (New York: W. W. Norton, 1987), 112.

69. James R. Rush, "The Philippine Church, Part II: Basic Christian Communities," (Hanover, N.H.: University Field Service Staff Report no. 32, 1984),
2; See also Earl Martin, "The Philippine Church amidst Revolution," *Peace
Section Newsletter* (Akron, Pa., Mennonite Central Committee). 12, no. 5
(September-October 1982).

70. Ibid., 4.

71. Youngblood, "Church Opposition," 513. The Task Force for Detainees
at times implicitly became a propaganda arm of the National Democratic Front.
Its literature, for example, is heavily weighted against the government. The
October 15-November 14, 1986, international edition of the Task Force's
human rights *Update*, for example, refers to NPA efforts to execute government
spies in its midst as "correcting errors" and characterizes Rodolfo Salas, chairman of the CPP, as a member of the "progressive movement." Even so, the
Task Force's statistics and case descriptions are highly accurate.

72. Gregg Jones, "Reconciliation Eludes Philippine Church," *Washington
Post*, October 19, 1985, 6–11. See also William Branigan, "Ferment in
Philippines Pressures the Church," *Washington Post*, November 24, 1981,
A14.

73. Tom Breen, "Church Rallies to Aquino in Peace Talks," *Washington
Times*, February 29, 1987.

74. Remarks made by Bishop Francisco Claver, S.J., at the Catholic University of America, on December 4, 1986, Washington, D.C.

75. *New Philippine Review* 1, no. 2 (August-October 1984): 51.

76. Lachica, for example, argued that Pampanguenos were marginally better off than other peasants and that their above-average literacy rates made
them more vulnerable to agitators.

77. Robert Redfield, *The Primitive World and Its Transformations* (Ithaca:
Cornell University Press, 1953), 125–126.

78. Stuart Creighton Miller, "Benevolent Assimilation," in *The American*

Conquest of the Philippines, 1899–1903 (New Haven: Yale University Press, 1982), 199.

79. Van der Kroef, *Communism*, 202. See *Daily Express* (Manila), July 21, 1980, 6, cited in *Joint Publications Research Service* (hereafter *JPRS*), August 29, 1980, 84.

80. Cited in Miller, "Benevolent Assimilation," 151.

81. Reynaldo Clemena Ileto, *Pasyon and Revolution: Popular Movements in the Philippines, 1840–1910* (Manila: Ateneo de Manila University Press, 1979).

82. John M. Gates, *Schoolbooks and Krags: The United States Army in the Philippines, 1898–1902* (Westport, Conn.: Greenwood Press, 1973), 259–260.

83. Sturtevant, *Popular Uprisings*, 141.

84. Lachica, *Huks*, 16. See also p. 257 for a discussion of Huk arms surrenders.

85. Ibid., 180.

86. Huk Study: Alvin H. Scaff, *The Philippine Answer to Communism* (Stanford: Stanford University Press, 1955), 116. NPAS study: Lachica, *Huks*, 238.

87. Gerard Chaliand, "Revolutionary Changes in the Third World: An Historical Perspective," paper presented at U.S. Defense Intelligence College Conference on "Revolutionary Changes in the Third World," Washington, D.C., June 28–29, 1988.

88. Quoted in Rush, "The Philippine Church," n. 31.

89. Ileto, *Pasyon and Revolution*, 200.

90. Kerkvliet, *Huk Rebellion*, 226.

Chapter 3. Strategy and Tactics of the People's Revolutionary Forces

1. Author's interview, Davao, October 4, 1985.

2. *Far Eastern Economic Review* (hereafter *FEER*) July 5, 1984, 13; also *FEER*, December 27, 1984-January 3, 1985, 27.

3. Author's interview, Davao, October 5, 1985.

4. Marty Villalobos (pseudonym for an NDF cadre in Mindanao), "Where the Party Faltered (An Analysis of the Snap Polls and the February Uprising)," mimeograph, n.d.

5. Amado Guerrero, *Philippine Society and Revolution: Specific Character-*

istics of Our People's War (Oakland: International Association of Filipino Patriots, 1979) 61, n. 10. A guerrilla front is "defined as an area which has its own organization, guerrilla forces and military command, and can function independently over a long period in the development of the guerrilla war" (*Liberation* [international ed.], March-April 1985, 2).

6. *FEER*, March 12, 1982, 40. The NPA itself claims to have had only eighteen "regular and over-sized platoons" and twenty-five "independent squads and small platoons" in all of Mindanao in 1982. See *Liberation*, March 1984. *International Liberation* (international publication of the National Democratic Front), May-June 1985, 5. *Business Day* (Manila), February 4, 1985, 10.

7. *Liberation* (Philippine ed.), September 1984, 8. American Embassy, Manila, "Counterinsurgency in Panay," *Airgram* (Confidential), March 2, 1977. In another confidential airgram, dated November 18, embassy officials report "widespread NPA activity." *Mr and Ms* (Manila), November 29-December 5, 1985, 18. *Foreign Broadcast and Information Service—Asia and Pacific* (hereafter *FBIS*), November 6, 1985, 30. Eduardo Lachica, *The Huks: Philippine Agrarian Society in Revolt* (New York: Praeger, 1971), 48 n. 16. *Ang Bayan*, in *FBIS*, November 5, 1985, 22.

8. *Liberation*, March 1984, 8. Guerrero, *Philippine Society*, 184, 61 n. 10. Guerrero claims NPA fronts in these regions were established by these dates: central Luzon (1969); Cagayan Valley (1970); southern Tagalog (1971); Bicol (1971); eastern and western Visayas (1973); Mindanao (1973); Quezon-Aurora (1975); Ilocos-Montanosa-Pangasinan (1976). The GOP claimed that NPAs were active in Ilocos Sur, central and northern Luzon, Bicol, Samar, western Nisayas, and Mindanao by 1972. See *FEER*, April 29, 1972, 14. See "Our Urgent Tasks," *Revolution* 1, no. 1 (July 1, 1976): 17. Twenty fronts were then said to have been opened in all regions.

9. *Business Day*, November 15, 1985, 11, reprinted in *FBIS*, November 19, 1985, 21. The NPA reportedly claimed that prior to 1976 50 percent of their support in the Cordilleras were native Igorots and by 1985, 90 percent. See also Richard Vokey, "Assaults on the Peaks of Power," *FEER*, June 13, 1980, 24–28; Rodney Tasker, "Philippine Communists Pose a Latent Threat," *FEER*, June 17, 1977, 36–37. See Sheilah Ocampo, "Breaching a Dam of Despair," *FEER*, June 13, 1980, 23. American embassy reporting for the period allows a partial reconstruction of the CPP's strategy. See especially Telegram, March 14, 1983 (Confidential), "Samar Update"; Airgram, November 5, 1974 (Secret), "NPA Assessment as of Mid-1974"; Airgram, October 1, 1975 (Secret), "NPA Assessment as of Mid-1975"; Telegram, Decem-

ber 23, 1980 (Confidential), "NPA in Samar"; Airgram, January 23, 1981 (Confidential), "Communist Insurgency in the Philippines"; Airgram, April 22, 1982 (Secret), "NPA Assessment"; Telegram, July 14, 1982 (Confidential), "NPA Activity in the Central Visayas"; Telegram, September 17, 1982 (Secret) "Views NPA Threat in Eastern Mindanao"; Airgram, October 26, 1983 (Confidential), "Peace and Order Conditions in Northern Luzon"; Telegram, June 18, 1984 (Confidential), "Government Authority Eroding in Northeastern Mindanao."

10. *FEER*, August 30, 1984, 29. The embassy used a 17-percent-of-total figure. In January 1986 GOP reported that 4–5 percent of the nation's barangays were influenced. See *FBIS*, January 17, 1986, 34.

11. *FBIS* report, January 17, 1986, 36, report of *Times-Journal* (Manila) of January 13, 1986, 1; *FBIS* report, January 13, 1986, 18; and *FBIS* report, July 18, 1985, 8, report of *Times-Journal*, July 16, 1985, 1. Larry A. Niksch, *Insurgency and Counterinsurgency in the Philippines* (Washington, D.C.: Library of Congress, Congressional Research Service, July 1, 1985), 3. U.S. Congress, Testimony before the House of Representatives, Committee on Foreign Affairs, Subcommittee on Asia and the Pacific, March 17, 1987, by Richard L. Armitage, assistant secretary of defense.

12. Guerrero, *Philippine Society*, 5. The hostility between the PKP and Sison-Guerrero can be seen in William J. Pomeroy, "Maoism in the Philippines," *Political Affairs, Journal of Marxist Thought and Analysis* 51, no. 5 (May 1972): 38–46; he charges that the "splitting and extremism of the Maoists have done great damage to the developing mass movement."

13. Guerrero, *Philippine Society*. At the same time he claims that the PKP did not have a strategic sense, only "tactical responses" (i-ii). Guerrero tends to be self-contradictory. See also Norman Lorimer, "Philippine Communism: An Historical Overview," *Journal of Contemporary Asia* 7, no. 4 (1977): n . 30, for another critique of Guerrero's inconsistencies.

14. *Philippine Society* begins with the observation that "the geographic position of the Philippines makes the Filipino people literally close to the center of the world proletarian revolution and part of a gigantic wave of powerful revolutionary movements in Southeast Asia" (1).

15. Ibid., 144–145.

16. Lachica, *Huks*, 299, citing *Rectify*.

17. Guerrero, *Philippine Society*, 185–186.

18. Lachica, *Huks*, 318, citing *Rectify*. Also Guerrero, *Philippine Society*, 195. In *Rectify* Guerrero proposed developing four types of armed units: regu-

lar mobile forces, guerrilla units, militia or self-defense groups, and armed city partisans (Lachica, *Huks*, 315). This organizational framework may have partly reflected a desire to prevent the party from being absorbed by Dante's unit.

19. David A. Rosenberg, "Communism in the Philippines," *Problems of Communism*, September-October 1984, 37–38.

20. Guerrero, *Philippine Society*, iii, 129, 131.

21. Guerrero defines Philippine society as consisting of six classes: landlords, bourgeoisie, (comprador, middle, and petit), the peasantry (rich, middle, poor), the proletariat (industrial workers), semiproletariat (unemployed), and lumpen proletariat (society's dregs) (132–153). Guerrero claimed that the leaders of the revolution were the proletariat, but the main force was the peasantry (157–158). In 1984 Sison indicated that he had decided that the "comprador big bourgeoisie has replaced the landlord class as the No. 1 exploiting class in 20th century Philippines." See Julieta de Lima-Sison, "Jose Maria Sison on the Mode of Production," *New Philippine Review* 1, no. 1 (May-July 1984): 30. Others have also argued that class analysis would be appropriate. See Jonathan Fast and Luzviminda Francisco, "Philippine Historiography and the De-mystification of Imperialism: A Review Essay," *Journal of Contemporary Asia* 4, no. 3 (1974): 349–352.

22. Benedict J. Kerkvliet, *The Huk Rebellion: A Study of Peasant Revolt in the Philippines* (Berkeley: University of California Press, 1977), 226, 177.

23. Ibid., 228, 235.

24. Alvin H. Scaff, *The Philippine Answer to Communism* (Stanford: Stanford University Press, 1955), 33–34.

25. Kerkvliet, *Huks*, 174.

26. Ibid., 177, 215–216.

27. Guerrero, *Philippine Society*, 187–188. The CPP would thus expand "wave upon wave" as each new base was consolidated.

28. *Liberation*, September 1982, 21. U.S. Embassy, Manila, Airgram (Secret), November 5, 1974, "NPA Assessment as of Mid-1974"; "Our Urgent Tasks," 10.

29. See Francisco Nemenzo, "Rectification Process in the Philippine Communist Movement," in Lim Joo-Jock, ed., *Armed Communist Movements in Southeast Asia* (New York: St. Martin's Press, 1984), 105, and Justus M. van der Kroef, *Communism in South-East Asia* (Berkeley: University of California Press, 1980), 185.

30. "Our Urgent Tasks," *Revolution* 1, no. 1 (July 1, 1976): 11.

31. Van der Kroef, *Communism*, 185–186.

32. *Liberation*, March 1984, 7. Niksch, *Insurgency*, 30. According to author's interviews in the Philippines in September-October 1985, a female DPA in the Mindanao Central Committee (KOMMID) was discovered. According to conflicting reports she either escaped or was tortured, tried, and executed. Her unmasking resulted in a complete reassessment of loyalties throughout the Mindanao party, causing a number of other individuals to be murdered. Partial reports of this later leaked out. See *Malaya*, October 7, 1985, 1, 11; *Daily Express*, December 9, 1985, 8; See *We Forum*, May 27-June 2, 1986, 10, 15, in which an NPA notes: "Education work was neglected to the extent that during the cleansing, we learned that those we had recruited in 1980–1981 had not undergone the basic Party courses. We did not have time to pay attention to their personal and political bio-data because, it seemed everything was in order; secondly, there were so many memos coming in especially during 1983–85. Too many mass organizations here and there." *New York Times*, June 26, 1986, A15; *Washington Post*, June 2, 1986, A17.

33. See U.S. Embassy, Manila, Airgram (Confidential), January 23, 1981, "Communist Insurgency in the Philippines."

34. There were five fronts in central Luzon, two in southern Luzon, seven in northern Luzon, eight in the Visayas, and eight in Mindanao. *FEER*, March 10, 1983, 21.

35. *Liberation* (Philippine ed.), September 1982, 22. See "Military Alarmed at NPA Activity," *Philippine News*, February 16–22, 1983, 8. *Liberation*, January-February 1985, 6.

36. Central Committee, CPP, "Summing up Our Experience after Three Years," March 3, 1972, mimeograph, 4.

37. See Phil Bronstein, "Revolution Is More Than Talk for Guerrillas, *San Francisco Examiner*, October 14, 1984.

38. U.S. Embassy, Manila, Telegram (Confidential), March 31, 1981, "CPP/NPA Activities." At the time of this report, the CC was said to have ten regular members and four alternative members.

39. *Ang Bayan*, October 6, 1975, "An Assessment of the Fascist Martial Rule after Three Years," 21.

40. "Our Urgent Tasks," 12. "Summing Up," 8, 15.

41. *Guide for Cadres and Members of the Communist Party of the Philippines*, 3d ed. (Central Luzon: Revolutionary School of Mao Tse-tung Thought, 1977), 7.

42. See *FBIS*, April 25, 1985, reporting a *Times-Journal* article of April 23, 1985, 1, 6, and see also *FEER*, November 21, 1985, 55, 57. See Paul

Quinn-Judge, "Insurgency," and Monica Feria, "CPP-NPA Reorganization," *Malaya*, June 1, 1986, 1; Monica Feria, "'Fragile Coalition Worries Communists," *Malaya*, June 2, 1986, 1; "Sum Up, Learn from Boycott Error," *Ang Katipunan*, July 1986, 7. In January 1988 the CPP began operating its own radio station, Radio Sierra Madre, and began expanding the number of its regional papers.

43. "Our Urgent Tasks," 8. "Summing Up," 5.

44. *Ang Bayan*, April 1984, 10.

45. *Liberation*, April-May 1986.

46. *Liberation*, March 1984, 24. See Philippines Research Center, *New People's Army of the Philippines* (Boston: United Labor Press, 1981), 17–20. U.S. Embassy, Manila, Airgram (Confidential), January 23, 1981, "Communist Insurgency in the Philippines."

47. *Liberation*, June-July 1987, 3. "Summing Up," 10. Interviews by author with Philippine military officers in Manila and Davao, September-October 1985; *Veritas*, March 25–31, 1984, 10; Niksch, *Insurgency*, 16–19; Republic of the Philippines, *The Communist Insurgency in the Philippines* (Manila: Ministry of National Defense, May 11, 1985), 20–21. See also Carolyn O. Arguillas, "A Look Inside NPA Country," *Philippine News*, October 2–8, 1985, 7, and Sheilah Ocampo, "The Communists' Growth Strategy," *FEER*, August 21, 1981, 23.

48. Scaff, *Philippine Answer*, 134.

49. Nemenzo, "Rectification," 82, 91–92, 80–81. "Our Urgent Tasks," 7.

50. The Huks had not tried to rebuild the social structure as they were less interested in changing the government than in the people governing. See Harvey Averch and John Koehler, *The Huk Rebellion in the Philippines: Quantitative Approaches*, RM-6254-ARPA (Santa Monica: Rand Corporation, August 1970), vi, and Lachica, *Huks*, 26.

51. Nemenzo, "Rectification," 96. *Mindanao Star*, November 7, 1985, 1, 6.

52. Author's interviews in the Philippines, September-October 1985. A peasant or a laborer may become a party member in six months, whereas it would take someone else as long as two years. There is a report that the CPP's inner core is growing more slowly than the party. See *FEER*, November 21, 1985, 55–56.

53. Guerrero, *Philippine Society*, 186.

54. See Ross H. Munro, "The New Khmer Rouge," *Commentary* 80, no. 6 (December 1985): 19–31; *FEER*, July 5, 1984, 14; *Christian Science Monitor*, November 26, 1985, 12; *FBIS*, January 27, 1986, 8; *FEER*, March 10,

1983, 22; *FBIS*, January 17, 1986, 36, citing *Times-Journal*, January 13, 1986, 1. "3 U.S. Officers Slain at Philippine Base," *New York Times*, April 14, 1974, 7. The NPA claimed to have killed twenty-two American military officers by March 3, 1972, although no independent confirmation of this figure exists (Guerrero, *Philippine Society*, 60 n. 7). A survey of Central Foreign Policy Records at the Department of State initiated by the author resulted in the discovery of only four documents pertaining to the 1974 case of which three were fully declassified and one partly. These cables do not support Munro's contention that Salas led the ambush. Technically, these documents indicate, the men were ambushed on a temporary road just outside the military reservation. "It appears quite likely that the ambush group happened to be in the vicinity as the jeep traversed the road. This group may have sighted (or at least heard) the jeep enroute to the construction site and decided to conduct the ambush upon its return under the false expectation that they could recover some weapons and ammunition, in addition to robbing the victims." The ambush squad is alleged to have been "led by Teofilo Valenzuela, a 28-year-old from Samal, Bataan." None of the reports identifies the group as NPA. See U.S. Embassy, Manila: "Ambush Killing of Three USN Officers," April 22, 1974 (Confidential), no. 4643; "Ambush Killings of Three USN Officers," April 22, 1974 (Confidential), no. 4642; "Killing of Three Naval Officers," April 16, 1974 (Confidential), no. 4328; "Ambush Killings of Three USN Officers," April 22, 1974 (Confidential), no. 4644.

55. See U.S. Embassy, Manila, Airgram (Confidential), January 23, 1981, "Communism Insurgency in the Philippines," which reports that the CPP sought support from Cuba and Nicaragua, but there was no evidence that it had received any.

56. Guerrero, *Philippine Society*, 191.

57. Ibid., 163. Nemenzo, "Rectification," 80–81.

58. Cited in Lachica, *Huks*, 167–168, from the 1969 *Basic Rules of the New People's Army*.

59. Ibid., 186, 315.

60. Guerrero, *Philippine Society*, 40. Nemenzo, "Rectification," 82.

61. Ibid., 193. *Liberation*, March 1984, 3, claims the first NPA unit in 1969 had thirty-five men.

62. *Liberation*, March 1984, 8. Interviews by author with Philippine military officers in Davao and Manila, September-October 1985. See also Frederick Z. Brown and Carl Ford, *The Situation in the Philippines*, staff report for the U.S. Senate Committee on Foreign Relations (Washington, D.C.: U.S.

Government Printing Office, October 1984), 32–33.

63. Kerkvliet, *Huk Rebellion*, 211–212. Lachica, *Huks*, 14, and Justus M. van der Kroef, "Philippine Communism and the Chinese," *China Quarterly*, April-June 1967, 143.

64. Guerrero, *Philippine Society*, 194.

65. *Business Times*, May 8, 1982, 11, cited in the *FBIS-JPRS*, October 23, 1984, 59–60. Quote on courting from *Time Magazine*, February 3, 1986, 37. Author's interviews in the Philippines, September-October 1985. Last quote from Steve Lohr, "For Filipino Rebels, a 'New Deal' via the Gun," *New York Times*, August 11, 1985, 18.

66. *Veritas*, April 29-May 5, 1984, 10. For additional information on "the proletarian relationship of the sexes," see Clayton Jones, "Dating Dos and Don'ts," *Christian Science Monitor*, February 12, 1987, 1. See also *Liberation*, February-March 1986.

67. *Ang Bayan*, April 1984; *Liberation*, March-April 1985.

68. *Liberation*, September 1982, March 1984.

69. Phil Bronstein, "Rebel Forces Grow in Philippine Forests," *San Francisco Examiner*, June 23, 1985.

70. U.S. Embassy official, Manila, in discussions with author, September-October 1985.

71. *Guide for Cadres*, 27.

72. Demonyos were also nicknamed "zombies." See Romy Marinas, "Secret World of Deep Penetrating Agents," *We Forum*, May 27-June 2, 1986, 10, 15. See also *Daily Express*, December 9, 1985, 1.

73. *Guide for Cadres*, 9.

74. *Business Times*. See also Phil Bronstein, "Rebel Army Grows in AFP Forest," *Philippine News*, July 3–9, 1985. A M-16 is reported to cost 6,000 to 12,000 pesos. See Bronstein, "Revolution Is More Than Talk for Guerrillas," *San Francisco Examiner*, October 14, 1984.

75. U.S. Embassy, Manila, Airgram (Secret), October 1, 1975; Airgram (Confidential), January 23, 1981.

76. See U.S. Embassy, Manila, Telegram (Confidential), April 25, 1983.

77. See *Business Times*, April 14, 1984, 11; *Malaya*, May 10, 1984, 1, and *Visayan Herald*, April 22, 1984, 8, for reports of sabotage, and *Bulletin Today*, April 1, 1984, 7, for reports on extortion rackets.

78. See U.S. Embassy, Manila, Telegram (Confidential), May 21, 1984.

79. *Manila Bulletin*, October 13, 1987, 18. Cited in FBIS-EAS-87-199, October 14, 1987, 35.

80. The Huks received their weapons by theft from U.S. government installations or through illegal purchases from the Philippine military. See U.S. Central Intelligence Agency, *National Intelligence Estimate*, 56–68, June 20, 1968. In 1983 the NDF admitted that the NPA's biggest problem was inadequate arm supplies. See *FEER*, March 10, 1983, 21.

81. Interview by author with U.S. Embassy officials and Philippine Ministry of National Defense officials in the Philippines, October-November 1985.

82. Jose de Vera, "NPA Trading Marijuana for Guns," *Bulletin Today*, April 10, 1984, 5, and P. Pelayo and Y. Malicse, "Navy Seizes Suspected NPA Fund-Raising Goods," *Daily Express*, March 11, 1984, 1. Other reports suggest that the NPA suppresses marijuana, even killing large growers who continue. See *People's Daily Forum*, August 21, 1984, 1.

83. *Liberation*, March 1984.

84. Guerrero, *Philippine Society*, 191. In 1985 the NPA was reported to have formed a New National Navy (Bagong Navy ng Bayan), although this seems an extravagant claim. *FBIS*, November 19, 1985, 16, citing *Bulletin Today*, November 13, 1985, 15.

85. Interviews, intelligence personnel, Philippine Ministry of National Defense, Manila, October 1985.

86. Interviews by author with Filipino doctors in the Philippines, October 1985, who claim to have personally helped wounded NPA cadres. In Mindanao a source added that the NPA treated him with respect and even paid for his services, whereas the AFP did neither. The Balweg story was confirmed by U.S. Embassy officials and Philippine intelligence officers.

87. Brown and Ford, *Situation*, 20.

88. The NPA is reported to have claimed that the Alex Boncayao Brigade killed Karingal. See *We Forum*, December 31-January 6, 1986, 7, 12. The naming of specific units is unusual. The Ferrer assassination was not so claimed, but the style of the killing strongly suggests it was the NPA. See also *Liberation*, June-July 1987, 3–5.

89. Interviews by author, Philippines, September-October 1985.

90. William Chapman, *Inside the Philippine Revolution: The New People's Army and Its Struggle for Power* (New York: W. W. Norton, 1987), 117.

91. The Lawyers Committee for Human Rights, *"Salvaging" Democracy: Human Rights in the Philippines* (New York: Lawyers Committee for Human Rights, 1985), 198–205. Nun's quote: Interview with author, September-October 1985. Mark Fineman, "Rebels Take Higher Toll," *Los Angeles Times*, May 8, 1986, 1. *Liberation*, March 1984, noted that the NPA's strategy is not

to kill the AFP soldiers but to gain their support. The NPA has challenged this account, stating that cadres moved bodies to the roadside to avoid oncoming traffic; leaking gasoline from an overturned vehicle then caught on fire, burning the dead.

92. Governor's sister: *Agence France Presse* wire story, June 16, 1985. Military man: *Bulletin Today*, October 14, 1984, 11, reported in *JPRS-FBIS*, October 24, 1984, 119.

93. Guerrero, *Philippine Society*, 161–162, 140, 138. Guerrero also saw the intelligentsia as being extremely oppressed with a limited fixed income and dependent upon menial jobs—perhaps a description of his own academic plight (139).

94. See Sturtevant, *Popular Uprisings*, 48.

95. See Kerkvliet, *Huk Rebellion*, 99–100, for a description of the Huks. Justus van der Kroef, *Communism in South-East Asia* (Berkeley: University of California Press, 1980), 64, argues that no Communist movement in Southeast Asia has been able to acquire power without mobilizing the middle class and developing an organization.

96. Van der Kroef, *Communism*, 136. Tillman Durdin, "Philippine Communism," *Problems of Communism*, September-October 1984, 40 n. 2, argues that this directive indicated a shift from a class analysis of revolutionary potential to one involving all groups. It is unlikely that CPP ideologues viewed it in such terms.

97. Nemenzo, "Rectification," 88–89.

98. Cited in Rosenberg, "Communism," 42.

99. P. N. Abinales, *Militarization: Philippines* (Manila: Nationalist Resource Center, Ecumenical Movement for Justice and Peace, April 1982), 13; also van der Kroef, *Communism*, 187–188. Quote: "A Revolutionary Blueprint for Unity," *Liberation*, January-February 1985, 7.

100. U.S. Embassy, Manila, Airgram (Secret), April 22, 1982, "NPA Assessment"; Airgram (Confidential), January 2, 1981, "Communist Insurgency in the Philippines"; Telegram (Confidential), March 31, 1981, "CPP/NPA Activities."

101. U.S. Embassy, Manila, Telegram (Confidential), May 12, 1982, "Recent NPA Activities"; Airgram (Secret), April 22, 1982, "NPA Assessment." Author's interviews, Manila, November 1986.

102. *FEER*, November 6, 1986.

103. *International Liberation*, March-April 1985, 3.

104. "Revolutionary Blueprint." See also *Program of the National Demo-*

cratic Front of the Philippines, Revised Draft (reprint of the NDF unit in North America, February 1985).

105. *International Liberation*, March-April 1985, 2.

106. Author's interviews, Manila, September-October 1985, with Bayan and moderate leaders. See also William Branigan, "Filipino Communists Shift 'People's War' to Cities," *Washington Post*, June 25, 1985, A8, 9.

107. In 1985 a bus that was operating in defiance of the strike was shot at; four were killed, including a mother and her child (*FEER*, November 21, 1985, 61).

108. Guerrero, *Philippine Society*, 114. *Liberation*, September 1982, 13. See also Ian Buruma, "The Church Militant Takes on a New Meaning," *FEER*, February 28, 1985, 77–79.

109. *Veritas*, April 29-May 5, 1984, 9–14. By 1984, Balweg was an NPA commander with a reward of 200,000 pesos on his head. See *Daily Express*, March 26, 1984, 3.

110. *New Zealand Herald*, December 7, 1983, 6. Sixteen other priests are estimated in this report to be NPA members.

111. *Liberation*, September 1982, 13. See also Robert L. Youngblood, "Church and State in the Philippines: Some Implications for U.S. Policy," paper presented at conference sponsored by the Washington Institute for Values in Public Policy, Washington, D.C., May 1, 1986.

112. *Liberation*, January-February 1985, 9. A Senate Intelligence Committee report estimates that 3–5 percent of the clergy are active NPA supporters. See U.S. Congress, Senate Select Committee on Intelligence, *The Philippines: A Situation Report* (Washington, D.C.: U.S. Government Printing Office, November 1, 1985), 13. Munro estimates that the CNL consists of 1,200 priests and nuns, an unsubstantiated claim. See Munro, "New Khmer Rouge," 26.

113. Lela Garner Noble, "Ethnicity and Philippine-Malaysian Relations," *Asian Survey* 25, no. 5 (May 1975): 460. *FEER*, March 10, 1983, 20. See also *FEER*, May 8, 1981, 40, and Rodney Tasker, "NPA Steps up Attacks, Seeks Links with Moros," *Philippine Times*, July 1–15, 1977, 6–7.

114. Van der Kroef, *Communism*, 94. Noble, "Ethnicity."

115. See Marites Danguilan-Vitug, "Philippine Communists Come Out," *Christian Science Monitor*, May 8, 1985, 12. This interpretation of the conference's hidden agenda is the author's.

116. See "CPP Politburo Member on Cordillera Situation," *Business Day*, May 17, 1986, 16, cited in *FBIS*, May 14, 1986, P-8. Balweg is a member

of the Tingguian tribe and was useful in helping the NPA establish a *bodong*, a peace pact between tribes, which allows the free movement of groups across tribal territories. The NPA has tried to introduce the bodong concept into Mindanao.

117. *Liberation*, January-February 1985, 8. The KM claimed that its membership had doubled between 1980 and 1981 and began forming agit-prop teams (APTs) of five to ten students to conduct impromptu teachings (*Liberation*, September 1982). In 1985, the young (twenty-four) secretary-general of the KM, Joven Peleador, announced the establishment of armed student defense units (SDUs) and a program of sending members to summer revolutionary integration programs. See *Mr and Ms*, October 11–17, 1985, 22–25.

118. *Liberation*, September 1982, 9. The CPP began publishing a youth magazine entitled the *Collegian Folio*. Belinda Olivares-Cunanan, "Moderates Take over UP Student Council," *Mr and Ms*, September 13–19, 1985, 10–14. The rise of student radicalism may have been less related to the CPP and more to increases in tuition. See *New York Times*, July 31, 1977, 8; *Philippine Times* (Chicago), September 1–15, 1977, 3.

119. Kerkvliet, *Huk Rebellion*, 181. The PKP's Committee of Labor Organizations (CLO) led by Felixberto Olalia is reported to have organized one-fifth of the Manila workers after the war. See Lachica, *Huks*, 119.

120. *Liberation*, September 1982, 18. The NDF claims that the turning point for labor militancy was the strike staged by the Association of Filipino Workers (BMP) on May 1, 1975—the first under martial law. See also *FEER*, May 14, 1976, 13–14.

121. Chapman, *Inside Philippine Revolution*, 129. "Our Urgent Tasks," 24.

122. For a description of the Philippine trade union movement, see Jaime T. Infante, *The Political, Economic, and Labor Climate in the Philippines* (Philadelphia: Industrial Research Unit, Wharton School, University of Pennsylvania, 1980); *FEER*, April 3, 1986, 52–53; *Ang Katipunan*, June 1985, 7; *Veritas*, October 6, 1985, 14–15; *FEER*, January 15, 1982, 46; *Mr and Ms*, October 11–17, 1985, 28–30; *Business Day*, October 9, 1985, 5.

123. See *Manila Paper*, January 24–30, 1984, 1, 3, citing discussions in *Ang Bayan*. Interestingly, the change in party line did not filter quickly to cadres in the field. One Panay NPA said in 1985, "A most glaring lesson from the 1972–1975 period was the shunning of empiricism." See *Mr and Ms*, "They're All around Us," November 19-December 5, 1985, 18.

124. *Business Day*, November 20, 1985, cited in *FBIS*, November 25,

1985, P-25.

125. *Ang Bayan*, December 1984. Villalobos, "Where the Party Faltered."

126. See Kerkvliet, *Huk Rebellion*, 101–102, 230, 181–183.

127. See reports in *People's Daily Forum* about problems in South Cotabato and also the *Metro Manila Times* for the same province cited in *FBIS*, November 29, 1985, 20. See "PC Soldier, Trader Slain," *Times-Journal*, May 22, 1985, 7; Nick Williams, "Philippine Insurgents Now Targeting Cities," *Los Angeles Times*, September 5, 1985, 1; Steve Lohr, "Filipino Insurgency: Out of Rice Paddies and into the Cities," *New York Times*, July 3, 1985, 1. Author's interviews, Manila, October 1985.

128. *Liberation*, special releases, January 31, 1986, February 26, 1986.

129. Villalobos, "Where the Party Faltered."

130. Political Bureau of the cc to Members of cc, "Resolution on the Party's Tactics Regarding the Snap Election," (confidential mimeograph), May 7, 1986, 1–3.

131. Ibid., 4–6.

132. See "Military Identifies 'Key' Communist Figures," *News Herald*, June 10, 1986, 1; cited in *FBIS*, June 13, 1986, 9; "Communist Party 'Officer-in-Charge' Named," *Malaya*, June 7, 1986, 1, cited in *FBIS*, June 16, 1986, 11; "Ocampo Says Cease-Fire Talks Not under Way Yet," *Business Day*, June 24, 1986, 5; "NDF Spokesman Interviewed on Cease-Fire Talks," *Philippine Daily Inquirer*, June 18–19, 1986, 13–14, both cited in *FBIS*, June 25, 1986, 4–13.

133. Interview with the author in Manila on October 30, 1986. For insights in the struggle by the NDF to pursue its strategy after the cease-fire, see E. San Juan, Jr., "New Dangers, New Opportunities," *Midweek*, March 4, 1987, 16–19, 44, in which he argues that "the movement has rectified a militarist or ruralist deviation" and that "left adventurism has been checked."

134. Lorimer, *Philippine Communism*, 477.

135. National Urban Commission, "When a Zigzag Turn Is Shorter Than a Straight Route" (Second Draft, March 24, 1986), 4.

136. Carl H. Lande and Allan J. Cigler, *Recent Philippine Elections: A Quantitative Analysis*, Interim Report, (Lawrence: University of Kansas, April 1988), 21.

137. BBC-TV Network, December 14, 1987, cited in FBIS-EAS-87-241, December 16, 1987, 45.

138. See Keith B. Richburg, "Manila Rebels Renew Threat against U.S.," *Washington Post*, November 10, 1987, A25; *FEER*, November 12, 1987,

52–53; "Rebels Say They Killed Americans," *Washington Post*, November 24, 1987, A17. Mark Fineman, "Philippine Rebels Target U.S. 'Meddlers' for Death," *Los Angeles Times*, November 20, 1987, 1.

139. Lawyers Committee for Human Rights, *Vigilantes in the Philippines: A Threat to Democratic Rule* (New York: Lawyers Committee for Human Rights, 1988), ix. Amnesty International, *Philippines: Unlawful Killings by Military and Paramilitary Forces* (New York: Amnesty International, March 1988), 1.

140. While some analysts have described the PKP as Soviet-oriented and the CPP as Maoist, both parties were less doctrinaire, and their external orientations changed over time. Nemenzo argues that the PKP was always more inclined toward the Chinese and critical of the Soviets, traditionally contacting the Chinese only through intermediaries. The PKP became critical of China, according to Nemenzo, only when the Chinese approvingly published Sison's May Day address and rejected PKP outreach efforts toward it. The PKP did not attack Mao Tse-tung thought until 1970 after the last vestiges of the Lava brothers were expunged and Felicismo Macapagal became party secretary. The PKP was also less critical of martial law and in 1974 members were publicly reconciled to Marcos. This reconciliation may have been engineered by the Soviets as part of their effort to open official diplomatic ties with the Philippines. See "The Philippines," in Richard F. Staar, ed., *Yearbook on International Communist Affairs 1984* (Stanford: Hoover Institution Press, 1964), 266. Nemenzo, "Rectification"; see also Kessler, *Philippine Foreign Policy*, 303–304.

141. Lachica, in *Huks*, 293, cites the CPP document. Guerrero, *Philippine Society*, 88.

142. *Ang Bayan*, "A Diplomatic Victory of the People's Republic of China: A Victory of the Philippine Revolutionary Struggle," October 20, 1974, 13.

143. "Our Urgent Tasks," 31.

144. Harold W. Maynard, "A Comparison of Military Elite Role Perceptions in Indonesia and the Philippines" (Ph.D. diss., American University, 1976), 467.

145. The MV *Karagatan I* and the *Dona Andrea*. See *News Herald*, June 10, 1986, 1, 6; *FBIS*, June 13, 1986, 9; *Malaya*, June 7, 1986, 1, 6, cited in *FBIS*, June 16, 1986, P-12. In 1982 the Philippine Air Force strafed a Japanese methanol tanker near Davao, believing it to be carrying military supplies. See *FEER*, January 22, 1982, 8. See also David Howard Bain, *Sitting in Darkness* (Boston: Houghton Mifflin, 1984), 399–400. Tillman Durdin, "Marcos Takes Multifaceted Foreign Path," *Pacific Community* 7 (July

1976): 576.

146. Guerrero, *Philippine Society*, 215. The establishment of diplomatic relations between the PRC and the Marcos government was a major embarrassment to the CPP which feared being sold out by Peking. Although the party initially criticized the action, Sison later sent "warm fraternal greetings" to Mao on the fifty-fourth anniversary of the Chinese Communist party's founding. While not helping the CPP, the break-off of Peking aid helped propel the CPP into adopting its "self-reliant" policy. See U.S. Embassy, Manila, Airgram (Confidential), July 3, 1975, "Philippine Communists' Dubious Reaction to Manila-Peking Ties," and Airgram (Limited Official Use), August 6, 1975, "Philippine Communists Send Fraternal Greetings to Chinese Communist Party."

147. Munro, "New Khmer Rouge," 36. Munro states that Morales admits receiving PLO aid. See *Time*, August 30, 1982, 16. For leather dealer's claim, see *Daily Express*, May 27, 1982, 1, 6, cited in *JPRS*, June 21, 1982, 121–122.

148. Author's interviews in Washington and in Manila. Also see official U.S. government testimony at congressional hearings that consistently deny the NPA received outside arms shipments until 1988 when Armitage testified that the Soviets were providing financial support. One CPP activist claims, however, that the NPA received less than 2 percent of its arms from abroad (he may be referring to existing stocks). See *Asian Defense Journal*, June 1985, 100.

149. U.S. Embassy, Manila, Telegram (Confidential), April 19, 1982, "NPA Assessment."

150. AFP dispatch dated November 20, 1985, cited in *FBIS*, November 21, 1985, P-15.

151. Chapman, *Inside Philippine Revolution*, 21. *FBIS*, January 7, 1987. Ocampo also denied the NDF was buying arms during the cease-fire. (*FBIS*, January 9, 1987).

152. Sison in the *New Philippine Review* 1, no. 2 (August-October 1984):52, 53.

153. Interview, U.S. Intelligence personnel, Washington, D.C. See also the exchange between Leif Rosenberger and David Rosenberg in "Correspondence: Moscow and Philippine Communism," *Problems of Communism*, July-August 1985, 84–87. *FBIS*, December 19, 1984, P-5.

154. On Soviet ships, see Kessler, *Foreign Policy*, 313–314, and "Sub, Copter Landings Reported," *Philippine News*, April 21–27, 1982, 1, 8. On

increased staff, see Niksch, *Insurgency*, 39 n. 42.

155. *Christian Science Monitor*, November 26, 1985, 1. The CPP reportedly had plans to increase the NPA by 40 percent over the next three years. In congressional testimony before the House Foreign Affairs Subcommittee on Asia and the Pacific, March 17, 1987, Assistant Secretary of Defense Richard L. Armitage reported that "there are unconfirmed reports that the communists are now receiving weapons from foreign sources, possibly from North Korea or Vietnam."

156. Chapman, *Inside Philippine Revolution*, 22.

157. Munro, "New Khmer Rouge," 37. Rome and Canada, according to the author's sources, were other fund-raising centers. "Foreign supporters [South Americans, German and Japanese leftists, and IRA members] do visit and give moral backing." There is also evidence of "large amounts of Scandinavian money" perhaps for arms manufacturing. See Phil Bronstein, "Rebel." Clayton Jones, "Filipino Communists," *Christian Science Monitor*, January 21, 1987, 1, reports than in Samar the CPP had established in 1986 "social economic teams" with ties to Western European private development groups, such as the Dutch. In 1987 a reporter in Negros found the NPA had Soviet rifles. See Joel Palacios, "Philippine Guerrillas," *Washington Times*, February 13, 1987. In 1988, M-16s with serial numbers identifying them as rifles provided by the United States to South Vietnam surfaced, but these appear to have come from an arms purchase made by Marcos in 1976 and later captured or purchased by the NPA from the AFP (Interview, American official, May 1988). For other information on external support, see Eric Guyot and James Clad, "Regaining the Initiative," *FEER*, September 22, 1988, 40–41, and James Clad, "The Left's International Lobby," *FEER*, December 17, 1987, 40.

158. Author's interviews with Bayan leaders, Manila, September-October 1985.

159. Nancy F. Rocamora, "R. P. Foreign Policy: Seeking New Options," *Anq Katipunan*, June 1986, 9. See also "Filipino Communist Leaders Infighting," *Philippine News*, May 6–12, 1981, 1.

160. Guerrero, *Philippine Society*, 205. The Huks on the other hand believed that the U.S. would not commit funds that would be "wasted by an administration which no longer enjoys popular support."

Chapter 4. The Role of the Military in Philippine Society

1. Bryan Johnson, *The Four Days of Courage: The Untold Story of the People Who Brought Marcos Down* (New York: Free Press, 1987), 158–168, recounts this story.

2. Jim Zwick, *Militarism and Repression in the Philippines*, Centre for Developing Area Studies, Working Paper Series No. 31 (Montreal: McGill University, August 1980), 13.

3. U.S. Congress, Senate Select Committee on Intelligence, *The Philippines: A Situation Report* (Washington, D.C.: U.S. Government Printing Office, November 1, 1985), 10.

4. Carolina G. Hernandez, "The Extent of Civilian Control of the Military in the Philippines: 1946–76" (Ph.D. diss., State University of New York at Buffalo, 1979), 259, 87, 146. A Congressional Commission on Appointments, composed of twenty-four members of the Senate and House, approved commissions and tour extensions for reserve officers beyond an initial two years. See also Carl H. Lande, "The Philippine Military in Government and Politics," in Morris Janowitz and Jacques van Doorn, eds., *On Military Intervention* (Rotterdam: Rotterdam University Press, 1971), 397–399.

5. Lande, "Philippine Military." Hernandez, "Extent," 62.

6. See Donald L. Berlin, "Prelude to Martial Law: An Examination of Pre-1972 Philippine Civil-Military Relations" (Ph.D. diss., University of South Carolina, 1982), 221–222, who makes the most persuasive case for this thesis.

7. Ibid., 135. Berlin attributes this view to too much attention being paid to the 1957–1965 period which was "historically atypical."

8. Hernandez, however, argues that Congress kept "political" officers from being promoted to general ("Extent," 146). Bernardino Ronquillo, "Clipping Marcos' Wings," *FEER*, March 27, 1971, 11. Ramos had recommended that the president be given the authority to confirm officers to general rank.

9. Benedict J. Kerkvliet, *The Huk Rebellion: A Study of Peasant Revolt in the Philippines* (Berkeley: University of California Press, 1977), 54.

10. See Vic Hurley, *Jungle Patrol: The Story of the Philippine Constabulary* (New York: E. P. Dutton, 1938), 22.

11. David R. Sturtevant, *Popular Uprisings in the Philippines, 1840–1940* (Ithaca: Cornell University Press, 1976), 26 n. 11, 115–117. Berlin, "Prelude," 5. Hurley, *Jungle Patrol*, 22.

12. Hurley, *Jungle Patrol*, 63.

13. Sturtevant, *Popular Uprisings*, 120–121.

14. Hurley, *Jungle Patrol*, 47.

15. Reynaldo Clemena Ileto, *Pasyon and Revolution: Popular Movements in the Philippines,* 1840–1910 (Quezon City, Metro Manila: Ateneo de Manila University Press, 1979), 236, citing notes by James LeRoy on "The Philippine Police," October 14, 1905.

16. For a discussion of this point, see Norman G. Owen, ed., *Compadre Colonialism: Studies on the Philippines under American Rule* (Ann Arbor: University of Michigan Press, 1971), 23. The centralizing trend continued. In June 1941 Quezon ordered the PC to take over the central Luzon's municipal police forces in order to attack "radical elements" (Kerkvliet, *Huk Rebellion*, 56).

17. Theodore Friend, *Between Two Empires: The Ordeal of the Philippines,* 1929–1946 (New Haven: Yale University Press, 1960), 167.

18. See Hurley, *Jungle Patrol*, 59, 96–97; Stuart Creighton Miller, *"Benevolent Assimilation": The American Conquest of the Philippines,* 1899–1903 (New Haven: Yale University Press, 1982), 82; and Edberto M. Villegas, "Modernizer or Anti-Developmental? A Study of the Armed Forces of the Philippines" (Quezon City: University of the Philippines, mimeograph, n.d.).

19. Berlin, "Prelude," 50, 56–58. See also Kerkvliet, *Huk Rebellion*, 104–105.

20. Hernando J. Abaya, *Betrayal in the Philippines* (New York: A. A. Wyn, 1946), 152.

21. See Alvin H. Scaff, *The Philippine Answer to Communism* (Stanford: Stanford University Press, 1955), 85.

22. Kerkvliet, *Huk Rebellion*, 196. Eduardo Lachica, *The Huks: Philippine Agrarian Society in Revolt* (New York: Praeger, 1971), 222.

23. Berlin, "Prelude," 157. The Philippine Military Academy's origins were in the Constabulary Academy, which was established in Manila in 1904 and moved to Baguio in 1908.

24. Ibid., 56–58, 44–48. Sherwood Goldberg, "The Bases of Civilian Control of the Military in the Philippines," in Claude E. Welch, Jr., ed., *Civilian Control of the Military: Theory and Cases from Developing Countries* (Albany: State University of New York Press, 1976), believes that the military opposed amnesty for collaborators in 1948, but this is based on a single interview with a retired officer (108).

25. Berlin, "Prelude," 44–48, 82, 105, 115. Kerkvliet, *Huk Rebel-*

lion, 205.

26. Berlin, "Prelude," 106, 108. By the third month of Magsaysay's administration eighty-five officers had been appointed to nonmilitary positions. No serving officers had been given civilian positions in the Commonwealth.

27. Ibid., 96, 142, 144, 158, 164, 166. Goldberg, "Bases," 105, argues that the military began presenting itself as a viable alternative to civilian rule in 1950 because some of its legitimacy had been restored. Berlin, "Prelude," 140–141, also argues that the military had less influence under Garcia and Macapagal because there were fewer Visayans and Pampanguenos promotable to senior levels. Lachica, *Huks*, 17, suggests that the AFP relaxed its pressure on the Huks between 1961 and 1965 because Macapagal was a Pampangueno.

28. Sturtevant, *Popular Uprisings*, 250; Kerkvliet, 250; *Huk Rebellion*, 161, 189–190, 196.

29. Melinda W. Cooke, "National Security," in *The Philippines*, Area Handbook (Washington, D.C.: Department of Army, 1984), 160; *FEER*, March 10, 1983, 18. Benjamin N. Muego, "The 'New Society' of the Philippines: A Case Study of a Developmental Movement Regime" (Ph.D. diss., Southern Illinois University, 1976), 133. General Ver was an ROTC graduate. Two PMA graduates defected to the NPA: PC Lt. Victor N. Corpus (PMA, '67) on December 29, 1970, and PC Lt. Rex B. Baquiran (PMA, '70) in February 1972. Corpus later rejoined the AFP as a lieutenant colonel after being released from prison. Baquiran also rejoined but was subsequently captured and brutally tortured and murdered allegedly by his former NPA comrades.

30. Ronald Guy Bauer, "Military Professional Socialization in a Developing Country" (Ph.D. diss., University of Michigan, 1973), 27–28 n. 3, 28 n. 2. In 1969 Marcos, at the request of the Military Academy, vetoed a bill that would have integrated a new officer group. Officers were retired either at the age of fifty-six or after thirty years of service.

31. Ibid., 70, 73, 76. See also Hernandez, "Extent," 179.

32. Cited in *Asiaweek*, November 9, 1984, 38.

33. See *New York Times*, January 23, 1986, 1; *New York Times*, January 29, 1986, A19; *Washington Post*, January 24, 1986, 1.

34. Berlin, "Prelude," 79.

35. U.S. Embassy, Manila, Airgram (Secret), April 22, 1982, "NPA Assessment."

36. See *Christian Science Monitor*, December 2, 1985, 6–8; *Christian Science Monitor*, June 14, 1983, 12; *Asiaweek*, December 13, 1985, 17; Carl Lande, "The Future of Philippine Politics and American Policy," manu-

script, n.d. [about 1980], 14.

37. Ileto, *Pasyon*, 235.

38. *Metro Manila Times*, December 2, 1985, cited in *FBIS*, December 9, 1985, 13.

39. See Lawyers Committee for International Human Rights, *The Philippines: A Country in Crisis* (New York, December 1983), 27, *FBIS*, November 5, 1985, 22; Jose M. Crisol, *The Armed Forces and Martial Law* (Makati: Agro Printing, 1980), 45–48; Jose M. Crisol, *Men and Arms* (Makati: Agro Printing, 1981), 72.

40. Crisol, *Forces*, 46. See also *Bulletin Today*, November 24, 1982, 5, cited in *JPRS*, December 15, 1982, 64. In 1982 the AFP began a program to organize the security forces of seven public and private firms considered vital to national security such as the power, telephone, and railway companies.

41. See Frederick Z. Brown and Carl Ford, *The Situation in the Philippines*, a staff report prepared for U.S. Congress, Senate Committee on Foreign Relations (copy of original report, dated September 30, 1984), 25. The examples of CHDF brutality have been extensively documented by human rights groups. The marines based in Davao first began pacifying the region by disarming the CHDF (author's interviews, Davao, October 1985). See also Eduardo Lachica and Lee Lescazo, "The Philippine Army: Tarnished Heroes, *Wall Street Journal*, May 14, 1986, 34.

42. See "Marcos Is Said to Admit to Spy Activity in U.S.," *Washington Post*, July 16, 1986, A19; *Philippine Report* 1, no. 3 (December 1984): 4–5; Cooke, "National Security," 276; Hernandez, "Extent," 233; Larry A. Niksch, *Insurgency and Counterinsurgency in the Philippines* (Washington, D.C.: Congressional Research Service, July 1, 1985), 69. Executive Order 829, dated September 11, 1982, ordered the creation of regional intelligence coordinating agencies. See *Bulletin Today*, October 9, 1982, 32, cited in *JPRS*, November 5, 1982, 75. On March 3, 1986, President Aquino abolished NICA and the PSC. See Lachica, *Huks*, 248. Ramos was a former chief of military intelligence. In 1966 and 1968–1969, he was military aide to Marcos and served as AFP vice chief of staff after August 1981. In 1985 he claimed to have been requesting retirement since 1982 (*FBIS*, November 22, 1985, 3).

43. Hernandez, "Extent," 203.

44. See Villegas, "Modernizer," 15; Lawyers Committee, *Crisis*, 141; Zwick, *Militarism*, 29; *Asian Defense Journal*, September 1982, 20. Related PDs include numbers 421, 482, 531, 585, and 641.

45. Lawyers Committee, *Crisis*, 141.

46. Harold Ward Maynard, "A Comparison of Military Elite Role Perceptions in Indonesia and the Philippines" (Ph.D. diss., American University, 1976), 400.

47. Ibid., 399.

48. For a fine discussion of these points, see W. Scott Thompson, *Unequal Partners* (Lexington, Mass.: Lexington Books, 1975).

49. Raymond Bonner, *Waltzing with a Dictator* (New York: Time Books, 1987), 52. Maynard, "A Comparison," 402. Bonner, *Waltzing*, 75.

50. Maynard, "A Comparison," 400.

51. Author's interview, former Philippine executive secretary Alejandro Melchor, Manila, 1979.

52. Berlin, "Prelude," 185, 201. Maynard, "A Comparison," 384.

53. Hernandez, "Extent," 217; Maynard, "A Comparison," 375. Three years after martial law had been declared these twelve were still in high positions, although some were past retirement age.

54. See *Malaya*, February 23, 1986, 1, 7, cited in *JPRS*, June 20, 1986, 41, where Enrile admits the attack was faked.

55. Maynard, "A Comparison," 348, 373; Hernandez, "Extent," 246.

56. Quoted in Reuben R. Canoy, *The Counterfeit Revolution* (Manila: Philippine Editions, 1981), 23.

57. Brown and Ford, *Situation*, 14.

58. See *Veritas*, November 10, 1985; *FEER*, April 30, 1982; *FBIS*, November 21, 1985, P-2; *FEER*, March 10, 1985, 16; *FBIS*, August 31, 1982, P-7; "Further Details on Marine Seizure of Illegal PC Logs," *Bulletin Today*, January 9, 1984, 28; "AFP Suspect in Sulu-Based Marijuana Syndicate," *Bulletin Today*, March 9, 1984, 8; *FBIS*, November 1, 1983, P-4. Metrocom Commander General Tomas Dumpit, also deputy chief of the PSC, was the car-theft ringleader; *FBIS*, May 3, 1984, P-5. Ver controlled the dollar blackmarket in Manila; *FEER*, March 12, 1982, 39; *FBIS*, December 14, 1984, P-6.

59. "Ver Admits Only 5 Percent Military Recall from Civilian Posts," *Bulletin Today*, February 28, 1984, 40. See also *Bulletin Today*, November 29, 1984, 10, cited in *JPRS*, January 4, 1985, 81. Under Executive Order 40, September 2, 1966, Marcos could detail military personnel to civilian offices provided that those assigned did not exceed 5 percent of the officer corps and 2 percent of the enlisted men. Ver noted that the order recalling military personnel assigned to civilian posts did not affect those appointed by Marcos (*FBIS*, January 16, 1984, P-6). Officers received both military pay and civil-

ian pay when assigned to civilian posts (*JPRS*, January 4, 1985, 81, citing *Bulletin Today*, November 29, 1984, 10). Cooke, "National Security," 253, argues that the military in the early 1980s played a "very limited role in the national economy."

60. See Crisol, *Armed Forces*, 74; Hernandez, "Extent," 223, 232; Brown and Ford, *Situation*, 26; Bruce Dover, "PC/INP Other 'Tactics' Reported in Bacolod Union Election," *West Australian* (Perth), March 6, 1984, 10; *Christian Science Monitor*, June 14, 1983, 12; Berlin, "Prelude," 2; Villegas, "Modernizer," 20; *JPRS*, December 21, 1983, 166–167.

61. Sheilah Ocamp, "Angels of Death, *FEER*, March 19, 1982, 21–22; Lawyers Committee, *Crisis*, 29; *Christian Science Monitor*, September 7, 1983, 1; *Philippine News* (San Francisco), April 10–16, 1985, 5; Mike Carrol, "NPA a Thorn to Paper Mill Giant," *Business Times*, April 14, 1984, 11. See also U.S. Embassy, Manila, Airgram (Secret), April 22, 1982, "NPA Assessment," and Telegram (Confidential), September 15, 1982, "*N.Y. Times* Article on Sag-Od Massacre."

62. *Bulletin Today*, December 2, 1984, 12, cited in *JPRS*, January 4, 1985, 80, and *Australian*, November 24–25, 1984, 13, cited in *JPRS*, January 16, 1985, 38. The PLO may have had its roots in a fifteen-thousand-man army under the western Mindanao regional command (RUC 9) under a former MNLF leader Al Hussein Kaluang (see *Daily Express*, June 7, 1980, 6, cited in *JPRS*, July 23, 1980, 70). See U.S. Embassy, Manila, Telegram (Confidential), March 20, 1981, "Rightist Vigilante Groups Target NPA."

63. Cited in *JPRS*, November 5, 1984, 47.

64. *Philippine News*, April 24–30, 1985, 6.

65. See *Asiaweek*, November 9, 1984, 31; *FBIS*, October 30, 1984, P-22; *FBIS*, November 15, 1984, P-1; *FBIS*, November 2, 1984, P-5; *FBIS*, July 11, 1984, P-2; and Edward F. Kobee, et al., *Small Craft and Counterinsurgency Blockade* (White Oak, Md.: Naval Ordinance Laboratory, February 3, 1972), B-7. See *Washington Post*, "Warning of Coup Causes 'Red Alert' in the Philippines," January 18, 1987, A25. The Guardians, although their titular head was a Maj. Efren Arayata, were mainly enlisted men.

66. Muego, "New Society," 197.

67. Maynard, "A Comparison," 485–487. See also Muego, "New Society," 138. *Philippine Times*, March 31-April 6, 1979, 16, citing a March 23, 1979, *FEER* article; *Bulletin Today*, March 15, 1979, 17, and *FBIS*, September 23, 1982, P-2.

68. Interview, published in *Manila Bulletin*, October 5, 1987, 1, 36. Re-

printed in *FBIS*, October 6, 1987, 36.

69. *FEER*, April 11–17, 1980, 46. See Canoy, *Counterfeit Revolution*, 230, and *FBIS*, November 5, 1985, P-20-21.

70. Marites Danguiland-Vitug, "AFP Officers Interviewed on Agrava Reports," *Business Day*, October 25, 1984, 22, cited in *FBIS*, October 29, 1984, P-13-14.

71. There are numerous reports on RAM. See especially *FBIS*, February 21, 1985, P-1; *FBIS*, December 4, 1985, P-19; *FBIS*, January 15, 1985, P-4; *FBIS*, November 16, 1984, P-2; *FBIS*, October 11, 1984, P-1; *Veritas*, November 10, 1985, 5; *FBIS*, August 19, 1985, P-7, citing *Business Day*, August 16, 1985, 10. A Metro Strike Force was announced in early 1985. See *Veritas*, February 3, 1985, 15. See *Malaya*, February 23, 1986, 8, transcript of an interview with Enrile.

72. Bauer, "Military Professional Socialization," passim. Bauer also found that cadets from higher-income groups were more accepting of authoritarian practices, whereas lower-income cadets became less authoritarian as a result of their academy experience. Cadets, however, were more "militaristic" than civilians. He also found a high attrition rate, which suggests that the process may have even shown a bias toward less authoritarian personalities. The cadets exhibited a strong continuity in attitudes, for the academy was not an "attitude-changing setting," he says.

73. See *Mr and Ms*, March 21–27, 1986, 19–21. See also Lewis M. Simons, *Worth Dying For* (New York: William Morrow, 1987), 257–278, for an excellent account of the various plots.

74. Walden Bello, "The Pentagon and the Philippine Crisis," *Southeast Asia Chronicle*, no. 95 (November 1984): 22.

75. Hernandez, "Extent," 161–162.

76. Quoted in "R.E.F.O.R.M. AFP—Greater Tasks Ahead," *We Belong* 1, no. 2 (May 30, 1985) (mimeograph).

77. This discussion is based on my observations when I was in Manila during the coup attempt and present outside Camp Aguinaldo during the assault.

78. Quoted in Maynard, "A Comparison," 448.

79. *We Belong*.

80. Felipe B. Miranda and Ruben F. Ciron, "Development and the Military in the Philippines: Military Perceptions in a Time of Continuing Crisis" Manila, Social Weather Stations Occasional Paper, August 1987. See also Carolina G. Hernandez, "The Multi-Faceted Role of the Military Lessons from the Philippines," paper presented at the 1988 Annual Meeting of the International

Studies Association, St. Louis, Mo., March 30-April 2, 1988.

81. Several factors may have contributed to this: Goldberg, "Bases, 112–113, argues that close ties to the civilian community and early retirement age kept the military from being isolated; Muego, "New Society," 136, states that officers were recruited from lower social classes; Lande, *Philippine Military*, 391, agrees that early retirement reinforced a disposition toward middle- and upper-class consensus.

Chapter 5. Insurgency and Counterinsurgency

1. Story recounted in Anne Nelson, "In the Grotto of the Pink Sisters," *Mother Jones*, January 1988, 49. See also other accounts and documentation in Amnesty International, *Philippines: Unlawful Killings by Military and Paramilitary Forces* (New York: Amnesty International, March 1988), and Lawyers Committee for Human Rights, *Vigilantes in the Philippines: A Threat to Democratic Rule* (New York: Lawyers Committee for Human Rights, 1988).

2. U.S. Embassy, Manila, Airgram (Secret), April 22, 1982, "NPA Assessment."

3. U.S. Congress, House of Representatives, Committee on Foreign Affairs, Subcommittee on Asian and Pacific Affairs, testimony by Richard L. Armitage, assistant secretary of defense, March 17, 1987.

4. Radio interview, Quezon City, December 27, 1987, cited in FBIS-EAS-87-249, December 29, 1987, 45.

5. Testimony by David Lambertson, deputy assistant secretary for East Asia and the Pacific, U.S. Department of State, at a hearing of the House Asian and Pacific Affairs Subcommittee, December 2, 1987.

6. Author's interviews with senior administration officials throughout the 1986–1987 period.

7. Economic Survey Mission to the Philippines, *Report to the President of the United States* (Washington, D.C., October 1950), 1.

8. U.S. Congress, House Committee on Foreign Affairs, *Hearings on Mutual Security Act of 1958*, Part IV, 85th Cong., 2d Sess. (Washington, D.C.: U.S. Government Printing Office, 1959).

9. U.S. Embassy, Manila, Airgram (Confidential), January 23, 1981), "Communist Insurgency in the Philippines."

10. See Eduardo Lachica, *The Huks: Philippine Agrarian Society in Revolt* (New York: Praeger, 1971), 49 n. 17, for discussion of a 1960's report on

peasant anomie in Negros.

11. See National Economic and Development Authority, *Philippine Statistical Yearbook* 1984 (Manila: Republic of the Philippines, August 1984), 110, and World Bank, *The Philippines: Recent Trends in Poverty, Employment and Wages* (Washington, D.C.: World Bank, June 20, 1985), 10.

12. Gary Hawes, "The Political Economy of Transnational Corporate Investment in Philippine Agriculture" (Ph.D. diss., University of Hawaii, May 1984), 4.

13. Frederick Z. Brown and Carl Ford, *The Situation in the Philippines*, a staff report prepared for the U.S. Congress, Senate Committee on Foreign Relations (copy of report released prior to publication, September 30, 1984), 15.

14. *Liberation*, March 1984.

15. *Bulletin Today*, December 21, 1982, 1, 2, cited in *JPRS*, January 19, 1983, 63; see also *JPRS*, January 12, 1983, 72; *FBIS*, July 8, 1976, P-2; *FBIS*, August 23, 1984, P-4; *FBIS*, November 26, 1984, P-4; *FBIS*, May 4, 1982, P-2; *Asian Defense Journal*, May 1985, 94. See also *Bulletin Today*, April 7, 1984, 5. Lachica, *Huks*, 33.

16. Khalid Abdullah, "The Philippine Armed Forces for the 1980s," *Asian Defense Journal*, June 1982, 28–29. See *Asian Defense Journal*, September 1985, 10; *Philippine Army Journal*, April 1984; *Sunday Express Weekend*, April 22, 1984, 23–25.

17. *Asian Defense Journal*, September 1984, 10; *Pelayo*, April 22, 1984, 23–25. *Asian Defense Journal*, September 1984, 10; *Bulletin Today*, March 10, 1984, 28; *Asian Defense Journal*, March 1984, 10. For some background on the army's civic action operations, see Lachica, *Huks*, 249–250. *FBIS*, March 3, 1982, P-1; *FBIS*, July 30, 1984, P-1; interviews by author with military officials, Manila, October 1985.

18. *FBIS*, October 22, 1982, P-1; *FBIS*, January 26, 1983, P-2; *FBIS*, August 2; 1984, P-4; *FBIS*, November 13, 1984, P-3; *FBIS*, March 16, 1982, P-1.

19. *FBIS*, March 18, 1983, P-1.

20. *FBIS*, September 20, 1982, P-3.

21. *FBIS*, October 26, 1982, P-1; *Times-Journal*, December 11, 1978, 1; *FBIS*, December 26, 1984, P-3; Carolina G. Hernandez, "The Extent of Civilian Control of the Military in the Philippines: 1946-76 (Ph.D. diss., State University of New York at Buffalo, 1979), 164, 221; *Bulletin Today*, December 11, 1978, 1; *FBIS*, March 22, 1982, P-3; *FBIS*, August 8, 1984, P-10;

FBIS, November 19, 1982, P-2; *Times-Journal*, December 11, 1978, 1; *FBIS*, August 9, 1984, P-5; *FBIS*, November 23, 1984, P-2; *FBIS*, December 1, 1982, P-1; *FBIS*, February 15, 1985, P-3; *FBIS*, December 17, 1984, P-6.

22. *FEER*, November 21, 1985, 58.

23. *Washington Post*, January 19, 1985, 17.

24. See Harold W. Maynard "A Comparison of Military Elite Role Perceptions in Indonesia and the Philippines," (Ph.D. diss., American University, 1976), 392; Lachica, *Huks*, 188–189, 231.

25. Lachica, *Huks*, 196.

26. *FBIS*, April 28, 1983, P-2; *FBIS*, March 23, 1983, P-2; *FBIS*, February 20, 1985, P-3; *Bulletin Today*, October 3, 1985, 10; *FBIS*, December 17, 1984, P-2; *FEER*, November 21, 1985, 58–59; U.S. Congress, Senate Select Committee on Intelligence, *The Philippines: A Situation Report* (Washington, D.C.: U.S. Government Printing Office, November 1, 1985), 7; *FBIS*, December 10, 1984, P-4; *FBIS*, November 20, 1985, P-4; *FBIS*, July 16, 1985, P-5; *FBIS*, August 10, 1984, P-5.

27. P. N. Abinales, *Militarization: Philippines* (Manila: Nationalist Resource Center, Ecumenical Movement for Justice and Peace, April 1982), 11, and Lela G. Noble, "Ethnicity and Philippine-Malaysian Relations," *Asian Survey* 25, no. 5 (May 1975): 463. On the napalm controversy, see *FBIS*, August 21, 1984, P-10; *FBIS*, September 17, 1984, P-4; *FBIS* October 1, 1984, P-1; *JPRS*, February 7, 1985, 92. Jim Zwick, "Militarism and Repression in the Philippines," Centre for Developing Area Studies, Working Paper Series No. 31 (Montreal: McGill University, August 1980), 141; Abinales, *Militarization*, 10.

28. *FEER*, July 5, 1984, 12.

29. *FEER*, March 12, 1982, 37–40; *The Philippines: A Country in Crisis* (New York: Lawyers Committee for Human Rights, December 1983), 72, 86; *JPRS*, March 5, 1982, 78; citing Agence France Presse report of February 7, 1982; *Business Day*, November 23, 1984, 5, 12, 21.

30. See, for example, "Fake NPA Surrenders Reported," *Bulletin Today*, March 5, 1984, 36. In Executive Order 1048, issued in 1985, Marcos created a presidential committee to implement a rehabilitation program for NPA members and their supporters (see *Metro Manila Times*, October 17, 1985). See also Larry A. Niksch, *Insurgency and Counter-insurgency in the Philippines* (Washington, D.C.: Library of Congress, Congressional Research Service, July 1, 1978), 63.

31. *FBIS*, December 27, 1984, P-4. See also Lawyers Committee,

Philippines: A Country, 20–21, 24.

32. Lawyers Committee, *Philippines: A Country*, 95, and Brown and Ford, *Situation*, 26.

33. *Washington Post*, January 19, 1985, A17; *Washington Post*, March 9, 1985, A14; Brown and Ford, *Situation*.

34. See *Manila Bulletin*, December 27, 1987, 22, cited in FBIS-EAS-87-249, December 29, 1987.

35. Cited in Maynard, "A Comparison," 360. Niksch, *Insurgency*, 5. Brown and Ford, *Situation*, 15.

36. Author's interview, Davao, October 1985.

37. *FEER*, March 10, 1983, 18.

38. Hernandez, "Extent," 62.

39. Brown and Ford, *Situation*.

40. See Lachica, *Huks*, 165, for discussion of Dante's support among the Aquino and Coguangco clans in Tarlac.

41. Jeffrey Race, *War Comes to Long An* (Berkeley: University of California Press, 1972), 141; page numbers hereafter cited in the text.

42. U.S. Embassy, "Communist Insurgency."

43. U.S. Embassy, "NPA."

44. Amado Guerrero, *Philippine Society and Revolution* (Oakland: International Association of Filipino Patriots, 1979), 144–145. For a discussion on the return to armed struggle, see James Clad, "Betting on Violence," *FEER*, December 17, 1987, 35–40.

Epilogue

1. As cited in Joseph L. Schott, *The Ordeal of Samar* (New York: Bobbs-Merrill, 1964), 62.

2. Henry Kissinger, "Too Much Euphoria?" *Washington Post*, March 14, 1986, A19.

Chronology

1521

March 16: Ferdinand Magellan lands in Cebu and claims the islands for Charles I of Spain, naming them after Crown Prince Philip. One month later Magellan is killed by a local chief.

1565

Islam spreads to the Manila area from the Malay Peninsula.
The First Spanish governor, Miguel Lopez de Legazpi, arrives in Cebu to establish the first permanent settlement.

1611

The University of Santo Tomás is founded in Manila.

1744

Francisco Dagohoy rebels in Bohol, expelling the Spanish. The Bohol region remains almost autonomous until 1829.

1762

October: British forces capture Manila during the Seven Years' War.
December: A Filipino rebel, Diego Silang, expels the Spanish from Ilocos and declares an independent government. Silang is murdered a year later.

1764

Manila is returned to the Spanish by the British under the Treaty of Paris.

1841

Cofradía de San José revolt, led by Apolinario de la Cruz. He is executed in November.

1872

January 20; Two hundred dockworkers and soldiers revolt against the Spanish in Cavite, but the Rebellion is suppressed two days later.
February 18: Three Filipino priests are garroted, allegedly for supporting the rebellion.

1878

The Sultan of Sulu surrenders to the Spanish, ending centuries of Moro rebellion.

1886

Jose Rizal publishes *Noli Me Tangere* (*Touch Me Not*), a sociohistorical novel about Philippine society.

1891

Jose Rizal publishes *El Filibusterismo* (*The Subversive*), a sequel to *Noli Me Tangere*.

1896

August 29: The Katipunan revolt breaks out, mainly in Cavite.
December 30: Jose Rizal is executed by firing squad for his alleged participation in the revolt.

1897

March: Emilio Aguinaldo is elected president of the revolutionary government.
May 10: Andres Bonifacio, a Katipunan leader, is arrested and executed by troops loyal to Aguinaldo.
December: Aguinaldo agrees to go to Hong Kong in exile in return for 800,000 pesos from the Spanish.

1898

April 25: The United States declares war on Spain.
May 1: American forces defeat the Spanish navy at Manila Bay and occupy Manila.
May 19: Aguinaldo returns to Manila aboard an American ship.
June 12: Aguinaldo declares Philippine independence.
September 15: A revolutionary congress convenes at Malolos.
December 10: Spain cedes the Philippines to the United States in the Treaty of Paris.

1899

January 21: Filipinos under Emilio Aguinaldo proclaim the Malolos constitution.
February 4: Fighting between American and Filipino troops begins.

1899–1903

Philippine-American War. Over 4,000 American and 16,000 Filipino troops are killed. Civilian casualties are estimated at about 200,000.

1900

December: Federalista party advocating independence is established. In 1905 it becomes the National Progressive party.

1901
July: Philippine Constabulary is organized, and military rule is terminated.

1902
July: U.S. Congress passes the Philippine Organic Act, providing for a legislature with two houses, a Bill of Rights, and a disestablished Catholic church.

1907
Elections held for the lower house of the first Philippine legislature.
The Nacionalista party is established.

1909
August: U.S. Congress passes the Payne-Aldrich Tariff Act, providing for the free entry of all Philippine goods, except rice, sugar, and tobacco, into the United States.

1913
Underwood Tariff Act removes all restrictions on Philippine exports to the United States.

1916
The U.S. Congress passes the Jones Act, which sets independence for the Philippines as an American goal and provides for a popularly elected upper house for the Philippine legislature.

1925
Florencio Entrencherado, a shopkeeper from Panay, declares himself Florencio I, "Emperor of the Philippines."

1927
Followers of Entrencherado launch an abortive uprising.

1932
Democratic party dissolves, leaving the Nacionalista as the only major political party.

1933
Benigno Ramos forms the Sakdal party.
January: Hare-Hawes-Cutting independence bill is approved over a presidential veto by U.S. Congress, but it is rejected by Philippine legislature.

1934
The U.S. Congress passes the Tyding-McDuffie Act, which provides for the

establishment of the Commonwealth of the Philippines and promises
independence at the end of a ten-year period.

1935

May: Sakdal uprising occurs but is quickly suppressed.
July: A Philippine constitutional convention drafts a constitution for the
Commonwealth; it is ratified by plebiscite.
September: First Commonwealth election is held.

1938

The Socialist party joins in a united front with Philippine Communist Party
(PKP).

1941

December 8: Japanese forces attack the Philippines.

1942

Filipino and American forces withdraw to Bataan Peninsula and Corregidor
Island in Manila Bay. Bataan surrenders in April and Corregidor falls in May.
March: The Army of Resistance against Japan (Hukbo ng Bayan Laban sa
Hapon) the Hukbalahap, is formed in Tarlac Province.

1944

October 20: American forces under Gen. Douglas MacArthur land on Leyte.

1945

January: American forces land on Luzon.
September 22: Japanese forces surrender. Manila is left one of the most
devastated cities of World War II. Over a million Filipinos are estimated to
have been killed.
Liberal party is organized.

1946

July 4: The United States grants independence to the Philippines and Manuel
Roxas becomes first president. U.S. Congress passes the Philippine Trade
Act (Bell Act), stipulating free trade until 1954 after which tariffs increase
annually until they reach full value in 1974. Peso is tied to U.S. dollar. U.S.
citizens are given full parity with Filipinos in ownership of property.
Philippine Rehabilitation Act of 1946, providing $620 million in war
damages, is made conditional on acceptance of parity provision.

1947
The United States and the Philippines sign a military bases agreement granting the United States twenty-three military installations for a period of ninety-nine years.

1948
Roxas declares the peasant guerrilla army, the People's Liberation Army (Hukbong Magpapalaya ng Bayan, the Huks), illegal and subversive.
April: Roxas dies of heart attack and is replaced by Elpidio Quirino.

1950
Ramon Magsaysay becomes secretary of defense.

1951
The United States and the Philippines sign a mutual defense treaty.

1953
November: Magsaysay, as a Nacionalista, wins the presidential election, defeating Quirino.

1954
May: Luis Taruc, the Huk leader, surrenders.
The United States and the Philippines sign the Southeast Asian Collective Defense Treaty (SEATO).

1955
Revised United States–Philippine trade agreement (the Laurel-Langley agreement) is negotiated, abolishing U.S. control of the peso, extending the sugar quota, making parity rights reciprocal, and extending the period for quota reduction and tariff application on Philippine goods.

1957
March: Magsaysay dies in a plane crash.
Carlos P. Garcia is elected president.

1961
Diosdado Macapagal is elected president.

1965
Ferdinand Marcos is elected president under the Nacionalista banner.

1966
The Philippines and the United States sign an amendment to the military

bases agreement, moving up the expiration date of the American lease to
1991.
The Philippines send a two-thousand-man civic action unit (PHILCAG) to
South Vietnam.

1967
Association of Southeast Nations (ASEAN) is formed.

1968
December: Communist Party of the Philippines (CPP) is formed.

1969
January: New People's Army (NPA) is established.
Marcos wins reelection, the first president to do so.
Nur Misuari forms the Moro National Liberation Front (MNLF).

1970
Delegates to a new constitutional convention are elected.

1971
June: Constitutional delegates begin meeting.
August 21: A grenade attack at a Liberal party rally in Manila kills nine and
wounds eight senatorial candidates. Marcos suspends the writ of habeas
corpus.

1972
September 21: Marcos declares martial law and suspends the 1935
constitution.
December: Marcos orders the creation of citizens' assemblies (barangays).

1973
January: A plebiscite staged on martial law allegedly demonstrates a 90
percent approval rating.

1977
December: A national plebiscite supposedly ratifies a new legislature, a
National Assembly.

1978
April 7: First elections under martial law are held to elect members of an
interim National Assembly.
Opposition wins only thirteen seats and claims fraud.

1980

January: Snap local elections are called by Marcos. His New Society party wins 95 percent of all seats.

May: Benigno Aquino released from prison to seek medical attention in the United States.

1981

January 17: Marcos formally ends martial law.

February: Pope John Paul II visits the Philippines.

April: Another plebiscite amends the 1973 constitution to permit a president to preside over a parliamentary system.

June 16: A presidential election is held—the first since 1969—with Marcos for all intents and purposes the only major candidate. He claims 88 percent of the vote.

Vice President George Bush visits Manila to attend Marcos's inauguration and declares, "We stand with you, sir. . . . We love your adherence to democratic principles and to the democratic processes."

1982

May: Elections are held for barangay officials.

1983

August 21: Sen. Benigno Aquino is murdered at Manila International Airport upon his return from exile.

1984

May 14: Elections held for the National Assembly are seen as defeat for Marcos's New Society party. Of 183 seats, the opposition wins 61.

1986

February 7: A presidential election is held between Corazon Aquino and Ferdinand Marcos. Both declare themselves victors.

February 22: Military elements with support from Defense Secretary Juan Ponce Enrile and Vice Chief of Staff Fidel Ramos launch a revolt against Marcos.

February 25: Marcos leaves for exile in Hawaii and Corazon Aquino is inaugurated president.

March 6: Jose Maria Sison and Bernabe Buscayno, CPP members, are released from prison as part of Aquino's amnesty program.

March 26: Aquino abolishes the National Assembly, claims all legislative powers for herself, and imposes a temporary "Freedom Constitution."

May 26: Aquino appoints forty-eight people to a Constitutional Commission.
July 6: While Aquino visits Mindanao, Marcos's vice-presidential
running mate, Arturo Tolentino, takes over the Manila Hotel with about 350
soldiers and declares himself acting president. Two days later, the rebels leave the
hotel peacefully.
August 5: Negotiations officially begin between the NDF and the Aquino
government.
September 15–23: Aquino visits the United States.
September 30: Rodolfo Salas, CPP leader, is arrested and the NDF suspends
talks.
November 13: Rolando Olalia, leader of the KMU trade union, is murdered.
November 23: The cabinet is dissolved after an alleged failed coup attempt.
Aquino replaces Defense Minister Enrile with retired general Rafael Ileto.

1987
January 22: The KMP leads ten to fifteen thousand people demanding land
reform on a march to Malacañang Palace. At Mendiola Bridge, gunfire
erupts with at least twenty killed.
January 27: Military troops attack military and civilian targets in an
attempted coup, occupying a television and radio station.
January 30: The NDF withdraws from peace talks.
February 2: About 85 percent of eligible voters turn out for a national
referendum on a proposed constitution which receives a 75 percent approval
vote.
February 7: The cease-fire between Communists and government troops
ends.
April 18: Military forces put down a small mutiny by Marcos loyalist soldiers
inside the army headquarters compound.
May 11: Congressional elections are held nationwide. Aquino-endorsed
candidates win twenty-two of twenty-four Senate seats and some 70 percent
of two hundred House seats.
July 27: The first session of the new Philippine Congress opens.
August 2: Local government minister Jaimé Ferrer is assassinated in a
Manila suburb, the first time in Philippine history that a cabinet member is
assassinated.
August 28: A rebel military group led by Col. Gregorio Honasan attempts a
coup with several thousand soldiers. The attempt is crushed the next day;
over sixty people die.
September 27: Lean Alejandro, leader of the People's party, is assassinated.

October 28: Three Americans are killed outside Clark Air Base by NPA assassination squads.

December 7: Former finance minister Jaimé Ongpin commits suicide.

December 9: Renegade rebel leader Honasan is captured.

1988

January 18: Local elections are held for mayors, governors, and other officials in sixty-two of country's seventy-three provinces. An estimated 136 people are killed in election-related violence, but 80 percent of electorate comes to polls.

January 21: Defense Secretary Ileto resigns and is replaced by General Ramos.

March: Romulo Kintanar, NPA chief, is captured.

April 2: Honasan escapes from a prison ship in Manila Bay.

November 12: Romulo Kintanar and his wife, Gloria, escape from military detention.

Glossary

Agaw Armas: Arms-grabbing raids by the NPA on AFP arsenals.

AKSIUN: A union of unemployed persons, associated with the NDF.

Alex Boncayao Brigade (ABB): An NPA urban assassination unit in Manila which first began operating in 1984.

Alliance of Concerned Teachers (ACT): A cause-oriented group essentially of Manilan schoolteachers with contacts in the NDF.

Alsa-Masa: Up-from-the-Masses, or Arise Masses; a Davao City–based anti-NPA vigilante group, established in 1986 with military support.

Amado Guerrero: Beloved Warrior, pseudonym for Jose Maria Sison; founded the Communist Party of the Philippines (CPP) in 1968.

Amazons: Female NPAS.

Amor propio: Personal dignity or esteem.

Ang Bayan: The Nation; the CPP's underground monthly newspaper which began publication in 1968.

Area of Operation (AO): Standard military term, also used by the NPA and AFP, to designate a particular unit's geographic responsibility.

Armado: An armed NPA regular.

Armed City Partisans (ACP): Armed City Partisan Units/Sparrow Units of the NPA of one to four members; also known as ACPUS or ACPU/SUS.

Armed Forces of the Philippines (AFP): Organized in 1935 by Gen. Douglas MacArthur, the AFP comprises four principal branches: the Philippine Army, Philippine Constabulary, Philippine Navy, and Philippine Air Force.

Armed Independent Group (AIG): Negros-based vigilante group.

Armed Struggle (AS): A term used by the CPP.

Army Literacy Patrol System (ALPS): Program begun by the AFP in 1982 for soldiers to provide educational, medical, and other services to local communities.

Associated Labor Unions (ALU): A moderate labor group affiliated with the TUCP.

Association of Major Religious Superiors of the Philippines (AMRSP): An association representing the interests of priests and nuns.

Babaylan: A spirit medium.

Baganian Area Subanon Anti-Communist Organization (BASACO):
    Zamboanga del Sur vigilante group.

Bagong Huk-bong Bayan (BHB): The NPA in Tagalog (very rarely used).

Bantay Banwa: People Wake Up; Negros-based vigilante group.

Barangays: Basic unit of local administration; a barrio or district.

Barrio Liaison Group (BLG) or Contact Group (Grupong Tagapaguguay):
    Formed of initial CPP sympathizers in a village.

Barrio Organizing Committees (BOC) or People's Organizing Committees
    (POC): Groups composed of CPP sympathizers recruited by Organizing
    Group cadres in one of the stages in penetrating a new village.

Barrio Revolutionary Committee (BRC): A basic village CPP unit, formed
    from sections of the Barrio Organizing Committees.

Barrio Self-Defense Units (BSCU): Civilian militias created by the AFP in
    1969 to deal with local disturbances.

Basic Christian Community (BCC): A development concept, initiated with the
    support of the Maryknoll Fathers in 1970, intended to empower
    villagers within the church and the community.

Bata Kang Bursong Pangpartido: A Handbook of the Communist party
    covering administrative and other matters.

Battalion Combat Teams (BCT): An AFP unit designation.

Bayan or Bagong Alyansang Makabayan: New Nationalist Alliance, or New
    Patriotic Alliance (a bayan is also a municipal center); established in
    1985.

Budong: A peace treaty formed among tribal villages; anyone protected by
    budong who is killed must be avenged.

Catholic Bishop's Conference of the Philippines (CBCP): Organization of
    Catholic bishops.

Central Committee (CC): Main governing body of the Communist Party of
    the Philippines.

Central Luzon Farmers Alliance (CLFA): A militant labor group begun in
    1981.

Christians for National Liberation (CNL): Founded in 1972 by Father Ed de
    la Torre as an offshoot of the PPI; one of the coalition members of the
    NDF.

Church-Military Liaison Committees (CMLC): Groups formed in the early
    1980s by government to promote dialogue between the military and the
    church.

Citizens' Army against Communism (CACA): Cebu-based vigilante group.

Civilian Armed Force Geographical Units (CAFGU): An organization that replaced CHDF in 1988.

Civilian Home Defense Forces (CHDF): Armed local militias formed by the AFP in 1976.

Civilian Volunteer Organizations (CVO): Military name for vigilante groups; first used in 1988.

Colorums: Generic term for peasant millenarian movements; derived from the Latin "per omnia saecula saeculorum" (world without end).

Communist Party of the Philippines (CPP): Founded December 26, 1968, in Pangasinan Province.

Contact Group (CG) or Barrio Liaison Group (BLG): Early organizing group of CPP cadres.

Cordillera People's Liberation Army (CPLA): Group controlled by Father Conrado Balweg.

Daba-Daba: An NPA newspaper in Panay.

Deep penetration agents (DPA): Spies for the AFP.

Demonyos: Government informers.

El Diablo Crime Busters Association: Group consisting primarily of enlisted military, vigilantes, and extortionists; apparently formed in 1982; later renamed the Guardian Brotherhood.

Executive Committee (EC): Provides daily direction for the CPP; composed of three permanent members and two alternatives.

Exposure: The visit by a political tourist to an NPA zone.

Federation of Free Farmers (FFF): A labor organization founded by Jesuits in 1953.

Federation of Free Workers (FFW): A labor organization founded by Jesuits in 1950.

Foreign Military Sales (FMS): U.S. military aid program.

Free Legal Assistance Group (FLAG): An organization of lawyers established to work on human rights cases.

Friends of the Filipino People (FFP): Anti-Marcos U.S.-based opposition group.

Gagmayng Kristohanong Katilingban (GKK): Small Christian communities.

Guardian Brotherhood: A military fraternity of enlisted men, initially located near American military facilities.

Guerrilla zone: A zone of operation surrounding a guerrilla base.

Hacendero: Plantation owner.

Hacienda: Plantation, farm.

Himagsik: Mass NPA newspaper in central Luzon.

Hiya: Shame.

Huks, Hukbalahaps, or Hukbo ng Bayan Laban Hapon: People's Anti-Japanese Army, later known as HMB, the Hukbong Mapagpalaya ng Payan, or People's Liberation Army; NPA members are sometimes referred to as Hukbos.

Ilagas: Anti-Communist religious cult based in General Santos City.

Ilustrado: Enlightened one; member of well-educated elite.

Institute for Social Order (ISO): Founded by Jesuits in 1947.

Integrated Civilian Home Defense Force (ICHDF): An AFP designation for local militias created in the late 1960s.

Integrated National Police (INP): Created to oversee all police work under the control of the Philippine Constabulary.

Integree: Reserve military officer integrated into the regular army.

Joint U.S. Military Advisory Group (JUSMAG): U.S. military logistical group based in Manila responsible for overseeing shipments of American military supplies.

Justice for Aquino, Justice for All (JAJA): Cause-oriented group established following Senator Aquino's assassination.

Ka: Abbreviated form of Kasama, or companion; an honorific title adopted by Communists to mean a comrade. The good guys, according to the NPA.

Kaaway, Kalaban Hapon: Japan, the enemy; also names for AFP soldiers. The bad guys, according to the NPA.

Kabataan Makabayan (KM): Nationalist Youth, of Patriotic Youth; a radical student group formed in 1964 by Jose Maria Sison and others.

Kabataan para sa Demokrasya at Nasyonalismo (KADENA): Youth for Democracy and Nationalism; claims 20,000 members of Bayan.

Kalatas: A CPP newspaper in southern Tagalog region.

Kalayaan: Independence, or enlightenment.

Kalihukan Alang sa Demokratikong Reforma (KADRE): Movement for Democratic Reforms; Cebu-based vigilante group.

Kapunungan sa mga Kabus Kontra sa Komunista: Organization of the Poor against Communists; related to Rock Christ, a Misamis Occidental vigilante group, also known as the 4Ks.

Katipunan: Highest and Most Respectable Society of the Sons of the People; nineteenth-century Philippine independence movement, formed in 1892 by Andres Bonifacio.

Katipunan ng mga Demokratikong Pilipino (KDP): An anti-Marcos opposition group based in California.

Katipunan ng mga Samahan ng Manggagawa (KASAMA): Association of Union Workers.

Katipunan ng mgu Gurong Makabayan (KAGUMA): Association of Nationalist Teachers, one of the NDF's founding coalition members.

Katipunero: Member of the Katipunan.

Kawal ng Barangay: Town soldier, civilian-military volunteers; AFP designation.

Kilusan, Ang: The movement, a CPP reference.

Kilusan ng Magbubukid sa Pilpinas (KMP): Peasant Movement of the Philippines; military/labor group formed in 1985.

Kilusang Bagong Lipunan party (KBL): Marcos's New Society movement.

Kilusang Mayo Uno (KMU): May First Movement; a labor group, formed with NDF support in 1980.

Kommid: The Mindanao Regional Commission of the CPP.

Kristiano Kontra Komuniso: Christians against Communism, also called Concerned Citizens Group Fighting against Insurgency; a Negros-based vigilante group.

Kuratong Baleleng: Misamis Occidental criminal syndicate and vigilante group.

Lapiang Manggagawa (LM): Workers or Labor party, founded by trade union organizer Ignacio Lacsina in 1962.

Larab: A CPP newspaper in Samar.

League of Filipino Students (LFS): Established in 1977 as an NDF affiliate.

Liberal party (LP): One of two traditional political parties.

Liberation: Newspaper of the National Democratic Front, begun in 1981; an international edition was started in Holland in 1985.

Loób: Inner self.

Lost Command: A paramilitary group of the AFP; also called Charlie's Angels.

Main Regional Guerrilla Units (MRGU): Units of 80 to 150 fighters, the largest-sized unit of the NPA.

Mala: Name of some NPA members employed in government agencies undercover.

Malayang Samahang Magsasaka (MASAKA): Federation of Free Farmers, or Free Farmers Union.

Malaysang Pagkakaisa ng Kabataang Pilipino (MPKP): Free Association of

Filipino Youth; founded from remnants of the KM.

Manila Crusaders for Peace and Democracy (MCPD): A vigilante group.

Military Assistance Program (MAP): American military aid.

Mindinao-Sulu Pastoral Conference (MSPC): A Catholic church–based organization established in Mindanao in 1971.

Ministry of National Defense (MND): Originally the Department of National Defense established in 1939.

Moro: Muslim Filipino.

Moro National Liberation Front (MNLF): Best known of three major Muslim groups; led major rebellion against government in early 1970s.

Movement, The: Ang Kilusan; a CPP reference.

Movement for an Independent Negros (MIN): A vigilante group.

Movement for the Advancement of Nationalism (MAN): Major left-wing group of the 1960s.

Nacionalista party (NP): One of two traditional political parties.

National Association of Health Workers or Patriotic Health Association (MASAPA): An NDF-created front to provide medical support to the CPP.

National Commission for Mass Movements (NCMM): Part of the Central Committee of the CPP politburo; responsible for infiltrating student, youth, labor, and peasant groups.

National Democratic Front (NDF): Associated with the CPP; founded in 1972 to control sympathetic organizations operating more or less overtly.

National Federation of Sugar Workers (NFSW): Founded in Negros with the aid of Luis Jalandoni as a radical offshoot of the FFF.

National Intelligence Coordinating Agency (NICA): The government's principal intelligence network.

National Military Commission (NMC): Part of the Central Committee of the CPP Politburo; controls the NPA.

National Propaganda Commission (NPC): Part of the CPP Politburo.

National Secretariat of Social Action (NASSA): Organized by the Catholic Bishops Conference of the Philippines in 1966.

New Armed Forces of the Philippines (NAFP): New name of the AFP following Marcos's overthrow in 1986; later changed back.

New People's Army (NPA): The regular armed forces of the CPP created in 1969.

Organizing Groups (OG): Groups representing various sectors of a village community once a Barrio Liaison Group of the CPP is in place.

Pakikisama: Getting along together; smooth interpersonal relations.

Pam basang Koalisyon ng Mangaggawa Laban sa Kahirapan (PKMK):
National Coalition of Workers against Poverty; militant labor group
formed in 1984.

Partido Komunista ng Pilipinas (PKP): Philippine Communist Party; founded
by Crisanto Evangelista in 1930.

Partido ng Bayan (PNB): People's party; a leftist political party formed in
1986.

Pasabilis: Rapid information units (reconnaissance) of the NPA.

People's Democratic Republic of the Philippines (PDRP): A CPP reference.

People's Liberation Organization (PLO): A paramilitary group; AFP unit.

People's Organizing Committees (POC) or Barrio Organizing Committees:
Formed by the CPP from the sectors represented in the initial
Organizing Groups.

Philippine Air Force (PAF): Formed in 1937 from the PC's air corps.

Philippine Alliance against Communism (PAAC): A Cebu-based vigilante
umbrella group.

Philippine Army (PA): Originated with the Philippine Scouts; formed in
1899 by the Americans as a local force to fight in the Philippine-
American War.

Philippine Army Civil Relations and Information Service (PACRIS):
Propaganda arm of the AFP.

Philippine Civic Action Group (PHILCAG): Philippine unit fighting in
Vietnam War.

Philippine Coast Guard (PCG): Established in 1967 as a secondary branch of
the AFP.

Philippine Constabulary (PC): The oldest branch of the AFP, formed in 1901
from remnants of the Spanish Guardia Civil, established in 1868; first
called the Insular Police Force.

Philippine Constabulary Forward Command (PCFC): Negros-based vigilante
group established by PC.

Philippine Military Academy (PMA): Nation's most prestigious four-year
college for military officers from which all services select cadres;
located in Baguio.

Philippine Navy (PN): Formed in 1939 from elements of the PC's naval units.

Philippine Priests Incorporated (PPI): An organization of diocesan priests
formed in 1968.

Philippine Society and Revolution: Written by Amado Guerrero (Jose Maria
Sison); the CPP's ideological guidebook, published in July 1970.

Philippine Transport and General Workers Organization (PTGWO): A moderate
  trade union affiliated with the TUCP.
Power Spirit–Alsa-Masa: Negros Occidental vigilante group; offshoot of
  religious cult, Power of the Holy Spirit.
Preservation of Democratic Institutions in the Philippines (PDIP):
  Zamboanga del Sur vigilante group.
Presidential Decree (PD): Power by which Marcos ruled during martial law
  period, giving him legal authority to legislate by decree.
Presidential Security Command (PSC): The AFP unit responsible for
  guarding the president.
Preventive Detention Actions (PDA): Special legal writs giving Marcos
  authority to arrest anyone with no legal restraint.
Proletaryo: Workers' paper begun by CPP on May 1, 1980.
PROPA: Propaganda; a neutral term with no pejorative connotations.
Pula-Puti: Red-White, or Body of Christ; Zamboanga del Sur vigilante
  group.
Pulang Bandila: Red Flag; NPA's own paper begun in 1985.
Rectify Errors and Rebuild the Party: Book on guerrilla warfare written by
  Amado Guerrero in 1968.
Reform the AFP Movement (RAM): A military reform group of middle and
  junior officers which surfaced in 1984; also known as "We Belong."
Regional Unified Commands (RUC): An AFP designation referring to the
  integration of all military units in one of the nation's twelve
  administrative units under one commander.
REVO: The Revolution; CPP reference.
Revolution: Short-lived internal theoretical journal of the CPP, begun in
  1976.
Revolutionary Peasant Association (SMM): One of the coalition members of
  the NDF.
Sagrado's Private Army: Misamis Occidental vigilante group
Sakdal: To strike, or to accuse; name of a peasant rebellion begun in 1935
  and that of a small newspaper begun in 1930 by the movement's leader,
  Benigno Ramos.
Samahan ng Makabayang Magsasaka (SMM): Revolutionary Peasant
  Association.
Samahong Demokratiko ng Kabataan (SDK): Democratic Association of the
  Youth.
Sandataang Yunit Pan Propaganda (SYP): An Expansion Group or armed

propaganda unit; CPP reference; also spelled Samahang unit Pampropaganda.

Sandigan ng mga Mag-aaral at Sambayanan (SAMASA): National Student Council; a radical student group based at the University of the Philippines.

Secondary Regional Guerrilla Units (SRGU): Forces of thirty to sixty regulars in the NPA.

Self-Defense Units (SDU): Armed militia formed by the KM.

Semi-legal Teams (SLT): Small bands of youths who propagandize; the basic CPP building block in a Communist village apparatus.

Silyab: A CPP newspaper in Bicol.

Sitio: Hamlet.

Socio-economic Military Program (SEMP): An AFP program designed to win people's support begun in 1958 as a military civic action program.

Special Action Force (SAF): Battalion formed in 1983 by the PC.

Specific Characteristics of Our People's War: Book written in 1974 by Jose Maria Sison on guerrilla strategy.

Students Cultural Association of UP (SCAUP): Radical student organization established at the University of the Philippines in 1959 by Jose Maria Sison and Francisco Nemenzo.

Subversive terrorist (ST): An AFP reference to the CPP.

Supremo: Leader.

Tadtad: Hackers, or chop-chop; a quasi-Christian group armed by the AFP.

Tao: Person; frequently used as "the common tao," meaning peasant.

Task Force Detainees–Philippines (TFDP): Human rights group established in January 1974.

TAYO: Jargon in the NPA for "Kom" or Communist.

Trade Union Congress of the Philippines (TUCP): A moderate trade union established with government support in 1975; some of its affiliates include the Associated Labor Unions (ALU), the Federation of Free Farmers (FFF), and the Philippine Transport and General Workers Organization (PTGWO).

Troika: Executive Committee in the CPP Politburo; also name given to command structure of an NPA unit consisting of a commander, vice-commander, and political officer.

TUGON: United Response; a moderate student group at the University of the Philippines.

Tulisane: Bandit.

U.G.: To go underground; a CPP reference.

United Farmers' Organizaton (UFO): Group in Cebu, affiliated with KMP.

United Front Commission (UFC): Part of the Central Committee of the CPP Politburo, controlling the NDF.

United Nationalist Democratic Organizaton (UNIDO): Political party of Salvador Laurel.

University of the Philippines (UP): The nation's most prestigious university which used to draw students nationally without regard to background.

Utang na loób: Debt of prime obligation.

Walang Patawad: No Mercy, or The Unforgiving; Leyte-based vigilante group.

War Dogs: Defectors from the NPA who work for the AFP as scouts.

We Belong: Name of RAM newsletter; the first name of the organization.

Welga ng bayan's: People's strikes; begun in late 1984 as a means of mobilizing opposition to Marcos regime.

Yellows: Moderate opposition to Marcos regime.

Youth for Nationalism and Democracy: One of the coalition members of the NDF.

ZONA: A liberated zone; also known as "Red Area"; previously used to mean zoning.

Zoning: An AFP house-to-house search after sealing off an area.

Index

Agrava Commission, 2, 142
Aguinaldo, Gen. Emilio, 8, 10, 26, 51, 112
Alejandro, Lean, 85, 86
Alliance of Concerned Teachers, 85
Alsa-Masa, 52, 97, 136, 137, 146, 153
Anti-Martial Law Coalition, 102
Aquino, Agapito, 86
Aquino, Benigno, 1, 2, 26–27, 81, 82, 85, 128, 142, 179
Aquino, Corazon Cojuangco, 27, 43, 57, 139, 151, 152, 158; election, 2, 3, 27, 55, 92; peace talks, 4, 89, 94–95; and Catholic church, 48; counterinsurgency policy, 49, 94, 103, 132–33, 146, 148; and CPP, 67; political role, 96, 147–48; opposed, 97, 131–32; supported, 97, 135, 152, 154; policies, 97, 160; human rights, 98–99; military, 106, 132, 135; paramilitary groups, 126; and USA, 138–39, 155; land reform, 148, 159
Armed City Partisan Unit, 92
Armed Forces of the Philippines. *See* Military
Association of Labor Unions (ALU), 90
Association of Major Religious Superiors of the Philippines, 47–48, 85
Association of Nationalist Teachers (KAGUMA), 80, 90
Association of Workers (KASAMA), 90

Baltasar, Julian, 8
Balweg, Father Conrado, 76, 88, 89
Barrio Self-Defense Units (BSDU), 120
Barros, Lori, 60
Basic Christian Communities (BCC), 47
Bayan, 85–96 passim, 102
Baylosis, Rafael, 69, 93–94
Bonifacio, Andres, 10, 37
Brotherhood of Farmers, 14
Brotherhood of St. Joseph, 6
Buscayno, Bernabe, 29, 41, 42, 50, 60

Casipe, Renato, 60
Castro, Pedro, 32
Catholic church: and social conflict, 23–24, 154; liberation theology, 24, 45–46; insurgency, 24, 45–48, 51, 76, 139, 184n112; CPP, 45, 47, 48; trade unions, 46, 47; poor, 47; Marcos, 47–48; radicalization, 87–88; military, 141
Central Luzon Farmers' Alliance (CLFA), 90
China, Peoples' Republic of: influence on insurgency, 38–39, 55, 57, 68, 70–71, 72, 170n41, 171n51; support of insurgency, 74, 99–100, 155, 188n146
Christians for National Liberation, 47, 80, 88
Civilian Home Defense Forces (CHDF), 110, 120, 127, 142
Clark Air Base, 4, 155, 158
Class formation, 12–19 passim, 21
Coalition for the Restoration of Democracy, 85